Illustrated Guide to
BIRDS
AND BIRDWATCHING

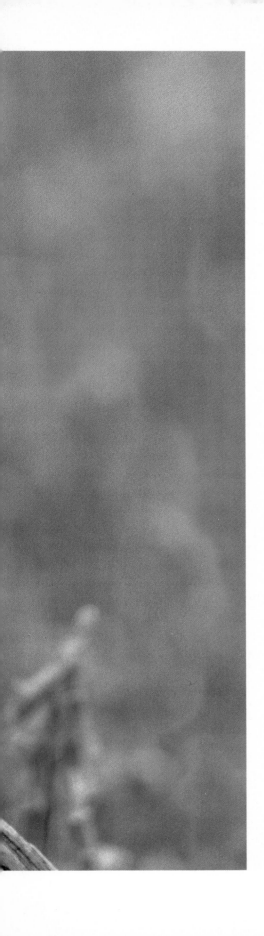

Illustrated Guide to
BIRDS
AND BIRDWATCHING

By Neil Ardley

KINGFISHER   BOOKS
WARD LOCK LIMITED

Page 5: A treecreeper climbs a tree trunk in search of insects hiding in the bark.

Previous page: A starling looks out over a field of bluebells.

Right: A gannet soars through the air, gliding on its outstretched wings.

The material in Part 3 of this book has been adapted from the *Kingfisher Guide to Birds*, first published in 1978

First Published in 1980 by
Kingfisher Books Limited
(A Grisewood & Dempsey,
Ward Lock joint company)
116 Baker Street, London W1

BRITISH LIBRARY CATALOGUING IN
PUBLICATION DATA
Ardley, Neil
  Birds and birdwatching –
  (Kingfisher illustrated guides)
  1. Birdwatching – Europe
  1. Title II. Series
  589.2'073'094   QL690.A1

ISBN 0 7063 6002 8

Printed and Bound in Italy
by Vallardi Industrie Grafiche

Contents

10

Foreword

The enormous increase of interest in natural history over the last thirty years has been astounding. Conservationists and biologists, professional and amateur, have hammered home their points for so long that few of us can now be unaware both of the variety of the animal kingdom and of the pressures which threaten it.

Birds have become particularly popular – possibly because of the large number of species easily available for observation, and because of their ubiquity. Even city-dwellers can observe the behaviour of sparrows, starlings and pigeons, and perhaps stop to consider how these ignored, (and often despised), species have adapted to achieve such success.

Neil Ardley has done his job well and thoroughly, and the range of his book is wide. The first part is devoted to birds in general – their structure and their behaviour in all its aspects. The second part shows how, when and where to study birds. This leads logically to the third part, the identification guide. The point is repeatedly made in text and picture that where the bird is, and how it is behaving are valuable aids to identification. This is a book to be enjoyed by beginners and old hands alike.

Peter Olney
B.Sc., Dip. Ed., F.L.S.; Curator of Birds, Zoological Society of London; Editor, International Zoo Yearbook.

Left: An avocet tends its eggs which are laid in a simple nest made on the ground. The avocet is one of several birds that have been helped by conservation measures.

Part One

The World of Birds

Left: A grey heron at its tree-top nest. Although they are among the largest birds of Europe, grey herons usually nest in trees.

The Bird's Body

Many people find birds the most interesting of all wild animals. The main reason for this is that birds are to be seen wherever people are likely to find themselves, for they are rare only at the icy poles and the summits of high mountains. Furthermore, birds are generally conspicuous animals; being easily able to keep their distance from man, they do not have to hide at our approach. Some birds are secretive by nature, but even they will reveal themselves to the patient or intrepid birdwatcher.

Birds also fascinate us because they are beautiful creatures and because they can fly; people have long prized the plumage of the more elegant birds and tried to emulate their prowess in the air. And even the most casual of birdwatchers must be aware that birds have an extraordinarily wide range of life styles. Some flutter around our houses and gardens while others are only to be seen on the coast or at lakes and rivers; some are mostly seen soaring high in the air while others keep to the ground; many are vegetarians while others are skilful hunters; some birds are active only at night while others disappear as soon as dusk arrives.

Although they live in so many different ways, birds are remarkably similar in their physical characteristics – so much so that no one has any difficulty in recognizing a creature as a bird wherever it may be found. Even so, a bird's life style is dictated by the shape of its body. The size and shape of its wings and beak, for example, can tell you how a bird flies and what it is likely to eat, and from this you can deduce how the bird lives. Every feature of a bird's body is governed by the need to survive in a particular environment. The bird suits the habitat in which it lives, and may not easily be able to survive in any other kind of habitat.

The Skeleton – A Framework For Flying

However different it may look to other vertebrate animals – animals such as reptiles, amphibians and mammals that possess backbones – the basic similarity between a bird and other vertebrates, including man, is obvious from the skeleton. In every case, the backbone supports a rib cage and to it are joined the bones of four limbs, neck bones and a skull. This basic similarity occurs because these animals evolved from common ancestors millions of years ago. Birds evolved from reptiles, and it is possible that they are the living descendants of dinosaurs. Feathers – the one feature that makes birds different to all other animals – evolved from the scales that cover the bodies of reptiles. Although reptiles that can truly fly have become extinct, birds and reptiles still have features in common. Their skeletons and muscles are similar, and both lay eggs. Newly-hatched reptiles and birds both have an egg tooth, a small projection on the beak that they use to break open the shell when they hatch.

The first known bird was more reptilian than today's birds, though still very bird-like. It is called *Archaeopteryx*, a name meaning 'ancient wing', and it lived in what is now Germany about 140 million years ago. Unlike today's birds, it had jaws with teeth,

Above: The skeleton of a bird has long arm and hand bones to which the wing feathers are attached, and a huge breastbone that anchors the wing muscles. This bird is a gull.

claws on the front of its wings and a long bony tail. But it was undoubtedly a bird because it had feathers. *Archaeopteryx* was about the size of a magpie, and opinions differ on how well it could fly. It long ago became extinct, and though we cannot be sure that it was the direct ancestor of modern birds, it certainly possessed the main features they have today.

Lightness And Strength

Birds have the same general kind of body because they can fly. The wings carry them through the air, but many other features of the body allow them to stay aloft. The body must be as light as possible – one of the largest flying birds, the mute swan, usually weighs no more than 14 kilograms while the smallest European bird, the tiny goldcrest, may tip the scales at less than $5\frac{1}{2}$ grams! Birds achieve this lightness by having hollow bones and air cavities in their bodies. They also digest their food and drop their wastes quickly, and eggs form and are laid rapidly, all to keep the body as light as possible. But lightness must not be achieved at the expense of strength, and the hollow spaces within the bones are criss-crossed with struts to make them tough.

Bird Bones

A bird's skull is basically like that of other vertebrates. However, the jawbones are long, sometimes very long, and form the bird's beak or bill. The shape varies greatly from one kind of bird to another, and is determined by the kind of food that the bird is normally able to find. There are no teeth, but the edges of the beak may have notches like the blade of a saw which are used for gripping slippery prey rather than for cutting. In the upper mandible or half of the beak are two nostrils, and the ear openings are in the side of the skull. The skull is joined to a long flexible neck having as many as 28 neck bones (by contrast, mammals, even the giraffe, have seven neck bones). A bird can therefore bend its neck and turn its head easily, which helps it get food and spot enemies as well as preen its plumage.

The neck bones are attached to the backbone, which supports a comparatively small rib cage. However, the breastbone in front of the ribs is huge, often bigger than the rib cage itself. This is because the breastbone serves to anchor the large and powerful wing muscles to the skeleton, and it is correspondingly reduced in flightless birds such as the ostrich.

The wing feathers are attached to long arm and hand bones. The upper arm and forearm bones are similar to those in human beings, but the hand and finger bones are very different. The hand bones are long and narrow, and there are only three finger bones. These can be moved to control the feathers in the wings when flying.

The backbone ends in the tail bones, to which the tail feathers are attached. The tail feathers can also be controlled to help the bird fly. The two legs have bones like our leg bones, but of different proportions. The thigh bone and knee are concealed beneath the plumage, and the first visible section is the shin. The first visible joint is the ankle and not the knee. Then comes the foot and four toes. As the bird cannot use its fingers for grasping, the toes have to

Below: A yellowhammer flies through the air, caught as it is about to land. The tail feathers are spread to slow the bird, and wing feathers are held together to push the air down and support the yellowhammer in the air. The bright yellow head serves to identify this yellowhammer as a male bird, for the female is light brown all over. The difference in colour helps to bring the birds together to breed.

hold things and they can be bent and are armed with claws accordingly. Most birds have strong leg muscles and can run or hop easily, as well as cling tenaciously to a perch. The legs are set beneath the centre of the body so that the bird can balance easily. In many sea- and water birds, the toes are webbed together or are paddle-shaped, and they are used primarily for swimming. The legs are often set far back to make the birds streamlined in the water. However, this hinders the birds on land, and many can only waddle when out of the water.

The Wings And Ways Of Flying

All birds have wings, but not all can fly. Some flightless birds depend on their modified wings as paddles (for example, penguins), and in some others the plumes can have a function in the male's courtship display. The reason that they have wings at all is because they evolved from birds that could fly and they have not lost their wings. All living European birds can fly (our only flightless bird, the great auk, is now extinct), though some are much better at flying than others. Birds use their wings to fly in several different ways; a few birds even use their wings as paddles to swim under water, and the extreme development of this can be seen in penguins.

In order for anything to fly, be it animal or machine, it must do two basic things. It has to lift itself up into the air, and it has to move itself forward through the air. Lift is achieved in two ways. The surface of the wing of both a bird and an aircraft is curved so that, as the wing slices through the air, the air moves faster over the top of the wing than it does beneath it. The fast-moving air has a lower pressure than the slow-moving air beneath the wing, which exerts a pressure on the wing and forces it upward. If this force or lift exceeds the weight of the bird or aircraft, it will rise. Lift is also produced by making air move downwards. The rotating blades of a helicopter do this, and so too do the flapping wings of a bird.

To move forward through the air, a bird or aircraft must push air backwards. The engines of an aircraft do this, but a bird moves forward by flapping its wings. It can also move by gliding. It holds

Left: A herring gull flies by flapping its wings and by soaring. The outer primary feathers and inner secondary feathers of the wing can be clearly seen.

Below: A house sparrow in flight. At the top of the upstroke (1), the wing feathers close and are held together on the downstroke (2), pushing air downward. On the upstroke (3), the feathers part to let air through the wings. To land (4), the wing and tail feathers are spread.

its wings outstretched and flies at a slight downward angle, gravity pulling it forward. Its speed must be fast enough to produce sufficient lift to keep it in the air. To gain height without flapping its wings, a gliding bird seeks up-currents of air to carry it aloft. Birds that soar high in the air, like eagles, glide in this way and so do seabirds, like shearwaters, that skim over the waves.

Some birds can also hover, flapping their wings in such a way that their effort goes into producing lift and no forward motion. Hovering is often accomplished by flying into the wind at the same speed as the wind blows the bird back, so that the bird remains above the same spot on the ground. Kestrels hover in this way. They can often be seen hovering beside motorways, slowly flapping their wings in a characteristic way.

A bird uses the feathers in its wings and tail to produce and control its flight. The wings have two sets of feathers. The set of feathers at the end of the wing, which can be spread separately, are called the primary feathers. These act to propel the bird forwards and to control flight. To push the air effectively, the feathers close as the bird brings its wings down. On the upstroke of the wings, the feathers part to allow the air through, otherwise the pushing effect of the downstroke would be cancelled out. The inner set of feathers are called the secondary feathers, and these provide lift. A small group of feathers near the wingtip known as the alula feathers help to control flight at slow speeds, like the slots or flaps on an aircraft wing. To turn, the bird can tilt its wings and body and also use its tail as a rudder for maximum manoeuvrability.

Below: Birds have different flight patterns depending on their particular ways of life, and the shapes of their wings are related to their flight patterns. We can therefore get some idea of a bird's life style from the shape of its wings.

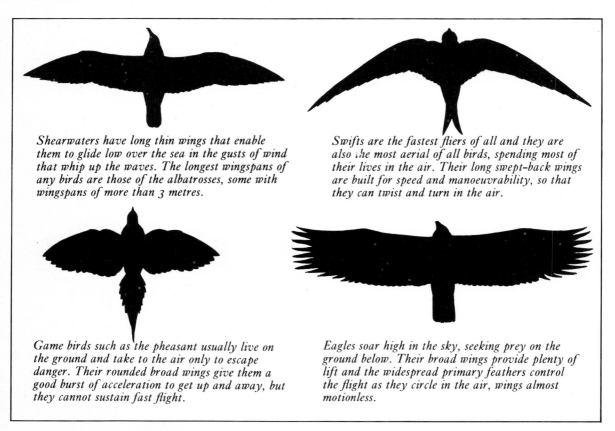

Shearwaters have long thin wings that enable them to glide low over the sea in the gusts of wind that whip up the waves. The longest wingspans of any birds are those of the albatrosses, some with wingspans of more than 3 metres.

Swifts are the fastest fliers of all and they are also the most aerial of all birds, spending most of their lives in the air. Their long swept-back wings are built for speed and manoeuvrability, so that they can twist and turn in the air.

Game birds such as the pheasant usually live on the ground and take to the air only to escape danger. Their rounded broad wings give them a good burst of acceleration to get up and away, but they cannot sustain fast flight.

Eagles soar high in the sky, seeking prey on the ground below. Their broad wings provide plenty of lift and the widespread primary feathers control the flight as they circle in the air, wings almost motionless.

Above: A spoonbill comes in to land. It spreads its wings and tail feathers to slow down, and extends its legs.

Getting into the air and landing are not always very easy. Small perching birds like thrushes and finches can simply jump into the air, but some water birds like swans have to 'run' along the water to get into the air and when not out at sea auks have to fall off a cliff. Swifts have great trouble getting off the ground as their feet are weak. They therefore try to avoid landing on the ground and instead cling to vertical surfaces. To land, birds spread their wings and tail to slow down and put their feet out to grip a perch or set themselves down on the ground. Water birds may find landing as awkward an operation as take-off and may have to splash down abruptly onto the water.

Plumage For Many Purposes

One feature makes a bird different to all other animals – its plumage. Other creatures may be able to fly or lay eggs, but no others have feathers. A feather is a remarkable structure, especially when you consider that it evolved from the scales of reptiles. Birds still have scales – on their feet – and a bird's beak is made of the same material as its feathers and scales. This material is called keratin, and it is the same material as that in human nails and hair. Like nails and hair, feathers can be tough or soft, and like hair, they come in many. different colours. These various properties give feathers several different uses.

A bird is thickly covered in feathers. A small bird such as a sparrow has about 2000 feathers while a swan may have as many as 25,000. These feathers are of two basic kinds: contour and down.

Contour feathers are those that cover the body of an adult bird. They are so called because they define the shape or contours of a bird's body. The wing and tail feathers are also contour feathers. A contour feather is designed to be strong though very light. It consists of a hollow central shaft, called a quill at the base, to which a vane of barbs is attached. The barbs lock together with tiny barbules that bear hooks, making the vane strong. Contour feathers have to be tough, because they provide the bird with an outer covering that must be able to withstand damage. The wing and tail feathers must also be strong if they are to produce and control flight.

Down feathers are the fluffy feathers that cover the bodies of young birds. They are similar to contour feathers, but the barbs do not lock together to form a strong vane. Adult birds also possess down feathers beneath the outer layer of contour feathers. They form an insulating layer that keeps the bird warm in cold weather. Birds are warm-blooded creatures and have to maintain a body temperature of 41°C, so the insulating layer must be effective in winter. Water birds possess dense layers of feathers, and can swim about happily in freezing conditions. Other birds fluff up their feathers if it is very cold. This action increases the insulation space beneath the outer feathers, trapping more body heat.

In summer, birds may be faced with the problem of ridding themselves of body heat. The plumage is also effective in this situation, for the bird can ruffle its feathers to allow cooling air to reach the skin.

Colour

A bird's outer feathers also give it a certain colour or pattern of colours. All the birds of a particular species usually have the same colours, though differences exist between the young and the adult birds and often between the males and the females. The colour patterns may also change from one season of the year to another.

Above: A close-up view of a duck's feather shows the barbs and barbules. The barbules hook over each other, and hold the barbs that make up the vane together.

Below left: Birds like this robin often look fat in winter. In fact, they are just the same size as at other times of year, but they fluff out their feathers to keep warm. This action increases the amount of air in the plumage, which acts as extra insulation against the cold.

The colours are usually produced by the presence of coloured pigments in the keratin that makes up the feathers. Pigment colours are generally red, brown, yellow, green and black. White plumage occurs where there is no pigment to colour the feathers. This happens in mainly-white birds such as adult gulls and terns, but white plumage may also be produced by mutation, giving rise to albino birds. This is fairly common in blackbirds which, despite their name, are sometimes piebald and occasionally pure white.

Colour is also influenced by the surface structure of the feathers. Fine grooves on the feathers cause the light waves reflected from the feather to interfere with each other, producing a glossy or iridescent colour, usually blue or green. The gloss on the green head of a mallard drake is caused by interference, and so too is the green-purple shine on a starling. You can see a similar play of colours reflected from the fine grooves of a gramophone record, and it is produced in the same way.

Although many birds are attractively coloured, the birds themselves are not concerned with colour purely as decoration. Colour has two very important and quite opposite uses. In birds that are liable to fall victim to hunting animals (which are often other birds), colour is used as camouflage and the pattern of the plumage serves to disguise and hide the bird. However, birds also use their colour patterns to find and identify one another. This brings birds of the same species together in the breeding season, and may also help to keep flocks of birds together, although call sounds are the most important way that flocks stay together.

Care Of Plumage

Feathers are therefore extremely important to birds, and they must be cared for with great devotion if the bird is to survive. A bird must be ready always to fly at a moment's notice, so it must keep its plumage in tip-top condition. This is why you can often see birds preening. They run their beaks through their feathers, pecking out dirt and pests and zipping up any vanes that have become disarrayed. Its flexible neck allows the bird to attend to its wings and tail as well as its back and breast, but, twist as it might, the bird cannot of course reach its head. Instead, it scratches at the head feathers with one foot while balancing on the other. Herons and some other water birds have special comb-like claws to help clean their plumage. Herons also produce a kind of dry shampoo from special down feathers that crumble into a powder. Combing this powder through the feathers easily removes any slime coating them.

Birds can often be seen bathing as well as preening. Many like to stand in a puddle or shallow pool and splash water over their bodies, while others such as kingfishers and swallows take a brief plunge into some water as they fly through the air. For water birds like ducks and grebes, bathing is simply a matter of diving and rubbing the feathers together. Pigeons and starlings are not so keen on water and bathe by spreading their wings out in the rain, while sparrows often take a dust bath and rub their plumage in some dusty soil. Dusting like this probably removes pests from the feathers, and bathing in water is done to moisten the feathers as much as to clean them. Dripping plumage would be as useful to a bird as wet hair is

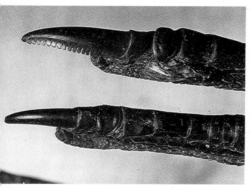

Below: Herons have an unusual comb-like claw that they use to comb a special powder through their feathers in order to soak up mud and slime.

Bottom: A mute swan preens its plumage. It runs its beak through the feathers to remove dirt and pests, and to arrange the feathers neatly. A swan has as many as 25,000 feathers, and has to keep them all in good order.

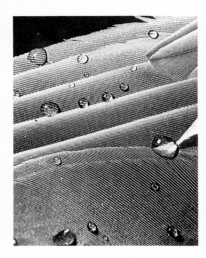

Above: This close-up of water droplets on a duck's plumage shows how waterproof it is.

Above right: A jay baths itself in a puddle of water. It has ruffled its plumage to allow the water to soak through the feathers.

comfortable to us, and the feathers are probably moistened to make them more pliable for preening and a third operation in feather care – oiling. Most birds oil their plumage by smearing a waxy substance over their feathers from an oil gland near the tail. The oil seems mainly to help waterproof the plumage, for most seabirds and water birds have a large oil gland. It may also help to provide the bird with vitamins.

Moulting

Tough though they are, feathers do not last for ever, and a bird has to renew its plumage at least once a year. Shedding old feathers and growing new ones is called moulting. Most birds moult gradually, a few feathers at a time, so that they do not have bare patches on their bodies and do not lose the ability to fly. Moulting usually takes place over several weeks in late summer, after the breeding season. Ducks, geese, swans and rails moult all their flight feathers at the same time and are unable to fly for a while. This places the birds in danger, and they may hide or gather in large groups for safety. Moulting time is very obvious in mallards, for the drakes lose their green heads and distinctive body patterns and become indistinguishable from the dull-coloured females. This change in plumage helps to camouflage the ducks at a critical time.

Moulting is done not only to replace worn plumage, but also to change colour. A special body moult may take place before the breeding season so that the birds acquire a colourful breeding plumage. This is true of divers, grebes, plovers and sandpipers, all birds which spend the winter in drab uniforms and brighten themselves for the spring and summer. In some cases, only the male changes, so that he will attract a female by his appearance when breeding time comes. This happens with some buntings and finches, especially the male chaffinch, whose head changes from brown to blue-grey as spring approaches.

Not all colour changes are caused by moulting. In some birds, the tips of the feathers wear away during the year and expose parts of a different colour. Starlings change their appearance in this manner, gaining white spots after moulting but losing them in summer as the feathers wear down.

The Feet Of Birds

The feet may not seem to be a very important part of the body for a flying creature. This is true of swifts, which spend the greater part of their lives in the air, eating and sleeping on the wing. When they do come down to breed, they cling to vertical surfaces and do not land on the ground if possible. Their four toes are arranged so that all four face forward, an unusual arrangement that helps them to cling on to something. If swifts do land, they are virtually helpless, for the legs do not have enough strength to allow them to jump back into the air.

However, swifts are unusual in this respect. Most birds spend a lot of time in trees, on the ground or on water, and their feet are adapted to help them survive in these places. The great family of perching birds, which includes many woodland birds and others that like to hop about on the ground, have feet with three toes facing forward and one backward. In this way, they can easily grasp a twig to perch or run and hop on the ground. Short legs allow them to move easily through trees and keep them low among the grass. Woodpeckers are tree-living birds with a different kind of feet. Because they drill into tree trunks, they have to grip the bark very firmly. Their feet have two toes facing forward and two backward so that they can balance evenly to do this, and they also brace themselves against a trunk with their tails.

Water birds have very special feet. Most use them as paddles to swim and dive and the feet are webbed, as in divers, gannets, cormorants, ducks, geese, swans, gulls, terns and auks. Some of these birds also use their wings to help them swim under water. Grebes and coots have feet that are very efficiently designed for swimming. Instead of being webbed, the toes have lobes that open as the feet push the water and close as the feet are brought back. However, most water birds are not very good at moving about on land, which they must do to breed and sometimes to feed. Grebes overcome this problem by building floating nests and so need never come ashore.

Some birds are at home on the land and in the water. Dippers are aquatic perching birds – a very unusual combination. Their perching-type feet enable them to get about on land and they use their wings under water. Wading birds such as herons, bitterns, plovers and sandpipers live by water and in marshes, standing in the shallows on long stilt-like legs or walking over the soft mud with long toes spread to take their weight.

Feet are also directly useful in feeding. Birds of prey can kill with their sharp talons and then hold their victims down as they tear them apart with their beaks. The talons of the osprey are especially adapted for catching live fish, which are its staple diet. Plunging down into the water, the bird grasps its prey with both talons, hooking them firmly into the fish. The four toes are of equal length, with spiky scales on the undersurface. Tits are very agile birds, and can use their feet to grasp food or hang upside-down to get at a morsel.

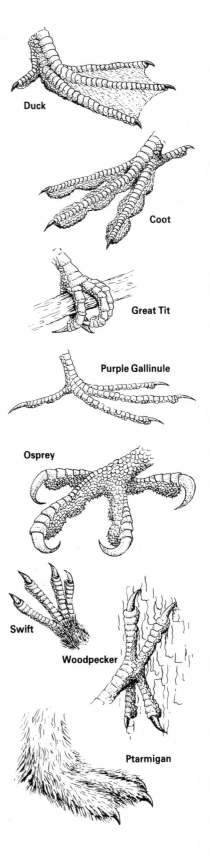

Duck

Coot

Great Tit

Purple Gallinule

Osprey

Swift

Woodpecker

Ptarmigan

23

Beaks And Eating

A bird has to use its beak like a hand as well as a mouth. It preens itself and gathers nesting material with its beak, and it may also use its beak to help get about (as a parrot does with the bars of a cage). But its most important use is in obtaining and eating food, and the shape of a bird's beak is closely related to its feeding habits. As the beak gets a lot of use, its surface does wear away; however, the beak grows continually to maintain its shape, just as human nails do.

Because birds of the same kind generally eat similar foods, they have a particular type of beak by which they can be identified. Birds of prey, from great eagles to diminutive falcons, and owls all have sharp hooked beaks to tear at the flesh of their prey. Finches, buntings and sparrows have stout beaks to crack open seeds and nuts. Fishing birds such as divers, grebes, herons and kingfishers have spear-like beaks to catch their prey, and wading birds generally have long beaks to probe in mud for food. Ducks, geese and swans have broad, flat bills that help them to pull at water plants. Warblers have small thin bills that are suitable for capturing insects in bushes, while birds that prefer flying insects have beaks that open wide to grab them in mid-air.

In some groups of birds that feed on the same general kind of food, the size or shape of beak may vary slightly so that each species can take a particular food but not others. In this way, the various kinds of birds can live alongside one another, as each searches for a different kind or size of food and competition is kept to a minimum. For example, a mudflat can support several different wading birds with beaks of various lengths. Each bird feeds at a different depth in the mud, finding its own particular kind of food. Seed-eating birds have beaks of varying size and strength. Some exist on large, tough seeds while others take smaller seeds that are easier to open. In this way, a small area of land may be home to several kinds of seed-eating birds because they all feed on different plants. In a garden in autumn, for example, you could easily see goldfinches taking seeds from the heads of thistles while greenfinches feed off the seeds in sunflowers.

However, few birds are limited to just one particular variety of food. Thrushes readily take worms, insects or fruit. If their favourite food becomes scarce, as it may well do in winter, many birds can turn to another source. Tits are principally insect-eaters, but flock around nut-feeders in winter. Some birds are omnivorous at all seasons of the year – they can eat just about anything they happen to find. Crows live in this way, their heavy beaks being shaped to allow them to deal with any likely source of food.

The illustration opposite shows in detail how beaks have adapted to the bird's way of life. The kestrel is a bird of prey and has a hooked beak to tear at flesh. The grey heron uses its long, sharp beak to spear fish, while the curlew probes deep into mud. The hawfinch cracks open tough seeds and nuts with its heavy bill, and the swift opens its mouth wide to catch flying insects. The great spotted woodpecker carves into wood with its chisel-like beak, while the treecreeper picks insects from the bark. The crossbill cuts open cones. The shoveler dabbles in water for food with its broad beak, while the puffin and goosander can both grip fishes with their beaks.

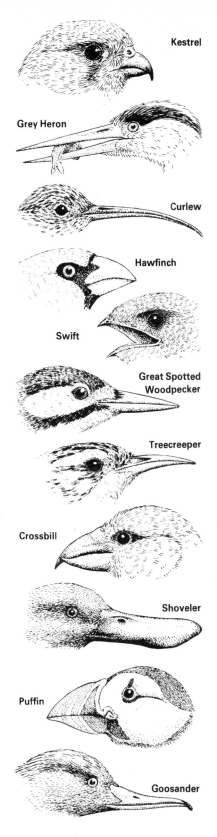

Kestrel

Grey Heron

Curlew

Hawfinch

Swift

Great Spotted Woodpecker

Treecreeper

Crossbill

Shoveler

Puffin

Goosander

Above: Wading birds, such as this black-winged stilt, have long legs and long necks that enable them to wade in shallow water and find food there. It feeds by probing the mud with its long straight beak.

Right: A kingfisher uses its long sharp beak to capture fish in swift dives into a lake or river. It then swallows the fish head first, so that the fins do not cause it to stick in the bird's throat.

Right: Birds have very keen vision. This golden eagle can spot a rabbit from a distance of two kilometres. We would have to use a telescope to see as well as an eagle. Eagles and all other birds of prey have sharply hooked beaks that they use to tear apart the bodies of their prey.

Right: Blackbirds spend much time on the ground, seeking worms in the soil. They have feet that allow them to move quickly on the ground, and sharp beaks that enable them to feed on insects and fruit as well as worms. Only the male is black; the female is dark brown.

Right: A greenfinch munches a peanut. Like other seed-eating birds, greenfinches have stout beaks that can crack open nuts and seeds. Their agile feet enable them to grip slender twigs and get at seeds that would otherwise be out of reach.

26

A Bird's Senses

A bird has the same kinds of senses as human beings have, but some are more highly developed and others are of less sensitivity in birds than they are in us. However, in their dependence on the various senses, birds are more like us than most other animals. Our most important senses are our sight and hearing, and birds rely heavily on these two senses as well.

Vision is the most highly developed sense in birds. Birds must have very sharp vision to enable them to find food, to find mates in the breeding season, to keep them together in flocks if necessary, and to avoid danger. A bird's eyeball is very large compared to its body size, and in big birds like eagles, the eyeball may be even larger than that of a human being. This gives such sharp vision that an eagle can spot prey such as a rabbit as far as two kilometres away – a distance at which we would need binoculars to see something of this size. Not all birds are hunters, but they also require good vision to detect the approach of enemies. In most birds, the eyes protrude and are set at the sides of the head, so they can see all around them and detect danger from any direction.

Woodcock

Owls have eyes at the front of their heads as we do, and their field of vision is restricted. However, they are hunters and seldom find themselves in danger, and they can turn their heads almost completely around to see things behind them. Most owls hunt by night and their vision is so acute that they can see things in light so dim that it would appear totally dark to us.

It is obvious from their colour patterns that birds can see in full colour as we do. Colour recognition is important in identifying other birds, and perhaps in finding food and rejecting inedible food sources. Water birds have a further aid to sight in the form of a transparent membrane that slides over the eyeball under water. This acts like a spectacle lens to keep everything in focus, whereas if we open our eyes under water, everything is blurred.

Owl

Birds use their voices to sing both a welcome and a warning to one another, and their sense of hearing is therefore well developed. It covers the same range as our hearing, but may be much more sensitive. Even when it gets so dark that their powers of vision fail them, some owls can still hunt by listening for the rustling sounds that a mouse or some other small nocturnal animal makes and then homing in on it.

The other three senses – of smell, taste and touch – are much less important to birds. Birds can smell – their nostrils are located at the base of the beak; however, this sense is not highly developed and seems to be little used in most birds. Taste seems to be of little use too. Colour vision helps birds avoid unpleasant or poisonous sources of food as these, like wasps, are often brightly coloured. Birds do have tongues, but hardly use them. Woodpeckers are an exception; they dart out a sticky-tipped tongue to capture insects.

Thrush

A bird's sense of touch seems to be much like ours. It probably helps birds to perch, and those that seek unseen prey, such as waders that probe in mud for worms and shellfish, have sensitive beaks to find their food. Some birds that pursue flying insects have bristles around their mouths, which may help the birds to sense vibrations produced by their prey.

Above: A woodcock has eyes at the top of its head so that it can see all round and spot danger coming from any direction. An owl has eyes at the front of the head so that the two fields of vision overlap and the owl can see in depth, as we do, and easily locate its prey. A thrush has eyes at the side of its head, so that it may both look for food and watch for danger at the same time.

27

Life Patterns

Birds have varied lives that are full of incident. In the course of a single year, an adult has to find a mate, nest and raise its young, moult its plumage and perhaps change colour and back again, and maybe migrate for the winter and return in the spring. Every day there is food to be found and the plumage to look after. Yet birds are creatures of habit. Within a season, a day will be much like the one before and next year is unlikely to differ overall from this year. Only unusual weather conditions are likely to force a bird to change its pattern of living, and many birds are unable to adapt to change – with severe consequences.

Living Together Or Alone

One of the most obvious features of a particular bird's behaviour is whether it lives in a group with other birds of the same kind or whether it likes to remain alone. In a garden, you will often see tits gathering around some food, each impatiently waiting its turn to peck at the food and get as much as possible as quickly as possible. At the same time, you may also spot a solitary robin or wren scurrying over the ground to find grubs or insects. When you travel through the countryside, you can look out and see flocks of lapwings or starlings feeding in the fields while perhaps a bird of prey, such as a kestrel, may be sighted hovering overhead, scanning the ground below with its keen eyes for rodents and the other small animals that go to make up its diet.

One factor is mainly responsible for a bird deciding whether it should seek the company of its fellows or whether it should remain aloof, and that is the availability of food. If a bird lives on food that is readily found in large quantities, then it will tend to live in flocks. Such food sources are trees laden with nuts, fruit or berries; fields ripe with corn; beaches or mudflats teeming with worms and shellfish; and bushes crawling with grubs and juicy insects. Flocks of birds can descend and each eat to their heart's content, though often to our detriment. Bullfinches can strip fruit trees of their buds and oystercatchers beat fishermen to beds of valuable shellfish. Flocking birds may also do us a service – gulls gather at rubbish dumps in the same way as they follow a ship or a plough and consume edible garbage as well as pests.

For many birds, food is not so readily available. The supply of worms in a garden is limited, and may not be enough to supply more than a single robin or blackbird that comes looking for food. Birds that hunt larger animals – birds of prey or owls seeking mice and other rodents or small mammals – may not find enough to eat if several birds depend on the same piece of land for food. Birds that feed in this way therefore tend to spread themselves out and seek food alone, giving themselves a better chance of survival. Another factor that makes them disperse is that a hunter is more likely to be successful on their own; a group of many birds is obviously more liable to warn potential victims of its approach and scare them away than if individual birds hunted alone.

Right: Birds like this robin are not social and never gather in flocks. In general, they have to spread themselves out over a particular area so that they each can get enough to eat.

Below: This group of guillemots (and one kittiwake) has gathered together in a colony on a cliff to gain safety in numbers while nesting. During the winter they disperse and roam the seas.

Safety In Numbers

Many birds also gather in flocks outside the breeding season because it is safer than living alone. Although the presence of a large group of birds is likely to attract the attention of birds of prey and other hunters, each individual bird within the flock has a better chance of survival than if it lived on its own. For every bird that is caught, many escape unharmed. The birds may also act together and confront danger. Small woodland birds will gang up and threaten a marauding owl or magpie, for example.

However, even the security of a flock is not a sufficient attraction to bring some birds together. If they do live in danger from hunters, they generally manage to survive by hiding. These solitary birds are often helped by being camouflaged so that they are difficult to see in their usual habitat. In a wood, you may hear the beautiful song of a thrush or warbler, but you will probably find it hard to spot. Birds that are hunters, such as eagles, falcons, owls and shrikes, have little to fear from other animals except for larger birds of prey, and generally can live alone with no worries.

Seasonal And Daily Changes

No species of bird can be entirely solitary. At some point in its life, it must form a pair with a bird of the opposite sex in order to breed. Once they are adult, almost all birds breed annually, and so regular changes occur in a bird's social life as the seasons come and go.

In fact, the breeding season may bring about a complete reversal of life styles. Seabirds such as auks spend the winter roaming the oceans on their own or in small groups and then, when the breeding season arrives, gather into huge colonies to raise their young. The birds spend the spring and summer living so close together that they can almost touch one another, while the autumn and winter sees them spread out over the seas, probably many kilometres apart. Conversely, birds that normally live in groups, such as tits and finches, pair off as the breeding season commences and remain paired until they have raised their young.

The reasons that these birds so abruptly change their life style include safety and the availability of food. Many seabirds gather in huge colonies instead of isolated pairs to breed. Most colonies are on cliffs or islands that are inaccessible to mammalian predators. Nevertheless, the eggs and young are always guarded by one adult while the other is away fishing at sea where it is more likely to catch enough to eat without competition from other seabirds. Therefore, as soon as they can safely leave their young, the birds disperse. The woodland birds, on the other hand, separate at breeding time, and the pairs of birds hide themselves away to nest in order to avoid danger. They also spread themselves out to ensure that there is enough food nearby to raise the young. During the rest of the year, they tend to gather in groups to find food because it is safer, and because food may be abundant – trees laden with fruits, berries and nuts, for example.

Birds may also have one way of life during the day and another at night. They may spend the daylight hours feeding alone and gather in groups to sleep at night. The starlings that flock to city centres as dusk falls have flown in from parks, gardens and the surrounding countryside after a day spent searching for food. They gather together to sleep for safety, and perhaps because it is warmer in the city than in the woodland where they would otherwise spend the night.

Keeping Together

If a flock of birds is to stay together, there must be ways for the birds to communicate with each other. Without communication, the birds could not act as a group and internal conflicts could not be resolved. The flock would rapidly split up as the birds began to behave in individual, different ways.

The birds must therefore behave in much the same way at the same time if the flock is to stay together and offer safety to its members. However, it is thought that birds have different roles within the flock. Some warn the group of danger, others may lead the flock in flight. Birds use their voices as they exercise their roles. They make alarm calls if danger is sighted and alert the rest of the flock. Other calls are given to get the birds into the air and follow the caller, while calls between the birds keep them together in the air.

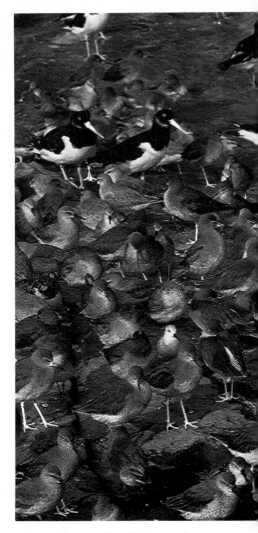

Above: Many wading birds – such as these redshanks, dunlins, knots, sanderlings and oystercatchers – congregate in large groups at the seashore in winter. They gain safety in numbers while feeding. During the breeding season they mostly disperse inland.

Right: Birds of prey are not social birds. They have to take their victims by surprise, and have more success if they hunt alone. The most common bird of prey in Britain and Europe is the kestrel, here seen dealing with a pheasant.

Such calls, which are completely different to a bird's normal song, are vital in keeping flocks together in the air at night – for example, during migration. But during the day, birds also rely on visual signals. The body pattern, particularly any bands of colour on the wings, help the birds to recognize their own kind and keep together in the flock. Ducks have brilliant patches of colour on their wings, and these are the same in both sexes, unlike the remainder of the plumage. The patches are more visible when the wings are spread than when they are closed. This is also true of the wingbars on birds such as finches, particularly goldfinches and chaffinches. As the bird takes flight, the stripes of colour immediately strike the eye. This sudden display serves to tell other birds still on the ground that they should immediately take flight, keeping the flock together when it has to make a quick departure to avoid danger.

Birds also use visual communication to keep the peace within the flock. Conflicts are likely to occur as the birds compete with each other for food or for somewhere to perch, for example. Coots seem to quarrel (constantly) whenever they gather together. However, although one bird must win such a quarrel and another must lose, the birds rarely fight. Instead, they use special postures that signify a threat and a submission. A bird will usually threaten another by pointing its beak at its rival, because its sharp beak is its main weapon. The opponent may reply with a similar threatening posture or it may back down, usually by turning its beak away or raising it in the air. This resolves the conflict without harming the birds involved, and without threatening the cohesion of the flock.

Mixed Flocks And Peck Order

When you see a group of birds, you will usually find that the birds in the flock are all of the same species – possibly even of the same sex. However, mixed flocks of birds of different species may be seen, especially in winter when food is scarce. Mixed flocks roam for food, and a source of food will attract birds of different species. This can be observed at a bird table.

If you study the various birds at a bird table, you will notice that they have a set of ranks. One species will generally be dominant, and will threaten the other birds so that it gets at the food first. Another species will come next, threatening all other species except the first one, and so on. This order of ranks is called a peck order. It varies from place to place, but you are likely to find that starlings feed first at the bird table, then house sparrows, followed by great tits and then blue tits.

A peck order also exists within a flock of the same species, some birds being more assertive than others. You can see this operation in a group of domestic chickens or pigeons, where the variations in plumage will help you to identify individual birds.

Day Birds And Night Birds

If you want to make a study of *all* the birds living in a particular area, you will have to be out at all hours of the day and night. You will be able to see many birds by day, but some birds are only active nocturnally.

Why should some birds prefer to sleep by day and be up and

about after dark, while others follow our general routine of working by day and resting at night? It might seem odd that a creature that has excellent vision should want to spend its waking hours in the dark. However, owls are able to hunt by night *because* they have very good sight, and can spot their prey in light so dim that it would appear dark to us. Other night birds do not depend on their vision as day birds do, and they may not in fact be able to see by day as well as day birds do.

Most birds are diurnal – that is, active by day. They are unable to find food in the night, and they use the cover of darkness to protect themselves when they are asleep. All the birds of prey are diurnal, though the hobby will hunt through the dusk for emerging bats and swallows going to roost. They seek live animals and have keen sight so they can spot their prey from a distance. Birds that hunt fish, such as ospreys and kingfishers, would also find it impossible to make a catch after dark. And birds that feed on seeds and fruits need light to search for food.

Nocturnal birds, apart from owls, do not rely so much on their sense of vision to find food. These night feeders include wading birds that probe in mud, sand or damp soil for worms, shellfish and other such morsels. Apart from woodcock, waders feed at night because they follow the tidal cycles. Birds that hunt flying insects, such as swifts and nightjars, often emerge at dusk and hunt on into the night, when the insects are most numerous. They may be able to sense the vibrations of the insects' flight to help them home in on their victims.

Some birds use the cover of darkness for activities other than feeding. It is thought that the nightingale and several other birds sing at night because the song is carried better and is more likely to be heard by a potential mate.

Although the night may bring safety, nocturnal birds are greatly at risk during the day when they must sleep. Owls have little to fear, though they may be woken from their slumbers by groups of angry woodland birds and made to move on and sleep elsewhere. Smaller birds avoid danger by hiding and using camouflage. The nightjar's brown-grey plumage makes it almost invisible against the dead leaves and branches in which it skulks away during the day.

Right: A barn owl flies back to its nest with a young rat in its mouth. Barn owls are able to hunt at night because they have sharp hearing that enables them to find their prey by the rustling noises it makes. Barn owls are also able to fly silently so that they cannot be heard.

Left: The hawfinch is a bird that lives by day. It needs the light to seek the nuts and seeds that it eats, and the bright colours of its plumage are designed to be seen by other hawfinches.

Above: Birds sometimes attack other creatures as a means of defending themselves, particularly at nesting time. This mute swan is about to attack a photographer who has intruded on its nest.

Attack And Defence

In the harsh world of nature, only the strongest and most able animals survive. A bird must be prepared to attack and defend itself at a moment's notice, if it is to live its full lifespan. The bird does not have to make a decision to act in its own interest. Its actions are instinctive, handed down by generation upon generation of forbears who each survived long enough to reproduce and pass on their abilities. In these, a bird is well served by its body and senses. An animal that can fly possesses the advantage of attacking from the air as well as being able to escape where no land-bound animal can follow. Its acute senses enable a bird to direct an attack efficiently, and also gain early warning that danger threatens. Furthermore, a sharp beak and claws make good weapons – to attack and fight back.

Fighting For Survival

Birds attack other animals, including birds of other species, mainly in order to kill and eat them. They are sometimes known to kill their own species. For example, in gull colonies it is commonplace for adults to eat wandering chicks, and nestling gannets are often killed, though not eaten, by adults other than their parents. However, not all birds are hunters; some are vegetarians and exist on a diet of seeds, nuts, fruits, berries or leaves. Pigeons and doves deserve their peaceful reputation in this respect, though they may turn to small animals such as grubs if necessary. Birds that are apparently placid by nature are not always to be trusted. Mallards, the common friendly ducks of park lakes and village ponds, normally content with pieces of bread, have been known to seize sparrows and drown them. Most birds are able to hunt other animals (including invertebrates), if only as a last resort when hunger drives them to it.

Birds of prey – eagles, hawks, buzzards, falcons and related birds – and owls habitually pursue larger animals such as rodents, other small mammals and birds. Many birds capture insects, grubs, worms, beetles, shellfish and other small animals, and several birds are adept at catching fish. In hunting their prey, birds employ a wide range of techniques.

Aerial Hunters

The most fearsome of hunting birds strike from the air. In this way, they can surprise their victims and fall on them at great speed – giving them little chance of escape. The attack is mounted in various ways. Large birds of prey such as eagles and buzzards search for prey by soaring high in the air and keeping a keen eye on the ground below. The sight of a reptile, amphibian or small mammal will bring them swooping down out of the sky, ready to deal a deadly blow with their needle-sharp talons and cruelly-hooked beak.

Harriers hunt at low level, patiently flying back and forth over marshland and moorland, and kestrels hover near the ground as they seek their food. Falcons such as the peregrine and merlin make spectacular attacks. Both prey on small birds, peregrines diving from above and merlins pursuing them near the ground. The peregrine swoops down on its victim at speeds of up to 130 kilometres an hour – so fast that if it misses its target, it may be unable to pull out of its dive and will hit the ground, killing itself. Normally, a peregrine kills with a slash of its talons and lets the body fall to the ground, where it feasts at leisure. A merlin speeds over moorland, taking small birds by surprise and twisting and turning in pursuit of them like a homing missile.

Above: Snowy owls live in the far north and prey mostly on lemmings, which are small rodents. This snowy owl has a lemming in its beak. Snowy owls have to hunt during the day because in summer in the far north, there is no night. The owl's unusual white colour could serve to camouflage it against the snow, but it is more likely that it helps the owl to remain unseen against the sky and surprise its prey.

35

Vultures are also birds of prey, but their hunting methods are very different. They rarely catch live animals and prefer to live on dead bodies or carrion, which they find by circling high in the air. Some vultures (of four species) live in southern Europe, but their numbers are declining as improved farming methods reduce the amount of carrion available.

Owls do not belong to the same order (group) of birds as the raptors, though they do seek much the same kind of prey. However, owls generally hunt by night, feeding on nocturnal animals such as mice. They have hooked beaks and sharp claws like the birds of prey, but they hunt in a different way. Owls have very keen vision and their eyes are mounted on the front of the head so that they can see in depth, as we do. These features enable owls to locate their prey with great accuracy in dim light. They can even hunt in what seems to be total darkness by listening for the noises made by prey animals. To avoid detection, owls can fly in total silence, having flexible wing feathers.

Flying insects are the target of such aerial hunters as swifts, swallows, flycatchers and nightjars. These birds have to be good fliers to capture the insects as they dart about in the air, combining speed with manoeuvrability. To ensure a catch, the birds open their mouths very wide. The swift is the fastest of all birds – indeed, of all animals. Spine-tailed swifts hold the record at 170 kilometres an hour. These birds live in Asia and their range does not extend to Europe.

Some birds get their food, or at least part of their diet, by robbing other birds of a catch. Skuas are adept at this, forcing sea birds like gulls and terns to drop a fish they have just caught. The skua then dives on its prey, often catching it before it strikes the ground or water below. If thwarted in its attack, it may force the other bird to the ground and rob it there.

Ground Hunters

Many birds hunt on the ground or in trees. Less ambitious than the birds of prey, they seek small animals, such as insects, grubs and worms. The treecreeper is one of several tree-living birds of woods and forests. It spends its days clambering up tree trunks and branches, continually probing into the bark with its long curved beak to find food. The woodland has its robbers too, generally birds of the crow family such as the magpie that readily take young birds and eggs from a nest.

The ground provides an important source of food for many birds. In a garden, you are likely to see wrens or dunnocks scurrying about looking for insects. Thrushes will land on a lawn and put their heads to one side as they peer intently at the ground, seeking worms. The seashore is another rich feeding ground. All kinds of wading birds may be seen there, digging in the mud or sand to find shellfish and worms. One of the more enterprising ground hunters is the turnstone, which gets its name from the way it turns over stones on the beach to seize any creature that may be sheltering underneath. The oystercatcher looks for common shellfish like mussels and cockles – for it is rarely able to feed on oysters. It opens the tightly-closed shells with a twist of its chisel-shaped beak.

Above: Birds of prey are masters of the air, striking fear into smaller birds. This sparrowhawk has seized a great tit and is preparing to eat it.

Water Hunters

Water birds face a fundamental problem when catching fishes and other underwater creatures. Being light so that they can fly, they tend to be buoyant in the water and find it difficult to stay beneath the surface.

Nevertheless, many birds do manage to survive by eating the animals that live in rivers, lakes and the sea. It is not always necessary to be able to swim or dive to live in this way. Long-legged birds like herons wade in the shallows and dart their sharp beaks down into the water whenever they spot a likely catch. However, most birds do take to the water to feed.

Being buoyant, many birds are good swimmers and some simply feed at the surface of the water. Gulls and dabbling ducks like the mallard live in this way, simply reaching into the water to feed. Other birds feed under water, forcing their way down into the water by diving from the air. Gannets dive into the sea with a huge splash, emerging a few seconds later with a fish. Terns also make brief dives from the air just off the shore. At lakes and rivers, kingfishers make a lightning plunge into the water to grab a fish with their large, sharp beaks, and ospreys make a catch with their sharp talons, splashing down feet-first into the water.

Several birds are capable of making long dives beneath the water and chasing fish. Grebes, divers and cormorants dive from the surface, and do not need the assistance of a headlong plunge from the air first. These birds are not as buoyant as other birds, and so can stay down more easily. They propel themselves with their feet, which are webbed or lobed, and steer with their wings. Auks, such as razorbills, guillemots and puffins, are also good divers and they swim underwater with their wings, using their feet like a rudder to turn. One of the most extraordinary diving birds is the dipper, which is a land bird and lives by mountain streams. It feeds on underwater insects by spreading its wings so that the current forces it down. Dippers can walk along the bed of a stream in this way!

Below: The grey heron feeds by attacking fish and other water animals. It stands or wades in shallow water, then stabs down into the water with its long sharp beak.

Above: Many birds employ camouflage as a means of defence, especially birds that live or nest on the ground. This woodcock is sitting on its nest among some rough grass, but its streaky brown plumage makes it almost invisible.

Above: In summer, the ptarmigan is brown and matches the low plants among which it lives.

Below: In winter, the ptarmigan becomes completely white so that it cannot be seen against the snow.

Defence Actions

Most birds will have to deal with several different enemies if they are to live their full span of life. They may come under attack by other birds, rats, snakes, foxes, cats, dogs or human beings. Birds are generally resourceful creatures, able to defend themselves when necessary.

However, many birds make sure that danger threatens them as little as possible. They keep out of harm's way by living in remote places, high up in trees or hidden away in bushes or reeds where an enemy is unlikely to find them. Auks nest in huge colonies on high cliffs where no land animal can threaten them, and rooks build their nests at the very tops of high trees for safety. Such precautions are most necessary in early life, for young birds are highly vulnerable. An adult bird can usually escape danger simply by flying away.

Nevertheless, birds may have to take action in their own defence and to protect their young. Attack is one form of defence, and nesting birds are sometimes driven to attack an intruder to drive it away from the nest. Birdwatchers who approach nesting skuas too closely are likely to be dive-bombed by the angry parents, and swans are reputed to be able to break an arm with a blow of their wings. The fulmar has a very unusual but effective defence action. It will spit a foul-smelling oil at any creature that threatens its young (a habit that gave the bird its name, as fulmar means 'foul gull' – fulmars resemble gulls). Smaller birds may have to band together to drive an enemy away. Aroused by an alarm call from one member of the flock, the birds take wing and mob or harass the animal – perhaps a sleepy owl or an inquisitive cat – until it goes away.

Some birds get rid of intruders in less direct ways. Several waders are well-known for the way that they will decoy a marauder such as a fox or dog away from their nests, which are made on the ground and hidden among vegetation. The parent bird attracts the raider's attention by walking away from the nest and dragging a wing as if it is broken. The intruder follows the bird until it has been led a safe distance from the nest, and then the bird simply takes wing and escapes.

Sitting It Out

Many birds employ a most effective defence method that involves them in no positive action at all. They hide away among leaves, grass or other vegetation and rely on the colour of their plumage to conceal them. These birds can be greenish in colour, as are many warblers, tits and finches, or brown to grey, or streaky in appearance, as are several thrushes and buntings, larks, sparrows and the wren. Such plumage makes good camouflage. Among the best matched birds are the nightjar (see page 159) and the bittern. When danger threatens, a bittern will freeze stockstill with its head pointed upwards. Its streaky light brown plumage then conceals it perfectly amid the reeds in which it lives. Should a wind ruffle the reeds, then the bittern sways to and fro with them, maintaining its disguise at all times.

Why then are some small woodland birds brightly coloured – like the bullfinch, goldfinch, chaffinch and yellowhammer? The colours of these birds are apparent to us because we usually see them in the open. Among the packed trees and bushes in a wood, it is rather gloomy and the colours do not stand out so much.

The most remarkable example of camouflage in a European bird is that of the ptarmigan, which lives in the far north and among high mountains. This bird spends the winter in a snow-covered landscape, and the summer on bare rock or among low plants that die off in the autumn. Patches of snow lie on the ground in spring and early winter. To keep up with these rapid changes in its surroundings, the ptarmigan moults three times a year. In winter it is white, and in summer it becomes brown (except for the wings). The bird assumes a grey colour in the autumn, and in spring and late autumn it goes patchy as it moults. These changes keep the ptarmigan adequately protected at all seasons of the year from such predators as the gyrfalcon, the most northerly bird of prey.

Below: When it feels threatened in any way, the bittern freezes stock-still among the reeds where it lives. Its plumage is exactly the same colour as the reeds, and it is very difficult to spot.

Storing Food And Using Tools

The winter can be hard for birds. Food may become scarce at a time when it is needed in quantity to provide warmth. Many birds avoid such hardship by migrating to warmer places or to places where food is easier to find, but a lot of birds stay put for the winter. A few of them overcome food shortages by storing food in the autumn to feed on during the winter.

The best-known and most accomplished of storing birds is the jay. Jays belong to the crow family, whose members all show a fondness for hoarding things. Magpies are renowned for their habit of taking shiny trinkets from houses and keeping them in their nests. Jays and nutcrackers, which are also members of the crow family, are more sensible and hoard food – jays store acorns, and nutcrackers store hazel nuts and pine cones. The birds can hold several acorns or nuts in their mouths at once, and during the autumn they gather thousands. Instead of eating them all, they store much of this food by burying it here and there in the ground. When winter comes, the birds go to their food stores and dig up the acorns, nuts or cones. They are able to locate the hidden supplies, even when the ground is covered with snow. They probably remember landmarks, such as nearby trees, to help them find the food again. However, they are not always successful and the buried seeds may take root and grow into trees. In this way, the birds help the spread of woods and forests.

A few birds have adapted to using 'tools' as another aid to eating. One of the Galapagos Island finches uses sticks to probe in tree trunks for grubs. The most interesting example of tool-using in a European bird is that practised by the Egyptian vulture, though it employs its particular technique only to the south of its range in Africa and not in Europe. There, ostrich eggs provide a good source of food for this species of vulture, but the eggs are tough-shelled and hard to crack open with the beak. The Egyptian vulture therefore takes a stone in its beak and drops it on the egg to break it open. Several common birds employ the reverse method to get at their food. Song thrushes will pick up snails and smash their shells by beating them against a stone, and gulls will drop shellfish and crabs on to a rock to break them open. The lammergeier, another vulture, similarly cracks open bones (to get out the marrow) by dropping them on to rocks from a considerable height.

Instinct Or Intelligence?

Such bird activities as food storing and tool using may appear to be intelligent, but they are in fact instinctive. The bird does not consciously think about how it can get at some food and then devise a method of doing so. It acts by instinct, driven by impulses that it inherits from its parents. However, the instinct may require some practice to make the resulting action perfect. Young Egyptian vultures will pick up a stone if they see an ostrich egg, but they may have to try dropping the stone several times before they succeed in hitting the egg.

Birds may develop apparently intelligent ways of finding food if the opportunity arises. An interesting example is the way tits have taken to opening milk bottles by pecking through the thin bottle

Top: A black heron (an African bird) raises its wings to shade the water so that it can more easily spot a fish. This action may indicate intelligence, for herons are quick to learn new ways of getting food.

Above: To protect its young, the skylark covers its nest with dead grass. This may shade the eggs or young from the hot sun, or help to conceal them from hungry predators.

Above: The song thrush breaks open snail shells by seizing the snail in its beak and striking the shell against a rock, called an anvil. This is an example of tool-using among birds, which is uncommon.

caps. Clever though this may seem, it must be remembered that tits are agile little birds that can clamber virtually anywhere to peck at almost anything. Given thin-capped milk bottles, they could hardly fail to succeed in opening them. Nevertheless, they do show great adaptability in taking so readily to a new source of food. A similar adaptability is shown by crows, which can turn to almost any source of food at any time. They accustom themselves quickly to new situations; for example, they soon realize whether a scarecrow or any other device for frightening them away from crops is likely to cause them harm.

Some actions performed by birds do seem to exhibit definite intelligence, however. Tits and crows are good at solving problems put to them, such as working out a series of actions needed to get at some food. Herons will raise their wings to shade the surface of the water and see any fish more clearly. In addition, faced with the problem of getting near the fish, they have been seen to place pieces of food in the water to act as bait. Moorhens will obtain food frozen in ice by sitting over the food and melting the ice with body heat.

41

Breeding

Breeding is the most important task a bird undertakes in its life. A bird may travel thousands of kilometres to breed, it may change colour, it may have to fight for the chance to produce young, and it will certainly have to work hard to raise them. Breeding requires a complete change in life style for almost all birds, but they could never shirk this particular duty. They are impelled to breed by instinct, however irksome it may be.

This inner compulsion to produce young has been handed down to birds by many, many centuries of evolution. If the instinct were not as strong as it is, breeding success would have declined and the species would have died out long ago. Every species now on Earth is here because it reproduces.

The Breeding Season

Birds do not spend all their time breeding. As the seasons of the year come and go, some times are better than others for raising young. It would not be sensible to try and bring up a batch of hungry, naked nestlings when the weather is cold and food scarce. Birds therefore confine their breeding activities to a particular season of the year, and follow this routine every year. In Europe, and most other (non-equatorial) parts of the world, birds set about breeding in early spring and continue until late summer. In the tropics, they may breed in the wet or dry season instead. By observing a set breeding season, the birds produce their young as the weather becomes warm and foods, particularly grubs and insects, are plentiful. The days are longer too, giving the parents more time to gather food for their young. In the far north, breeding birds can work virtually non-stop in the perpetual light of mid-summer. They must raise their young quickly, for the summer will be short.

The exact timing of the breeding season depends on the kind of food the birds feed to their young. Robins and blue tits give them caterpillars, which appear early in summer, whereas young spotted flycatchers need flying insects, which do not appear until later. Robins and blue tits therefore breed earlier than spotted flycatchers. The weather may also affect the timing of breeding, and birds will start early if there is a warm spring. Other factors that affect the availability of food will influence the onset of the breeding season. For example, tawny owls breed early in spring because it is easier to catch a large quantity of mice and voles to feed their young at this time than in mid-summer when woodland plants have grown and hide the owls' prey. Also important in the timing of breeding seasons is the extra food needed by the female to form her eggs. This is one reason behind courtship feeding.

Numbers And Survival

Birds may breed two or even three times in a single season if the weather and food supply are very favourable. Each brood usually contains several young – though some seabirds and large birds of prey are content to raise only one. However, these birds generally

Above: Among the courtship actions performed by birds is a kind of ritual feeding in which one bird feeds its mate as if it were a young bird. Here, two rooks are indulging in courtship feeding.

live longer than birds that have more young every year, and in their lifetime may produce as many young. Certainly, a pair of birds will produce far more than the two young birds needed to replace them when they die. But life is hard, especially for young birds, and not many of them will live long enough to become adults and themselves breed. No more can survive than the food supply and weather conditions permit, unless the birds are prepared to move, which few are. But by producing more young than can live to breed or acquire territories if they do live, the parent birds ensure that their species will remain at its maximum possible level and not decline. Moreover, this annual surplus of young can make up for excessive adult deaths, for example in cold weather or an oiling incident, and this is how bird populations can recover fairly quickly from short-term disasters.

In captivity, where birds do not live with any of these risks, they may live a long time. A caged parrot may live as long as its keeper and survive for 70 years. Even in the wild, a few birds will complete their full natural lifespan. Large seabirds such as gannets and fulmars are thought to be capable of reaching the age of fifty, and even small common birds such as tits, sparrows, chaffinches and starlings may survive until they are about ten years old. However, these are the lucky ones. The average lifespan of each bird is only about a year and a half even for those birds that survive to become adult. Larger birds do better. A blackbird can expect to live for two and a half years and a herring gull six years on average. Swifts live as long as herring gulls, a tribute to their aerial mode of life.

Below: In many birds, the male and female have plumage of different colours. This pair of pheasants are very unalike, the male having very bright colours and the female being a dull brown. However, the female raises the young alone, and being drab in colour helps to conceal her when she is at the nest. If the male were also at the nest, his bright colours would attract enemies.

Finding A Mate

As a rule, birds are suspicious creatures. They have to be continually on the lookout for danger, and it is only sensible for them not to trust other animals. This wariness extends to birds of their own species, even though they need not fear attack from them. But the birds have the same tastes in food and must compete with each other to eat. Quarrels over food are inevitable. If the birds are not forced to live together for safety, they will go their own way and seek food alone.

All this has to change as the breeding season approaches. Male and female birds must form pairs to mate, and then they usually have to stay together for the remainder of the breeding season to raise their young. They are faced with the task of sharing duties and cooperating with each other to a high degree. Yet at the same time, the male bird must become more, not less, aggressive towards other males in order to prevent rival birds breaking up the pair or otherwise trespassing on a feeding territory. Then, at the end of the breeding season, the birds must revert to their former behaviour until the following spring.

Birds alter their behaviour in these ways as a result of hormone changes in their bodies. These changes seem to be triggered mainly by the length of daylight, so that they accurately follow the seasons of the year. But chemical changes are not enough to bring about such great differences in behaviour. They must be reinforced with special actions that reassure and convince the birds as they seek to get together. These actions make a special bird 'language' called courtship.

Displays And Dances of Birds

In almost all species of birds, it is the male who has to court the female and persuade her to be his mate. She of course may encourage him and respond to his courtship, but he generally has to make the first move. The phalaropes, which are dainty wading birds, are an exception. The females not only court the males but are more brightly coloured, which is very unusual. Two species, the grey- and red-necked phalaropes, are found in northern Europe.

As birds have good vision and can see in colour, they often conduct their courtship in the form of colourful visual signals. In many species of birds, such as ducks, pheasants and most finches, the male is brighter in colour than the female, which is often drably dressed. The male's plumage may intensify in hue as the spring approaches, and he may even develop a special patch of colourful feathers especially for the breeding season. The male chaffinch grows a blue-grey crown to his head, and the brambling goes deep black. One of the most spectacular courting plumages of any European bird is that grown by the male ruff. This bird gets its name from the broad collar of coloured feathers that adorns its neck during the breeding season, as it resembles the elegant ruffs that people wore in Tudor times, about four hundred years ago. The colour of the ruff varies from one bird to the next.

These differences in colour not only help the male and female birds to find and recognize one another, but help to make the female bird feel more at home with the male. Several male birds put on a

Above: A ringed plover stands in front of a mirror, reacting to its reflection as if it were another bird. It raises its tail feathers in a fan, an aggressive display intended to threaten a rival bird.

Right: Mutual preening, in which each bird preens the other with its beak, is another common courtship action. These spoonbills are preening each other as part of their courtship.

Right: The male red-breasted merganser, a species of duck, performs its courtship. This consists of a strange posture known as the 'curtsey' display.

Far right: Male ruffs gather in groups to court the females or reeves. They grow special collars of plumage called ruffs, and parade in a field or some other open ground before the females.

44

Above: The courtship dances of pairs of great crested grebes may start with bouts of head shaking.

Above: The courtship actions are often similar to everyday actions. Here one bird preens itself.

Above: The dances become more involved in the later stages of courtship. One bird may offer the other a fish.

Above: In the 'cat' display, one bird spreads its wings before the other, helping to reduce aggression between the birds.

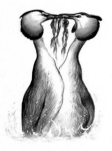

Above: In the 'penguin' dance, the birds dive and swim towards one another, rising from the water with weed in their beaks.

really special show for their prospective mates by making postures that display a particularly colourful part of their plumage. No British or other European bird can match the breathtaking displays of the peacock or the birds of paradise, which are among the great marvels of the bird world. However, the ruff's display in which it raises its colourful collar to frame its face is extraordinary, and so too is the display of the great bustard. This bird, sadly now rare, seems to turn itself inside-out to raise great fans of white plumage before its mate. A more frequent sight is the display of the black grouse or blackcock, a moorland and upland forest bird. The black males raise their white tail feathers in a fan to entice the brown females to mate.

Of course, not all birds have special courtship plumage and in many species, the males and females are exactly alike. Nevertheless, these birds still make special displays at courting time to cement the developing relationship between them. It has been shown that a male penguin does not know the sex of the bird he is displaying to, until he gets the behavioural response.

The display consists of a series of special postures or movements that convey the birds' feelings and intentions towards one another. The display varies from one species to the next, but it will contain poses that invite the female to mate with the male and postures that calm the aggressive feelings they may still have towards other birds. The male bird may spread his wings or shake or dip his head to 'advertise' for a female, and then the birds may cross their bills or face away from each other to reduce their suspicions. This calming display is often similar to actions that the birds take to resolve quarrels peacefully.

Many birds go further than mere poses or postures to attract and reassure a mate. Special actions may be required, some so lively that they amount to courtship dances. Many of these active displays involve the birds in movements similar to those that they will later use in raising their young. For example, many finches have a courtship ritual in which the female sits on the nest and begs food from the male bird. This action may produce parental feelings in the birds and maintain their tenderness towards one another. Actions like nest-building are another feature of courtship. Great crested grebes perform extraordinary courtship displays that involve many kinds of postures and culminate in the 'penguin' dance. The pair of birds dive and then swim towards one another before rearing up out of the water, facing each other with pieces of weed in their beaks. Grebes build floating nests of water plants, and the climax of the dance anticipates nest building for them. The most vigorous of courtship dances are those performed by cranes, in which they leap crazily up and down, grabbing sticks or blades of grass in their beaks and throwing them up in the air. Young birds and females also dance and leap in the air.

Songs And Sounds

The language of courtship is not entirely visual. Birds have keen hearing and strong voices, and they make good use of them in the breeding season. Birds may use their voices at any time of the year to utter calls of alarm and calls with similar social purposes. These

Right: No bird can match the magnificent courtship display of the peacock (the male peafowl). This bird is not a wild bird of Britain and Europe, but can be seen in captivity in parks and zoos.

Below: A male black grouse or blackcock courts a female by raising a beautiful fan of white feathers. Black grouse live on high moors, and courtship may start while snow is still on the ground.

are short phrases designed to convey information quickly to other birds – for example, that danger threatens, or to keep together.

But during the breeding season, some birds extend their repertoire by singing. Few birds sing throughout the year, and the songs seem to be designed for courtship and advertising their territory, though birds may also sing for the joy of it.

A song consists of a particular phrase or a series of phrases that is repeated over and over again. It may be musical, like the liquid notes of the songthrush, or it may grate on our ears, like the harsh sounds of the great reed warbler. The song may sound totally unlike anything that could be produced by a bird, as in the foghorn-like booming of the bittern.

But however it sounds, the song will be music in the ears of the female bird – for it is mainly the male that sings and not the female. In courtship, birdsong has a rather different purpose to visual display. It is produced principally to proclaim a male bird's presence on his territory – the area in which he intends to breed – and to attract a female bird to the territory. It is effective over a greater distance than a visual display designed to advertise for a mate. Singing is therefore most important at the beginning of the breeding season. However, birds continue to sing when they have formed pairs and carry on through the breeding season, though they will become less vocal once the young have hatched. Apart from the enjoyment gained from singing, a male bird's song also serves to warn rival males away from the territory. It may therefore be necessary to continue singing to prevent raids into the territory by rivals.

These warnings may be answered by a nearby male, producing a duet of phrases. The song may sound like one of love as you hear two birds singing to each other, but it is more likely to be a fanfare to

Below: Birds sing as the breeding season approaches in order to attract a mate. They may also continue to sing throughout the season in order to reassure their mates, and the song also serves to warn off rival birds. Here a blackbird sings at the top of a hedgerow, making sure that it will be heard and seen.

battle. However, some pairs of birds sing duets in which the male and female answer one another. Most of these birds are only to be found in the tropics, but pairs of owls may call each other in the night. The famous 'to wit to woo' of the tawny owl is made by two birds singing, either a male and female or perhaps a young and an adult bird.

A bird that seeks a mate will have to make its presence known to all the other birds around, whether it advertises itself by singing or by displaying. Many birds have song posts – exposed branches or high perches from which they can easily be heard and seen. There they will sing to their heart's content – like the yellowhammer, which can be seen perched at the top of a hedge or bush, singing out its famous refrain of 'a little bit of bread and no cheese'. Some birds make song flights so that their songs will descend from the air. Larks flutter up from the ground and ascend into the sky, singing all the time.

Pleasant though such an activity may be, it is also dangerous, for birds of prey or other enemies may be looking and listening. This is why birds tend to stop singing when their young hatch and later when they moult – though they may also be too busy finding food for their young to sing then. Earlier in the breeding season though, the birds may seem to throw caution to the winds and ignore the possibility of danger, but this may not really be so. Much bird behaviour involves opposing impulses. The bird's desire to breed will conflict with its natural wariness and, for a time at least, the strong drive to breed will overcome its fears.

Some birds do exhibit caution, however, and do not make themselves visible when they sing. A nightingale will sing at night for this reason, and a bittern booms from the safety of a reed-bed. The sounds carry far; the nightingale's song echoes in the stillness of the night, and the bittern's strange low notes have great penetrating power. To such timid birds, song is all-important for they dare not show themselves off to attract a mate.

Song may also be all-important for birds to identify one another. The chiffchaff and willow warbler are two species of warbler that look superficially alike, and they both live in woodland. One way to tell them apart is to listen for their songs. The chiffchaff gets its name from its unmusical two-note song, whereas the willow warbler sings a musical, liquid phrase. Sounding so different, the songs bring birds of the same species together and ensure successful breeding.

However musical or unmusical they may sound to our ears, most birds use their voices to seek a mate and proclaim that they are in business for breeding. Some birds make inviting sounds by other means that do not involve singing. Woodpeckers are given to drumming. They use their beaks to make a rattling noise on a piece of dead branch, producing a loud drumming sound that immediately alerts any other woodpecker in the surrounding woodland. Each species has its own particular rhythm of sounds just as songbirds have their set phrases of notes. The snipe makes a strange bleating sound by diving through the air with its tail feathers held out, and woodpigeons perform display flights in which they clap their wings together to call attention to themselves.

Above: The willow warbler (top) and the chiffchaff (bottom) are two species of warblers which resemble one another so closely that it is almost impossible to tell them apart. However, their voices give them away instantly. The willow warbler has a musical song of descending notes, whereas the chiffchaff has a monotonous two-note song from which it gets its name.

Taking A Territory

To get through life, birds find it necessary to establish some kind of territory that they can call their own. The territory is an area that 'belongs' to a bird. If another bird of the same species should try to enter the territory, then it will be repulsed. Seabirds that roam the seas during the winter months, and uncommon birds that are thinly spread throughout a region, may not have to defend their territories as no other birds of their species will normally come within striking distance. However, every bird has to admit another of its own kind in order to breed, and the territory will then usually belong to the pair of birds for the breeding season.

Territorial behaviour is most evident during the breeding season, but birds may continue to exercise territorial rights after they have split up and gone their separate ways once the young have been raised. A robin will chase other robins out of a garden during the winter, behaving just as pugnaciously as it does during the breeding season. Birds that roam in flocks during the winter may keep a small area around themselves and stop other birds from approaching too closely. Similarly, birds that roost in flocks, such as starlings thronging the ledges of buildings in city centres, may keep a certain distance apart throughout the night.

Two basic factors determine the kind of territory that a bird requires, and these are the same two factors that decide its general social life – the need to find food and the need to be safe. These needs are much greater in the breeding season when the birds have young to look after as well as themselves. Several birds use the territory as an exclusive area of ground that will provide a safe nesting site and sufficient food to raise a family. Robins, wrens and blackbirds depend totally on their territories in this way, and they will defend them fiercely. Robins of either sex become enraged at the sight of a red-breasted intruder – even a pink-breasted chaffinch – and will attack mercilessly. Both robins and blackbirds have been seen to attack their own reflections in car hub caps, so strong is the instinct to defend their territory. Birds that use their territory as a feeding ground each require a comparatively large area of land. With small birds like robins, a garden should suffice while large birds of prey may guard several square kilometres.

Many birds have territories that provide places in which to nest but not to feed. The birds fly away from the territory to gather food, but defend the area around the nest. Seabirds that gather in huge colonies to nest – such as auks – behave in this way. The sea provides them with a vast larder of food, and so there is no need to defend a feeding area. The nest has to be defended from aerial raiders such as gulls that will snatch the eggs and young if they are not well protected. The birds therefore gather together to find safety in numbers. They do not get so close that incubating and brooding adults can peck at one another though there may be vocal squabbling, but they are near enough together to mount a concerted attack on any intruders.

Several woodland birds, including finches such as the goldfinch, also use their territories only for nesting and leave them to find food for their young. They do not pack themselves together like auks do, for this would invite the attention of predators. Safety is gained by

Above: Many birds take territories at nesting time. Around this single marsh warbler's nest, hidden away for safety in some bushes, will be an area defended from other marsh warblers. The parent birds find food for their family in their territory.

concealment and so the birds space themselves out over small areas, for they do not need to reserve such large areas as birds that feed in their territories.

Meeting Places

The proclamation of a piece of ground as a particular territory is generally the act that opens the breeding season. The male birds generally take up their territories first and then set about finding a mate. However, some birds that migrate to their breeding grounds may begin courting one another on the journey there before the territory is reached. Others, such as ducks, pair during the winter.

Once a territory has been established, courting begins in earnest. By singing and courting displays, the male will try to attract a female bird to his territory. His behaviour at this time also serves to warn off rival males from the territory, and he will defend its boundaries vigorously. The female may join in defending the territory once she has settled there. Apart from its value in providing a safe nesting place and possibly food as well, the act of keeping a territory may help to bind the pair of birds together and so help them to raise their young.

Some birds become so attached to their territory that they return to it when the breeding season comes round every year. For example, gannets usually return to the same colony, and many raptors return to their same nesting sites. Territories, however, do vary in size, and may be large when population density is low, and small when there are more males competing for the space. Nevertheless, the same birds often pair up again the following year. But they part as the breeding season ends and go their separate ways until the following year. A few birds may pair for life, spending all their time together. Swans, geese and jackdaws are believed to live in this way.

Some birds display no fidelity to each other whatsoever, and use the territory merely as a place in which to meet and mate. They include black grouse, pheasants and ruffs. As the breeding season arrives, the birds gather at their courting grounds. These are areas of land on which the males do their courting in groups and not singly. However, each male defends a small territory within the courting ground. There he sings and displays to attract a female bird, though the performance is also intended to preserve the territory against encroachment by rival males. The females look on, and each eventually decides upon a partner. Mating takes place there and then, after which the females disperse to nest and raise the young alone. The males remain, eager to gain the favours of other females.

This behaviour may seem callous in that the female is left to raise the family without help. However, like all forms of behaviour, it has survival value. In the species which act in this way, the male is generally brightly coloured and the female is drab, which helps to bring the birds together for breeding. However, his gaudy plumage would expose the young to danger if he were to help raise them, for it would attract predators to the nest. Being dull brown in colour, the female can live in safe concealment among the bushes or low plants in which these birds generally like to nest.

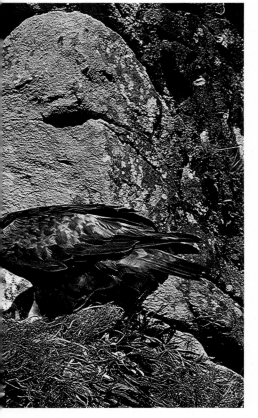

Below: Birds of prey have large territories because their food is not abundant. This golden eagle is raising its two young on a cliff ledge, where they will be safe from foxes and other marauding animals. The parent birds will find food in the valley below.

Nest Building

Even before it is born, a bird has to face danger. A bird's egg is a delicate object, easily broken, and it must be kept warm if the embryo inside is to develop into a fully-formed bird. Furthermore, the contents of the egg are tasty and eggs are sought after by other animals as food. Once safely hatched, the young bird is usually helpless and an easy target for any determined hunter. Other animals will be raising their own young at the same time and seeking food with great vigour, so the first weeks or months of life are very hazardous indeed.

If a bird is to breed successfully, it must provide its eggs and young with protection – to keep them warm and sheltered, and to prevent predators getting at them. Birds do this by making a nest for the eggs and young. The kind of nest that a bird builds and the place it chooses vary greatly from one species to another. But the purpose is always the same – to maximize the survival of the young.

A bird shelters its eggs and later its young in one of two main ways. It either builds a construction from materials that are readily available to house the eggs, or it places the eggs in a hole, which the bird may make itself. Danger in the form of other animals comes from two directions – from the ground or the air. Mammals such as rats, weasels, foxes and squirrels, and possibly snakes, will prowl about and perhaps climb into trees in search of eggs and young birds. Birds of the crow family – crows, magpies, jackdaws and jays – will raid nests from the air, and so too will gulls. In fact, gulls are so given to nest-raiding that they sometimes attack their neighbours in the nesting colony.

Kinds Of Nests

Many birds find that the best way to keep their eggs and young out of danger is to conceal the nest. A small bird would stand little chance of fighting off a marauding fox or weasel, and so tries to make sure that its nest will not be found in the first place. Woodland birds, such as thrushes, finches and warblers, hide their nests among the leaves of bushes and trees. They generally build a cup-shaped nest by weaving grass or other plant fibres or twigs together, and lining the cavity with feathers, fine grasses or mud to make the nest comfortable. The nest is anchored to a fork in the twigs or branches. The parent birds are mostly greenish or brownish in colour, so that they do not give the position of the nest away should any predator come near. Birds that are more vulnerable, such as the brightly-coloured bullfinch and linnet, tend to hide themselves among brambles or thorny bushes such as gorse. Even if the parents' plumage should act as a beacon for any raider, it may not be able to penetrate the thorns and get at the nest.

Many birds nest on the ground, a situation that would seem to expose them to danger. However, many successfully conceal their nests among the vegetation on the woodland floor or among the

Left: Both male and female tits are brightly coloured. They therefore hide their nest away in a tree or bush, so that their bright plumage does not attract enemies to the nest.

Little Tern

House Martin

Woodpecker

Nest Box

Reed Warbler

Great Crested Grebe

Song Thrush

Long-tailed Tit

Robin

Golden Eagle

grasses, heathers or other low plants of more open locations, such as fields and moors. The nests are made from the plant materials in which they are concealed, such as grass and dead leaves, and are very hard to spot. Many ground nesters, like larks and pipits, are a dull brown and match their surroundings as closely as do their nests. But the nests have no protection other than concealment, and so the parent birds often have ways of defending their eggs and young, such as the decoy tactics employed by plovers.

Many seabirds make virtually no nest at all. They lay their eggs on the ground, perhaps digging a hollow for them and decorating them with some scraps of vegetation. This may seem a foolish thing to do, and yet the birds survive. In many cases, the eggs are blotched and look more like pebbles than eggs so that they escape the attention of any raiders. Also, such birds tend to breed in isolated places – beaches, cliffs and islands – where danger is likely to come only from gulls or other seabirds. Most of them deal with this threat by nesting in colonies and finding safety in numbers.

Freshwater birds may also place their nests in inaccessible locations as seabirds do. Swans and ducks will make for an island in a lake or river if there is one to be found, while grebes build a floating nest of water plants and anchor it to reeds.

Several birds conceal their eggs completely by building a nest with a roof, leaving only a small entrance hole to get in and out. Magpies and wrens weave these dome-shaped nests, and house martins use mud to construct a nesting chamber against the wall of a building. Even if they were to find such a nest, predators would not necessarily suspect that it contained eggs or young. Long-tailed tits go one stage further and conceal their domed nests by covering them with lichens to camouflage them in the bushes and trees where they build.

Many birds like to hide their eggs in nesting chambers, but do not go to the trouble of building one. Instead they use holes. Hollows in trees or crevices in walls or rocks provide nesting places for many birds, among them owls, starlings, jackdaws, tits and sparrows. Kingfishers and sand martins nest in holes in river banks or sand banks, and puffins and shearwaters use holes in the ground. The birds may use natural holes in trees as well as any they may find in walls or rocks, and they may even take over disused rabbit burrows. But some birds prefer to excavate their own nesting chambers, notably woodpeckers, which have sharp beaks that can carve out a nest hole in a tree trunk, usually a decaying one.

Birds that breed in holes do not need to make any kind of nest within the hole; they simply lay their eggs at the bottom of the cavity. The hole gives full shelter to the eggs and young, and is almost completely safe from raiders. Climbing animals like squirrels may be able to get into large tree hollows, and woodpeckers can open up tree holes to get at the young birds inside, but there are few other hazards.

Some birds do not bother to build a new nest every year and return to the same nest, although they may have to repair it. Eagles use the same nest every year, adding sticks to it so that it grows in size. Eagles' eyries may reach a size of three metres in diameter. Others, such as kestrels and sparrowhawks, prefer to take over the

Above: Many birds gather in groups or colonies to breed. Rooks build a group of nests, called a rookery, at the top of a clump of trees. There, the nests will be safe from ground raiders such as rats, and the rooks can band together to deal with threats from the air. The rooks can feed in the surrounding fields.

nest of another bird rather than build or find their own. Sparrows can often be seen flying in and out of house martins' nests and will evict the original occupants, and starlings may chase away woodpeckers when they have completed their nest holes and take them over. Nuthatches counteract any such possibility of eviction from their nest holes by plastering up the entrance with mud until the opening is too small to let in any invaders.

Making The Nest

Birds that return to an old nest, as swallows do, are not faced with the tasks of choosing somewhere to nest and then building the nest. Most birds do have to find a site and construct the nest, though these tasks are often left to one of the prospective parents and not both. In birds that weave nests, such as the blackbird, the female usually decides where the nest will be built once she has settled in the territory. However, with hole-nesting birds like the redstart, the male may decide where the young are to be raised even before the female arrives.

Each particular species of bird has its own requirements when choosing somewhere to nest, and birds may have to compete for the best site if they are not already separated by territorial behaviour. Within the territory, one site will prove better than others and although the birds may have to choose where to nest, they are likely to settle in the same spot every year. In this way, a particular tree may serve as a nesting place for generation after generation of the same species.

The choice of nest site and the building of the nest is left completely to the female with birds like black grouse, in which the male takes no part at all in raising the young. This is also the case with many birds that breed in pairs, but often the two birds share the duty of nest building. It can be hard work and time-consuming, taking many weeks in some species. A pair of swallows, for example, may have to make a thousand trips to gather enough material to make their nest. Only in a few species does the male bird do most of the nest-building. The male wren constructs the outer part of the nest and the female then lines it. So strong is the male's urge to make nests that he constructs several in his territory, and then the female wren chooses one and completes it. The domed nest makes a good shelter, and the male wren may sleep in it outside the breeding season.

Eggs And Incubation

An egg is a flimsy object, and may seem to be a precarious home for the developing embryo inside. However, the eggs are designed for the survival of their occupants as well as the mother birds that lay them, and thereby for the continuance of the species.

Every spring, a female would be placed in great risk if she had to carry a load of developing young birds in her body. The extra weight would make flying difficult, and the bird would be likely to be caught by a predator. Thus would perish not only the mother bird but also the unborn young. This risk is removed by surrounding each embryo with a shell and enough food to see it through to the time when it has developed sufficiently to be born.

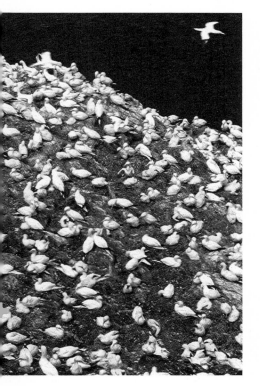

Below: Many seabirds breed in colonies at cliffs on the coast or on islands. They gain safety in numbers, and can find food in the sea nearby. These colonial nesters are gannets.

The embryo will still be at risk inside the egg, but even if it should be destroyed in an attack, the mother bird is likely to escape and lay other eggs, possibly in the same year but if not then certainly in the following year.

The egg forms inside the oviduct of the mother bird. A sac of yolk and albumen surrounds the embryo, serving to feed the developing bird and to cushion it inside the shell. The shell itself is composed of a thin layer of calcium carbonate, the same compound as chalk and marble. This compound is white, and pigments may be added by glands in the oviduct to colour the egg. If the egg remains stationary while colouring takes place, then coloured spots form on the shell. But if it moves, streaks are produced. An overall blue or green colour may also be given, with or without spots or streaks.

Eggs are speckled or blotched in this way to serve as camouflage. A parent bird may defend its eggs if they are laid in the open. Some try to decoy away enemies, while others will stay sitting on the nest as danger approaches. However, this last method is likely to work only if the parent is camouflaged. The female pheasant is a dull brown and hard to see among the low plants where she nests. She will therefore stay at the nest until she is forced to flee to save herself. Other more conspicuous birds abandon their eggs. They leave the nest the moment danger threatens, knowing that they are otherwise likely to draw attention to the eggs. The eggs are left on their own, but their spots or streaks match the vegetation or stones around them. With any luck, they will not be noticed. Ducks and grebes are less trusting and help to conceal their eggs by scattering plant debris or feathers over them to make them less visible.

Birds that lay their eggs in nest holes, such as owls and woodpeckers, generally produce white eggs. Being hidden from view, there is no need for the eggs to be camouflaged. Furthermore, it is probably easier to locate white eggs in a dark burrow or hollow. Birds that build open nests hidden in bushes and trees, such as thrushes and finches, often lay blue-green eggs, usually speckled. This colouring may act both as camouflage to would-be predators and as a beacon to the parents.

Apart from some seabirds and large birds of prey, the majority of European birds lay more than one egg during the breeding season. A clutch of eggs is produced, each being laid at an interval of one or two days. Common garden and woodland birds such as thrushes, warblers, finches, sparrows and starlings lay about three to six eggs in a clutch, though tits are more prolific at seven to twelve eggs. Hole-nesters like owls, woodpeckers and kingfishers are a little more productive, laying about four to seven eggs. The biggest layers are ducks – the mallard producing from ten to twelve eggs – and game birds, the pheasant and partridge laying as many as fifteen or sixteen. Even larger clutches are sometimes found, but are probably the product of two females laying in the same nest.

The number of eggs that a bird lays is equal to the largest number of young that the bird will be able to provide, on average, with enough food to live. A bird doesn't waste eggs by laying more than it can cope with. The number in a clutch may therefore vary from one place to another or one time to another, depending on the food supply. In Britain, swifts lay two or three eggs in a clutch but

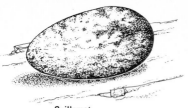

Guillemot

Blackbird

Tawny Owl

Above: Eggs vary in shape from almost completely round to oval and even pear-shaped. Owls lay round eggs, whereas the egg of guillemots and razorbills are pear-shaped. The owls' eggs are laid in holes, but the guillemot and razorbill lay their eggs on bare rock ledges. Being pear-shaped, they roll in a circle if disturbed. If they were round, they would roll in a straight line and fall off the ledge.

elsewhere in Europe where it is warmer during the summer and insects are more plentiful, the clutch increases to three or four eggs. If the weather is poor and food scarce, the parent birds will probably be unable to raise all their young. Some birds, including owls and kestrels, can respond to this possibility and reduce the size of their clutches if food is hard to find at egg-laying time. With a few exceptions, birds are able to lay more eggs to replace any that are destroyed, even a whole clutch if necessary. And should the weather be good during the breeding season and food abundant, a second or even third clutch may be laid if there is enough time left to raise another brood of young.

Although it takes several days to lay a clutch of eggs, in most nests the young hatch at about the same time. This is because the female bird does not begin to incubate the eggs until the last one has been laid. By this time, she has developed brood patches on her underside. These are patches of warm bare skin that fit over the eggs as the female sits on them. The warmth enables the embryos inside the eggs to develop. The female may sit on the eggs all the time and be fed by her mate, or she may leave the eggs to feed and the male will take over while she is away. But the eggs can be left for periods without them coming to any harm, so that the parents can safely leave the nest if danger threatens and a female without a male partner can search for food.

In some birds, the female begins to incubate the eggs before she has finished laying and the young hatch at different times. The first

Below: A baby snowy owl emerges from its egg to face the world. The white egg tooth on the end of the beak has helped it to break through the shell.

birds to be born have a greater chance of surviving than their younger and weaker brothers and sisters. This is an advantage in cases where the food supply is uncertain, as with birds that hunt other animals. Birds that produce their young in this way include owls, birds of prey, swifts and herons. Although the younger birds may starve, those born first will not – eating the younger ones if necessary. If all the young were the same age they would tend to share the available food equally, and more of them would not get enough to eat.

Incubation takes as little as 10 to 12 days for warblers like the blackcap, and 11–13 days for the hawfinch. Most garden and woodland birds sit on their eggs for about two weeks. Owls, ducks, geese and swans take about a month, but the fulmar and manx shearwaters as long as seven to eight weeks.

Hatching And Fledging

Breaking its way out of the shell that imprisons it is the first task that a bird has to face in life. A bird is well equipped by nature for this dramatic entry into the world. It develops a strong neck muscle to peck at the shell from within, and a short spike known as an 'egg tooth' forms on the end of the upper bill to help pierce the shell. Both the neck muscle and egg tooth disappear shortly after hatching.

Hatching is no easy business for a young bird, and it takes from an hour or two to as long as two or three days to break out of the egg. The parent birds immediately remove the broken eggshell or eat it,

Below: The inside of an eggshell is white, and pieces of broken shell may attract enemies to a nest. The parent bird, here a greenshank, may therefore remove the pieces as soon as its young have hatched.

Cuckoos lay their eggs in the nests of a variety of other birds, mainly small species such as pipits, warblers and the dunnock. During the breeding season, a female may visit many nests and lay an egg in each one. However, she always chooses nests of the same species, and the eggs often resemble the eggs of the other bird in colour. She waits until the other bird has left its nest and then acts quickly. She lays her egg in a matter of seconds, and removes one of the other eggs (1), either by dropping or swallowing it. The cuckoo then leaves. It never returns and will never see its own young. The other bird then comes back to its nest, usually unaware of the substitution. There are the same number of eggs in the nest as before, and they all look the same. The cuckoo's egg usually hatches first, needing a shorter incubation period than the other eggs in the nest. The new-born cuckoo sets about removing all competition, and heaves the other eggs and any nestlings out of the nest (2). Soon, it has the sole attention of its foster parents. Being normally able to collect enough food to feed a batch of several young birds, they can stuff the cuckoo with great quantities of food. It grows quickly, soon taking up the whole nest and outstripping its foster parents in size. The birds continue to feed the young monster because they are impelled by instinct to do so (3). The charade goes on for about three weeks, after which the young cuckoo is able to fly and leaves the nest (4).

as it is white inside and could attract predators to the nest. The young bird now faces the most dangerous part of its life. Although its parents will do their best to defend it, the young bird will spend some time on its own while the parents find food or as it seeks food itself. Until it can fly, it is virtually defenceless and it will be lucky to survive, especially if it has to compete with other young in the same brood.

Most young birds therefore waste no time and develop quickly, often learning to fly in about the same time as it took the egg to incubate – about two to three weeks for most garden and woodland birds. The hawfinch fledges (gains the ability to fly) in as little as ten days after hatching – and so can leave the nest in about three weeks after the egg was laid. Young game birds such as pheasants and grouse grow a special set of wing feathers within 10–14 days of hatching. These little wings enable the chicks to fly away from their nests, which are on the ground, when danger threatens. Other birds take much longer to fledge. Swifts take six weeks, mallards eight weeks, barn owls ten weeks and swans as long as 13–15 weeks. However, early life is generally safer for these birds.

Learning to fly does not necessarily mean that a young bird has to leave its family. Although the nest may be abandoned, it generally stays with its parents a little longer, learning and practising new skills. The family may keep together for the remainder of the breeding season, and little family groups of birds can often be seen in mid- to late summer. However, with most smaller birds especially passerines, the parent birds will have time to raise another brood if their young fledge quickly and can be left to look after themselves. A robin, for example, may find that it has to lead its own life when it is as little as three weeks old!

Caring For The Young

Birds develop to different degrees while in the egg, and may hatch in an advanced or a primitive state. The more advanced hatch with their eyes open and are already covered with coloured down that serves to camouflage them. Within a matter of hours, they are able to run or swim so that they can leave the nest and join their parents in seeking food. These birds are called nidifugous, which means nest-fleeing, and they include many ground and water birds, such as ducks and the moorhen, as well as waders and the domestic hen. For a day or two the young return to the nest at night, when the parents shelter or brood them. The amount of parental care varies from one group of birds to another. Ducklings and young waders are capable of finding their own food, and only need guarding as they do so. In game birds, the parents may lead their offspring to food whereas young grebes wait at the surface as their parents dive to find food for them. Young grebes may ride on their parents' backs instead of swimming about, and pop up like corks should the parents suddenly dive. Young gulls are even more dependent and though they are able to leave the nest, they immediately hide and wait for the parents to bring them food.

Most birds that can keep their young safely hidden away in a concealed nest or a hole bear young that are totally helpless after hatching. These birds include common garden and woodland birds such as tits and thrushes. The young birds are naked and, until they grow feathers, they must be kept warm by the brooding parent. They are usually blind at first and unable to move much, and so cannot leave the nest to feed; they are therefore known as nidicolous, meaning nest-living. The parents bring food to the nest, stimulated by the gaping red mouths of their young into making frantic efforts to find enough morsels to satisfy them. Their efforts

Above: Many young birds are helpless at birth, like these young blackbirds. They are blind and naked, and have to be fed by their parents. The young birds instinctively open their beaks, and the red gaping mouths stimulate the parents into pushing food into them.

Below: Other young birds are born in a more developed state. They can immediately leave the nest and seek food. However, the parent birds guard them as they explore the world around them. This pair of Canada geese are keeping a close watch on their trail of young goslings.

may be prodigious; a pair of blue tits, for example, will make 500 or more trips a day to obtain food for their young.

Although they are born in a comparatively undeveloped state, nidicolous birds grow rapidly and are ready to fly before birds that are well developed on hatching. This is just as well, because the parents' activities in bringing food to their young may well attract predators to the nest. The longer they remain helpless, the longer the young are at risk. Nidifugous young that can look after themselves are able to scatter if danger threatens. They usually live in large family groups, and each individual young bird has a good chance of escaping danger. It may therefore grow more slowly before it has to face the hazards of leaving the family and living its own life.

Most young passerines are not faced with fending for themselves immediately they learn to fly. Swifts are an exception, for the young become independent as soon as they take to the air and leave the nest never to return. However, swifts spend a comparatively long time in the nest first, and are fully grown on leaving. Other birds range wider and wider from the nest or family group once they are able to fly. They practise the skills they inherit, instinctively seeking food and avoiding danger. Eventually they become independent and leave, fully able to look after themselves.

The young bird, though independent, is not yet an adult and cannot itself breed. It must usually wait until the next breeding season, the following year. Large birds may have to wait several years to become mature and breed. At the seashore, you can often see brownish gulls among the white and grey ones. These are immature birds that cannot yet breed. They remain in this state for as long as three to four years before they assume their adult plumage and begin to breed.

Above: Several species of gulls, including this great black-backed gull, have a red spot on their beak. The gull chicks instinctively peck at this spot, and are rewarded with food from the parent's beak.

Right: Several weeks after hatching, the young birds are ready to fly. These young jays have grown the blue wing feathers of their parents, and are ready to take wing and leave the nest. Flying is instinctive. The young birds do not have to learn how to fly, but they may need some practice before they can fly well.

Migration

Once the breeding season is over and the adult birds have raised their young, they are faced with the problems of surviving the winter. It is not the cold that is likely to harm them in temperate latitudes at least. Birds can fluff out their feathers and tuck in their bills and feet to prevent heat escaping from their bodies – the ptarmigan even has feathered feet to keep it comfortable in the snow. Birds may also huddle together for warmth when roosting, gathering in a hole or a tree during the cold winter nights.

The main cause of death in birds during the winter is lack of food. Being colder, birds need more food to stay alive but, as the days are short, there is less time in which to find it. Sources may still be plentiful. There should be a rich crop of seeds, nuts and berries available from the autumn on into winter, and worms, grubs, fishes and other animals may be no less abundant than during the summer – though flying insects may no longer be available. However, the crop will diminish as the winter goes on and little may be left by early spring. If the ground and lakes and rivers freeze, or snow covers the land, then many birds will find their food supply cut off.

Many birds can survive such conditions for a time, though water birds stand little chance in a prolonged freeze-up. Some are able to turn to almost any source of food that is available. Tits go for insects in the summer, but will readily take seeds in the winter – as anyone putting out nuts will find. Crows are also very adaptable, and jays and nutcrackers will store food for the winter. Seed-eaters tend to fare well, and flocks of finches and sparrows roaming for food are a common sight in winter. Woodpeckers continue to gather food from trees, pecking at the bark for grubs.

Surviving The Winter

Depending on how severe the winter is, other birds may find it difficult to survive. Birds that hunt flying insects, such as swifts, swallows and flycatchers, are unlikely to find anything to eat even if the winter is mild. Freshwater birds such as herons and ducks, and waders like sandpipers, will be in danger if it gets so cold that the water freezes. And a really severe winter that covers the land in ice and snow will threaten birds such as thrushes, wrens and tits that in Britain we think of as resident.

Most of these birds are unable to stay and survive such conditions. With the exception of the poorwill, an American nightjar, no bird is able to pass the winter in a state approaching hibernation. But birds can fly. Faced with possible starvation, the birds therefore migrate; they leave the regions where they spent the breeding season and fly to places that will be warmer during the winter and provide them with the food they require.

Seabirds are faced with similar problems. The cold northern and polar seas teem with fish, and attract seabirds to breed along their shores in great numbers. But the savage winter forces the birds to disperse, and they fly out over the oceans or move to warmer shores.

Above: The best-known or most-awaited migrating bird in Britain and Europe is the cuckoo. Although the cuckoo is seldom seen, its call is unmistakable and is a sure sign that spring has arrived.

Population Changes

In any part of Britain and continental Europe, the population of birds changes as the seasons pass. Insect eaters like swifts and swallows arrive in the spring to breed and depart in late summer or early autumn to spend the winter in Africa. As winter approaches birds such as geese, redwings and fieldfares arrive to escape the rigours of the far north where they have been nesting in the brief summer there. At the coast, the cliffs that are crowded with breeding seabirds in summer are practically deserted in winter, their occupants having left to roam the oceans.

The bird population of a particular place may also change because other kinds of seasonal movements occur. Long-distance travellers fly from one country to another or even one continent to another to survive the winter. Many birds meet the challenge of winter by migrating shorter distances and moving to a different kind of habitat that can provide them with food. Many wading birds breed in marshes and moors, and then survive the rigours of winter by moving to the coast, where they can dig for shellfish and worms at mudflats and beaches. Gulls may move in the opposite direction, leaving their seashore nesting grounds and moving inland, particularly to towns and farmland where they can scavenge for food. Birds that live in mountains during the summer may move down to the valleys for the winter.

Bird populations may also change at migration time because of short visits by migrating birds that are passing through a region. Waders flying from the far north to more hospitable climes in the south begin their migration flights early, because the summer is so brief in the Arctic. They have had no time to moult, and so stop over in Britain and western Europe to moult before continuing their journey. Visits may also occur by birds that are blown off course during migration. Migration time is therefore a particularly fruitful season for birdwatchers, and unusual sightings are likely to be made.

Migration also causes bird populations to change in ways that will be much less apparent to birdwatchers. Regions that enjoy mild winters will receive an influx of migrating birds from colder areas. In their winter quarters, they will mix with birds of the same species that have no need to migrate. The population of resident birds may therefore apparently swell during the winter as immigrants join the resident birds.

In one area, some birds of a particular species may decide to leave while others prefer to stay. These birds are known as partial migrants, and they are mainly wagtails, finches or thrushes. In such cases, the winter may not be so harsh as to force all the population of the region to face the hazards of migration. The birds that are more able to find food may stay. The migrants consist mainly of females and young birds, which are less successful at competing for food than the more dominant males and older, more experienced birds.

Long-Distance Travellers

Some birds migrate enormous distances. The swallows that breed in Europe winter in southern Africa, making a twice-yearly journey of about 8000 kilometres in each direction. Wheatears that nest in

Below: Migrating birds often band together for safety, and fly in flocks. Geese are known for their formation flying. This huge V-formation is made up of white-fronted geese.

Greenland pause for a rest in Spain and then continue south to West Africa where they spend the winter. Birds flying from Britain or central Europe to northern Africa, as many warblers do, face a journey of at least 2000 kilometres.

Seabirds may make even longer journeys. Manx shearwaters leave their breeding grounds on British coasts and fly across the Atlantic Ocean to winter off Brazilian and Argentine shores. The Arctic tern makes the longest migration flight of all, for it may breed along Arctic coasts and winter in Antarctic waters, as much as 12,000 kilometres away. Birds that make long north-south journeys, like the Arctic tern and swallow, enjoy two summers every year. Indeed, in the case of the Arctic tern, it may travel from one land of the midnight sun to another and spend most of its life in perpetual daylight!

Seabirds are able to feed from the sea as they travel, and swifts and swallows will encounter flying insects as they migrate and so can continue to feed on the journey. Other birds may not be so fortunate. The little wheatear must make its vast flight across the ocean with no chance of landing to rest or find food. Birds travelling from Britain and continental Europe to Africa, as most summer migrants do, first face the arid Mediterranean region, then the Mediterranean Sea itself, followed by the Atlas Mountains and the Sahara Desert beyond. There is little prospect of finding food on the way, and so the birds eat well before leaving their staging posts in France, Spain and Portugal, fattening themselves for the journey. Small birds, like warblers, may even double their weight. The birds consume these reserves of fat as they migrate, having to use up vast amounts of energy in non-stop flights lasting two or three days as they cross the physical barriers below.

The timing of the migration flight is important. The bird must leave its winter quarters in time to be able to raise its young on the breeding grounds as food becomes available there. And it must leave before the food supply begins to fail. The journey may also have to take place when there is sufficient food available for the bird to fatten itself in preparation for a long flight ahead. While the weather may affect the departure date – for birds would not want to leave in stormy weather – the main factor that sets them on their way is the length of daylight. This tells the bird exactly what time of year it is and when it should migrate.

The migration flight is likely to be hazardous, and many birds band together and fly in migration flocks. Some fly in formation, geese making a big V or long line in the sky. The birds gather together as migration time approaches and become increasingly restless. Swallows and martins can be seen perching on telegraph wires at this time of year. Suddenly the birds depart. Radar observations have shown that some birds migrate at great heights of 6000 metres or more, but most cruise at about 1000 metres. Great height makes for safety, but flying in the thin air consumes energy. Birds may migrate at night because it is thought they navigate by star patterns, but this can be dangerous as they may strike obstacles – some even fly into lighthouses, presumably dazzled by the light.

Birds migrate from Britain and continental Europe to Africa and back in vast numbers every year. At least a thousand million, and

Right: Swallows are summer visitors to Britain and continental Europe. They come to nest under the eaves of houses, and arrive when insects are becoming abundant enough to feed their young.

Far right: At the end of the breeding season, in early autumn, the swallows return to Africa for the winter. Here, young swallows gather on telegraph wires before making their first migration journey.

Right: Having flown all the way from Europe, swallows arrive at their African winter quarters exhausted. This swallow has just arrived in South Africa, and is resting on the ground.

possibly two or even three times this number, fly back and forth. A well-placed observer may therefore see thousands of birds at migration time. Few species follow narrow set routes that the arrows on migration maps tend to suggest, but geographical features such as mountains and coastlines may act to funnel them along the same broad path. The Straits of Gibraltar and the Bosporus, at opposite ends of the Mediterranean Sea, are like bridges to and from Africa, and migrating birds can be seen in their thousands there. The coast of Holland is another place where migrating birds concentrate. In overcast conditions migrating birds land in their thousands on the newly-built oil-rigs in the North Sea. Many are exhausted, and it seems likely that sea crossings take a high toll of migrating birds.

Unusual Movements

Whole populations of birds may migrate irregularly, leaving their usual quarters for perhaps a few weeks at a time or possibly just one winter now and then. These unusual movements take place in response to bad weather conditions or food crop failures. If it becomes so cold in central and eastern Europe that ice and snow cover the ground for prolonged periods, then the birds that normally feed there migrate to the south and west while the cold spell lasts. These birds include starlings, lapwings, ducks and thrushes and blackbirds, and flocks of them are a common sight in winter, especially of the first three. The new arrivals will face fierce competition for food from the local inhabitants, and they return as soon as the weather improves.

A few birds may face greater hardship if they depend on certain seeds and berries, for such crops sometimes fail completely. Then the birds are forced to spread out from their normal winter range,

Below: The migration routes of six species of bird are shown on a world map. Distances covered are vast.

Above: The arctic tern may fly from the Arctic to the Antarctic and back again every year.

Above: The swallow migrates from Europe to spend the winter in the warm lands of southern Africa.

Above: The barnacle goose comes to Europe for the winter. Many birds fly across the ocean from Greenland.

66

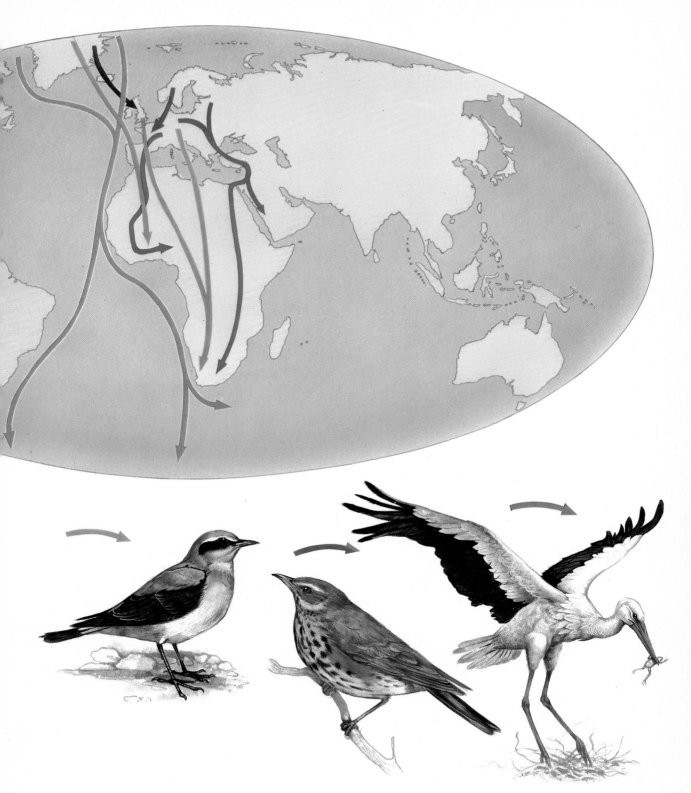

Above: The wheatear makes a vast, non-stop journey across the Atlantic from Greenland to Europe and Africa.

Above: The redwing breeds in the far north during the brief summer, then migrates south to the warmer parts of Europe.

Above: The white stork migrates between Africa and Europe via the Straits of Gibraltar and the Bosporus.

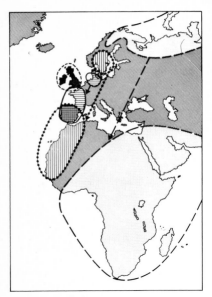

Above: The migration pattern of the little-ringed plover (see text opposite).

seeking food wherever they can find it. Every few years, invasions of birds such as waxwings, crossbills, redpolls and siskins may occur in regions where these birds are normally scarce. These invasions are called irruptions. The birds depart in spring, and may not appear again for several years.

One other kind of migration is not linked with feeding at all, but with moulting. Ducks moult all their flight feathers at the same time, and cannot fly. Some gain safety by gathering together in large groups at moulting time, and they may migrate to special moulting grounds to do so. In Europe, shelduck from Britain and north-west Europe gather in July to moult in the Heligoland Bight off the coast of West Germany. When the moult is complete, the ducks return to their breeding grounds for the remainder of the season.

The Origin And Direction Of Migration

Migration is obviously a most necessary activity for many birds, but how did it arise in the first place? The answer probably lies in the ice ages produced by the advance and retreat of the polar ice cap. Until the end of the most recent ice age, about 11,000 years ago, much of Europe was covered in ice. All the birds would have been crowded into the southern half of the continent and Africa. But as the ice retreated, the birds nearest the ice would have found new living space opening up for them, though they could only survive there during the summer. The birds would have begun to travel to and fro between their previous homes and the uninhabited breeding grounds opening up to the north. And as the ice retreated over the next 5000 years or so, then longer and longer journeys would have been necessary.

In some birds, such as the ringed plover, this seems to have given rise to unusual migration patterns known as leap-frog migration. The birds at the southern end of the breeding range, in Britain, are mainly resident, while those that breed a little farther north, in Holland and Denmark, migrate short distances to North Sea countries and Spain. Birds that nest in southern Sweden migrate to northern Africa, and those that summer in the Arctic winter in southern Africa. Hence the farther north the bird breeds, the farther south it migrates, 'leap-frogging' over the less travelled birds.

Finding The Way

Most long-distance migrants that breed in Britain and in northern and central Europe fly south to Africa for the winter, though a very few species may head in a south-east direction and make for the warmer parts of Asia. Many proceed in the right general direction, and simply press on until they reach their destination. Others take account of mountains and seas, and follow a definite route. White storks, for example, do not like flying over the Mediterranean Sea because they cannot find the up-currents of air that help them fly. While a few hop from island to island as they migrate, most make for Gibraltar or the Bosporus on their way to Africa. Seabirds may follow coastal routes, along continental shelves where fishing is more rewarding. The eastern American population of the Arctic tern first flies across the Atlantic to join up with the European population, before flying south down the west coast of Africa, finally reaching the Antarctic.

Western continental Europe receives many winter visitors originating from further north and east. Their route lies to the west or south-west, and the birds may follow definite paths. There are three breeding populations of barnacle geese in the Arctic. One in eastern Greenland migrates to the north-west coasts of Ireland and to the Scottish Hebrides; one in Spitsbergen or Svalbard, north of Norway, winters on the Solway Firth on the western border of England and Scotland; and a population from Novaya Zemlya in northern Russia migrates to Holland. Although all three populations fly towards the same general area of Europe, none meets with another. They all know exactly where they are going.

All migrating birds know the general direction that they must take to reach their breeding grounds or winter quarters, but the navigating ability of some birds is phenomenal. Swallows, for example, return to the very same mud cup nest every year after their vast journey from southern Africa.

Birds know instinctively the right direction in which they should head at migration time. Many orientate themselves according to the position of the sun or stars in the sky and may drift off course if it is cloudy. However, some are able to carry on in the right direction, and experiments have shown that, like a compass, birds may possibly be sensitive to the Earth's magnetic field. Certainly, migrating birds must have a very good sense of time if they can deduce directions from the position of the sun or stars.

However, a good sense of direction is not always enough to guide a bird to its breeding ground or winter quarters. It may be blown off course by strong winds, and some birds are unable to compensate for this and so get lost. Experiments have shown that migrating birds which are captured and taken some distance before being released may carry on as if nothing had happened; they continue migrating parallel to their original route, and end up to one side of their intended destination.

Left: Once every few years, a species may spread out from its normal range and invade neighbouring regions. This kind of movement is not really a migration, and occurs because of a sudden shortage in the food supply. It is called an irruption. In Britain and central Europe, waxwings may suddenly arrive in autumn or winter to feed on berries. They roam in search of food, and return as soon as the spring arrives.

Extinction and Conservation

Life is full of danger for birds, and it is unlikely that many will live out their full lifespan and die of old age. They are more likely to starve, to become the victim of a predator or disease, or simply to die by accident. A young bird will starve to death if its parents cannot bring it enough food, and older birds will die in this way if the food supply fails – for example, because of bad weather. A bird consumes great amounts of energy in flying and needs to eat often and well.

Disease usually does not affect birds very much, and other causes are likely to kill them before disease can get a grip. Except for birds of prey, seabirds and other large birds, the danger from predators is very serious. Unless the winter is very severe, producing widespread starvation, smaller birds are just as likely to die during the summer as in the winter. Birds that are busy defending territories, sitting on nests or frantically seeking food for their hungry young are good targets, and many lose their lives in this way.

Although individual wild birds, with the exceptions of waterfowl and gamebirds, are likely to live out their lives without much threat from man, human activities do affect the ways in which whole species of birds live in a particular country or continent. While our influence may sometimes be beneficial and help a species to increase in numbers and spread its range, often we do the opposite. Several kinds of birds come into conflict with us, and suffer at our hands. There are three main ways in which we harm birds – by destroying their habitats, by hunting them and by polluting their environment.

Destruction Of Habitat

Five thousand years ago, Europe, excluding the glaciated north, was mostly covered in trees. Mountains broke through the forests in places, and the trees gave way to tracts of marshland here and there. Now, on a flight across the continent, you will still see bare mountain tops but gone are the great forests and marshes. Instead, a vast patchwork of fields stretches in all directions, interrupted by cities and towns.

This fundamental change in the landscape has been wrought by man. Since prehistoric times, woods and forests have gradually been cleared to produce land for farming and living as well as materials for building. The marshes have been drained to make farmland and living space. Now, except in the inhospitable climate of the far north, there is little extensive forest or marsh left. In other continents, especially in the tropics, alteration of the land in these ways is still going on, but in Britain and Europe, any changes are now on a small local scale. Farmers, for example, may cut down hedgerows to create bigger fields that are easier to work. Lakes are created by flooding valleys to make reservoirs, and small forests may reappear in the form of plantations of trees for timber.

Above: The great auk is the only species of bird that lived in Europe and is known to have been wiped out by man. The story of its decline and extinction is a sad one, for it was a very interesting and unusual bird. The great auk could not fly, but was very good at swimming. On shore, it stood upright and walked awkwardly – like the penguins of southern oceans. Great auks lived in the North Atlantic Ocean, and bred in colonies at its shores, as other auks do today. The birds were hunted for their meat and feathers. Because they could not fly, great auks could easily be captured at their breeding grounds. Hunting began in prehistoric times. By 1750, the great auk was restricted to a few colonies off Newfoundland and Iceland. It soon disappeared from Newfoundland and, in 1830, a volcanic eruption destroyed the main breeding island. A few survivors moved to a nearby rock, where the last pair of birds were killed in 1844.

All these changes affect bird populations. The clearing of woods and forests takes away nesting places and food sources for all kinds of small woodland birds as well as birds of prey and owls. The removal of hedgerows makes it difficult for small birds like warblers to find secure nesting places. The drainage of marshes seriously affects wading birds, which feed in shallow water or on damp soil and may hide away in the reeds. Reservoirs are not like natural lakes, being deep and having steep sides that do not produce the same kinds of shores that lakes have. They may not therefore suit birds that normally live by water. Similarly, plantations may not contain the right kinds of trees for woodland birds that have lost their original homes, since the tendency is to replant conifers rather than deciduous trees. Seabirds may also be at risk, especially those like terns that nest on the open shore. The birds are mainly affected by our desire for recreation by the sea, and are disturbed by holidaymakers.

Although most great forests have disappeared, woodland birds have not been affected disastrously. Many of the smaller birds have taken to living in parks and gardens, and woodland birds such as robins, song thrushes, blackbirds, tits and some finches are completely at home living alongside man in this way. Swifts and swallows have turned from breeding in trees or cliffs to nesting on buildings. Enough woodland still exists in the countryside to support forest birds like owls and woodpeckers that are not so common in gardens, though they may now be less numerous than they were before man began to change the face of the land.

By planting regions with trees for timber, new 'forests' may be created and attract woodland birds back to their former haunts. However, these plantations are mainly of conifer trees, which are much less attractive to most birds than broad-leaved trees. Nevertheless, some species prefer conifers, such as the crossbill, goldcrest and coal tit, and the plantations will help these birds to survive.

The destruction of any habitat creates a new one and, although the original occupiers may not be able to live in the new habitat, other birds may be able to take advantage of it. Some birds, such as many finches and warblers, like to live at the edges of woods where light conditions allow the growth of a shrub layer. Before forests were cleared, this habitat would not have been very common. Now, the countryside is scattered with little woods instead of thick forest, and these birds may exist in greater numbers than before. This change would also have favoured birds that nest or roost in woodland but feed in open country such as fields. These birds include starlings, crows and woodpigeons, and they too would find today's landscape more to their liking than the natural forest of prehistoric times.

Most of the land where great forests once stood is now empty of trees. Instead we have fields, downs and moors, which cannot support woodland birds. However, many birds are at home in this kind of open country and thrive there. They include small ground-living birds such as larks, pipits and wagtails, and many plovers and sandpipers nest in open country. It is unlikely that these birds were common in Britain and Europe before the landscape changed.

Overall, then, the clearing of forests has created a landscape of greater diversity that can support a greater number of species of birds than existed before. This is not true of the drainage of marshland. The birds that live in this habitat cannot adapt themselves to living in parks and gardens, where there is seldom any shallow water or soft ground in which to find food nor any thickets of reeds in which to find shelter. Areas of marsh are not scattered throughout the countryside as woods are, and so there are few places to which the birds can retreat. Marshland birds have therefore been seriously affected by man's activities, and there are many parts of Britain and Europe in which they are either now absent or very rare. These birds include cranes, spoonbills, bitterns, harriers and bearded tits.

Birds of open water have been less affected, as lakes and rivers exist now much as they did before man began to make an impact on the land. In fact, our activities have improved their lot in some ways, for the building of reservoirs and gravel pits that have flooded has benefited various species of diving birds such as grebes, coots and diving ducks.

Hunting

Hunting, mainly by shooting but also by trapping with nets, is responsible for the deaths of many birds. In the past, hunting has threatened entire species of birds. It played a significant part in the extinction of the dodo and passenger pigeon, and hunters were totally responsible for the demise of the great auk and of the flightless Pallas' cormorant which used to breed in the Bering Sea.

It is unlikely that hunters could completely wipe out a bird species in Europe today, for hunting is largely controlled by law. Some birds that are regarded as pests by farmers may be killed without any penalty. These birds include crows, sparrows and pigeons. Game birds such as pheasants and partridges may be hunted during the autumn and winter, but are protected by law during the breeding season. In many European countries, but particularly in Britain, other wild birds have the full protection of the law and may not be killed, nor may their eggs be taken or their nests disturbed.

Hunters in the past looked upon birds as a source of income. They killed them for food and for their plumage. The great crested grebe came near to extinction in Britain during the 19th century because of the demand for its plumes. Only action by conservationists saved it. Nowadays, in several Mediterranean countries, hunters are allowed to shoot or trap birds as they pass through on migration. In Italy, it is estimated that about 100 million birds are killed every year in this way. Birds also run a similar gauntlet in France, Spain, Portugal, Cyprus and Belgium. The carnage has reduced the number of breeding birds in these countries, but fortunately does not seem to have had a great effect elsewhere. However, this does not mean that the bird populations of Europe are not in danger from hunting. If you consider that the most common British wild bird, the wren, numbers only about 20 million, then the annual Italian slaughter of 100 million birds may well soon begin to make its mark on populations in Europe.

Above: A pair of peregrine falcons pass some food to their young. The nest has been built on a rock ledge high above a valley, where the eggs and young are safe from most raiders. The peregrines' territory extends out over the valley around the nest. There they can seek food for themselves and their young without having to compete with other peregrines.

A further threat faces birds that become uncommon. Rare birds are also placed in peril by egg collectors and by people who capture the birds for their private zoos. Birds of prey are prime targets for these collectors, and also for farmers and gamekeepers who shoot the birds in the mistaken belief that they threaten their domestic animals and gamebird stocks.

Pollution

Pollution poses a threat to several kinds of birds. Lakes and rivers may become so polluted with industrial waste that no animal or even plant life may be able to survive in the water, and water birds will have to fly elsewhere or die. However, the most powerful of polluting substances have not been waste materials but used deliberately. These are DDT and other toxic chemicals, which since World War II have been applied to crops in large amounts to kill insects.

DDT also affects higher animals in sufficiently large doses. Several bird species began to receive large doses of DDT after this had been in use for some years. These were birds of prey, which were consuming animals that in turn had fed on the treated crops; every time a bird of prey made a kill, it consumed more and more DDT. Fish-eaters such as grebes and herons were also affected because their prey had become contaminated with DDT washed off the land and into lakes and rivers. The chemical did not necessarily kill the birds outright, but it either made them sterile, or caused them to lay eggs with thin shells that were crushed before they could hatch. Either way, breeding became less successful and numbers began to fall.

The cause of this problem was identified in 1958 before it was too late, although many birds had become seriously affected, especially

Left: A rare photograph of the great bustard Otis tarda *taken in Portugal in 1976. Both sexes have pale lavender-blue heads and necks, white underparts, with black and gold in close barring on the back and tail. In spring, the males give incredible displays, cocking their tails to expose a cascade of brilliant white feathers. Scattered across the plains or hillsides, these males are one of the most exhilarating spectacles in nature. With a world population of some 25,000 — mainly in Hungary, Portugal and Russia — this is one of the rarest of the bustards. At Porton Down in Wiltshire, efforts are being made to re-establish the great bustard in England and so help to save this most fascinating and threatened of birds.*

73

the peregrine falcon and sparrowhawk. DDT and the related chemicals were withdrawn in the 1960s and the birds began to recover in numbers, though very slowly.

Seabirds face an individual threat, though scarcely a danger to any complete species, in the form of oil pollution. The discharge of oil from tankers, which occurs deliberately as well as by accident, produces a floating layer of sticky oil on the surface. Seabirds have to dive or settle on the sea to feed and so become coated with oil. Their feathers matted together, they are unable to fly and this usually means their death. A few lucky birds get to the shore and are rescued and cleaned by bird lovers, but even then survival prospects are poor since cleaning destroys the natural water-proofing of the plumage. Auks such as guillemots and puffins are highly vulnerable to oil pollution, and it is a danger that seems likely to increase as more oil rigs are built out to sea.

Endangered Birds In Europe

Of the 500 or so species of birds that live in Europe, only one can be described as endangered; this is Audouin's gull, which lives exclusively in the Mediterranean and Aegean Seas. Several other species are rare in Britain and Europe, and it is quite possible that they may cease to exist there. However, these birds are also found in Asia or Africa, where they are not threatened. The four species of vultures found in Europe are examples. They are all declining in southern Europe because it is no longer so easy for them to find the bodies of wild or farm animals to consume, but they continue to thrive in Africa and Asia.

Audouin's gull is slightly smaller than a herring gull and has the white, grey and black plumage typical of gulls. Its beak is distinctive, being red with a black band near the yellow tip. It nests mainly on islands off the north coast of Morocco, but there are several other island colonies elsewhere in the Mediterranean Sea and in the Aegean. It has always had a restricted distribution, and some colonies are raided by fishermen who take the eggs. The total world population numbers about 800 pairs and it could be in danger of extinction if the colonies are not protected.

Another European bird that is seriously endangered is the Spanish imperial eagle. This bird is a subspecies of the imperial eagle. It is found only in Spain, where it is isolated from the main race, which lives in eastern Europe and Asia. The Spanish birds differ from the others in having white patches on their shoulders. Only about a hundred of them exist, and very few of these are in reserves where they can be best protected. Like other eagles, the Spanish imperial eagle has been the target of hunters and collectors as well as dangerously exposed to poisoning by insecticides such as DDT.

Several spectacular birds have declined in Europe, mainly because of the drainage of marshes. Marvellous birds such as cranes, avocets, spoonbills, ibises and pelicans were once common throughout much of Europe, including Britain, but are now scarce there. Cranes nested in Britain until about 1550, and spoonbills did so until about 1660. They are long gone, and very unlikely to return as nesting species, though both still occur here as rare migrants.

Above: Oil spills from tankers at sea are a threat to seabirds, especially those like auks that dive to fish. This guillemot became completely covered in oil.

Above: The avocet is one of several birds that have been helped by conservation measures. In Britain, it died out early in the 1800s as a result of hunting and disturbance. However, it has now returned to nest in special reserves. The avocet is the symbol of the Royal Society for the Protection of Birds, which has helped the bird to breed again in Britain.

The Great Bustard

Another spectacular bird that was once common throughout most of Europe is the great bustard, one of the largest flying birds. It lives on open grassy plains, where the males gather to display before the females in the spring. The display is magnificent, for the birds raise great fans of white plumage that billow out over their bodies. The great bustard is large and tasty, and in its open habitat an easy target for hunters. Hunting accounted for a dramatic decrease in its numbers during the 1800s, when it disappeared from most of western Europe. The planting of hedges to form fields also drove it away, and farming machines have destroyed the eggs and chicks of this groundnesting bird. Now there are only three populations left in Europe, and they contain about 3000 birds in all. They are in Spain and Portugal, Poland and East Germany, and from Austria through Hungary and Czechoslovakia into Romania. The latter population extends into Asia, where there may have been some local increases where forests have been cleared.

Right: The mandarin duck was introduced from China to brighten up lakes in parks and the grounds of stately homes. Several escaped from captivity, and there are now some wild populations in Britain and continental Europe. Only the male is multicoloured; the female is brown.

Conserving Birds

Action has to be taken if more birds are not to follow the great auk into extinction. If no checks had been placed on the use of DDT, it is very likely that the peregrine falcon and possibly some other birds of prey would be extinct by now. The great crested grebe, a beautiful bird commonly seen on lakes and rivers in Britain, would have disappeared here about a century ago if a few people had not protested and taken action to save the bird from hunters and collectors.

The conservation of wildlife is important to all life on Earth, and not just to animals that are endangered. We stand at the top of a pyramid of living things, depending on them to feed us. If we place these lower animals – and plants – in danger then we could eventually find ourselves in trouble. Had not the plight of birds of prey alerted us to the dangers of DDT, then we might have poisoned ourselves. Mercury pollution harmed people in Japan, for example, because people turned out to be more sensitive to mercury than the contaminated fish that they were eating.

People can help to save threatened birds personally, for example, by cleaning oiled seabirds or by guarding the nest of a rare bird from the attention of egg collectors. But to have an effect on dwindling numbers, action has to be taken by governments and conservation organizations, such as the World Wildlife Fund and the various bird societies. Governments must pass laws to protect birds and enforce them. Conservation organizations must set up reserves where birds can live in safety, and run campaigns to bring the plight of endangered birds to public attention.

In Britain, both these approaches have been very effective. Laws exist to protect most wild birds, certainly all those in need of conservation, and are generally effective. Organizations such as the Royal Society for the Protection of Birds look after birds with enthusiasm and concern.

The protection of wild birds in reserves is an effective way of conserving small numbers. To save birds on the brink of extinction, conservationists may capture some of them and breed from them in reserves until their numbers have increased. Then the birds can be taken back to their original home and released. The Wildfowl Trust at Slimbridge in England played an important part in preventing the extinction of the Hawaiian goose by breeding these birds. This captive breeding has also been successful in increasing numbers of peregrine falcons in the United States.

Protection of breeding birds in the wild and captive breeding have been successful in saving the rarest bird of prey, the Mauritius kestrel. Numbers were down to single figures during the 1970s, but have now begun to climb – though the bird is still very rare. Captive breeding is not easy. It is often difficult for the captive birds to take to the wild, and they may not survive for long. So some conservationists take eggs from the nests of endangered species, rear the chicks and then take them back to the nest. The young are accepted by the parents and learn to fend for themselves. This technique is effective with eagles, and has been applied to the Spanish Imperial Eagle.

Success Stories

Since the demise of the great auk in 1844, no other British or European bird has become extinct. Some have withdrawn from parts of the continent, but none have died out completely. Action has been taken to halt the decline of several birds, such as the peregrine falcon. In general this has been effective, even though numbers may take a long time to climb back towards their former levels.

In several places, birds that ceased to breed there have been reintroduced. In Britain, these birds include the goshawk and capercaillie. Other birds have come back of their own accord, such as the avocet, bittern and ruff. New birds have been introduced that never lived here before. These include exotics such as three species of pheasants, Canada goose and mandarin duck, all of which originally lived in other continents and now breed in the wild in Britain and elsewhere in Europe. Then there are birds which extend their range naturally and colonize new regions. In Britain, about a dozen of these new birds have arrived since 1800; they include such common birds as the tufted duck and the collared dove.

New birds, whether they are introduced by man or arrive of their own accord, will be able to spread if there is a habitat available for them and if that habitat is not filled by other species that take all the food there. The collared dove was originally restricted to south-east Europe and Asia, but in 1930 it began to extend its range to the north-west. It soon spread through central Europe, reaching Britain in 1955 and moving to most parts of Britain and Ireland over the next ten years. It has recently reached Iceland.

Another group of European birds that have generally increased their numbers are the seabirds. The fulmar, gannet and several sea ducks and gulls have expanded during this century. The reasons for these increases are not clear. It is possible that fulmars have taken to following fishing boats and found a new food source in waste fish.

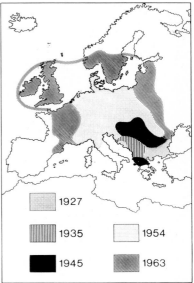

	1927
	1935
	1945

	1954
	1963

Above: The collared dove (top) began a remarkable expansion into central Europe in the 1930s. As the map shows this expansion is still continuing, and the bird may soon find its way across the Atlantic Ocean via Iceland and Greenland and reach North America.

Part Two

Studying Birds

Left: Many birds, such as this robin, live in trees. They mostly have three toes facing forward on each foot and one facing backward, which enables them to grip a twig or branch. This arrangement of toes also enables a bird to hop or run, and robins are often seen on the ground. Its prey shows this robin to be an insect eater, and most insect-eating birds have similar small, sharp beaks.

How to Use this Guide

Many people find that birds are fascinating creatures, and yet really know very little about them. The aim of this book is to help them get to know more about birds, so that they can enjoy and appreciate birds more than ever. Birdwatching is for many people a rewarding hobby, for birds are to be seen almost everywhere. Being able to identify any bird is satisfying, but even more interesting and worthwhile is to be able to understand why a bird is behaving in a

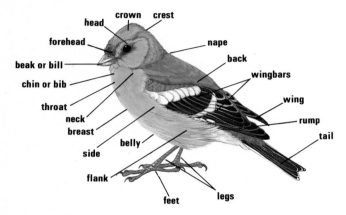

Left: The parts of a bird and their names are shown in this illustration of a male chaffinch. These names should be used in describing a bird.

particular way. Some birdwatchers go on to become professional ornithologists or naturalists, making their living by carrying out research into birds for scientific organizations and institutes, or possibly by photographing birds or writing about them. Few people take birds this seriously and perhaps few would want to, fearing that a diverting hobby might become a chore – though ornithologists would not agree. Nevertheless, the amateur birdwatcher can play a useful role in furthering our knowledge of birds. By taking part in studies of bird populations, he or she will be able to contribute work of value and may help to improve the lives of birds.

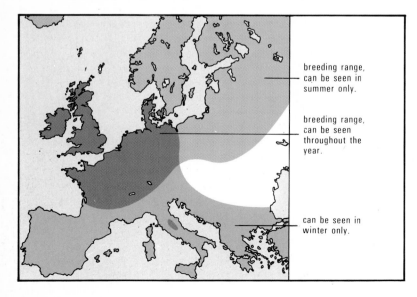

breeding range, can be seen in summer only.

breeding range, can be seen throughout the year.

can be seen in winter only.

Left: The maps in this book show at a glance in which parts of Europe a bird is likely to be found and at which times of the year. A pink area is that in which a bird is to be seen after migration to its breeding grounds in the spring, and then throughout the breeding season until it returns to its winter quarters in the autumn. A blue area indicates its winter quarters, and is inhabited from autumn to spring. A purple area is inhabited throughout the whole year. The bird is unlikely to be found in a white area, except perhaps during migration.

Above: The fulmar (top) and the herring gull (bottom) look very alike, having much the same shape and both being white with grey wings. However, they belong to different orders of birds because the structure of their nostrils is very different. The fulmar's nostrils protrude over the beak, the herring gull's nostrils do not.

Above: The crane (top) and the coot (bottom) could hardly be more unlike each other, and yet both birds belong to the same order. The birds of this order are long-legged wading birds. Cranes are at one extreme with very long legs, while coots are at the other with legs hardly longer than normal. All other features of the birds in this order vary greatly.

Naming Birds

Several different features can help you to identify a bird. Its shape, size and pattern of colours are usually enough to be sure of its name, but some birds look rather alike. In these cases, it may help to know the kind of countryside in which the bird is found and in which countries it lives. The way in which it moves and flies and the kind of song that it sings may also help to name a bird.

In this guide, the birds are placed in groups called *orders* or *families*. Each group has a short introduction that gives its Latin name, and describes the general features of the birds in each group and any interesting points about them as a group. On the same page are full-colour paintings of each bird in the group. The paintings show any differences between the male and female, and any changes in colour that occur in different seasons of the year. If the caption to the painting does not say that the bird is a male or female, then the male and female look alike and cannot be told apart. On some pages there are also colour photographs that show some of the birds in characteristic activities. In the text accompanying each painting is a description of each bird giving its usual English name, its Latin or scientific name (genus and species), its size from the tip of its beak to the end of its tail in centimetres (cm) and inches (in), and a description of its habits and the kind of places in which it is likely to be seen. Any special points of interest are added.

Classification

The arrangement of groups of birds in a field guide may not seem to be logical. However, if you look quickly through any guide, you will see that similar kinds of birds are placed together. Three species of swan can be seen in Britain and Ireland during the winter, and by placing them together it is easiest to compare and name them. Geese are similar to swans though smaller, so they come next to swans; ducks are similar to geese, though smaller still, and they are included next to geese. Now, it is easy to tell a swan from a goose, and a goose from a duck, so it is not really essential for these groups to be placed together. However, the three kinds of birds have very similar bodies (especially beaks and feet) even though they are of different sizes. Scientists group animals together according to their physical structures and adaptations, even though they may be of various sizes and of different external appearance. Swans, geese and ducks are all members of the same family group, and this is the reason that they appear together in guides. Some groups, for example the buntings or warblers, contain birds that are very similar in appearance whereas others, such as herons and their allies, may contain birds that are quite different to look at. Nevertheless, their body structures are similar and so they are grouped together.

The order of the groups may look very odd. Why should divers come first and sparrows last? However, you will see that grebes come next to divers and that they are both similar water birds. Buntings come next to sparrows, and they are both similar seed-eating birds. This general order of groups is intended to reflect the order in which birds are thought to have evolved long ago. Birds at the beginning of the list are more primitive than those at the end.

Listing birds in this way is called 'classification', and its various components are considered in more detail in the following section. Ornithologists do not always agree on the precise order that should be followed in a classification. This guide follows the order recommended by the British Trust For Ornithology.

Scientific Names

The scientific (Latin) names that birds have are not just an international code that can be understood by ornithologists throughout the world; they do have meanings. For example, the strange Latin name of the wren – *Troglodytes troglodytes* – is derived from the word 'troglodyte', which means cave dweller. It refers to the way wrens like to hide away in cave-like nests and holes. But why use the same word twice? And why use *italic* letters? There are good reasons, and these are connected with the necessity to place similar birds in the same group.

All animals and plants are placed in several kinds of groups, which are given Latin names to prevent confusion between different languages. All the birds together form one *class* of the animal kingdom. It has the Latin name Aves, which simply means 'birds'. Within this class there are several large subdivisions called *orders*. Each order comprises birds that are broadly alike in structure and have a common ancestry. For example all the shorebirds – plovers, sandpipers, auks, gulls and terns – make up one order which has the Latin name Charadriiformes. All order names end with the suffix '-iformes' and begin with a capital letter. Charadriiformes simply means the order of water-birds, derived from the Greek word 'kharadrios'. Ornithologists divide all the birds of the world into about 30 separate orders, and 20 of these are represented in Europe.

The birds placed together within one order may then be subdivided again into smaller units called *families*, to further define degrees of affinity. Thus the smaller wading birds, including snipe, woodcock, curlew and the true sandpipers, make up the same family which has the name Scolopacidae (derived from the Greek word 'skolops' = pointed, a reference to the long beaks of these waders). However, the superficially similar plovers are sufficiently different in body structure to be placed in a family of their own (the Charadriiadae), as are the gulls (Laridae), terns (Sternidae) and auks (Alcidae). All family names begin with a capital letter and end with the suffix '-idae'. Thus Laridae simply means the family of gulls.

Within a family, the birds are subdivided again into smaller groups called *genera* (singular: *genus*). Each genus contains birds that are very alike and obviously closely related. For example, in the wading birds of the Scolopacidae family, most snipes are in the genus *Gallinago*, most of the coastal sandpipers in the genus *Calidris*, and most of the freshwater sandpipers in the genus *Tringa*.

All these subdivisions may sound very complicated, but they are essentially ways of expressing the differences and similarities that have resulted from millions of years of bird evolution. One can draw an analogy with a tree. The trunk is the *class*, the main branches are the *orders*, the slimmer side branches are the *families*, the yet-

Above: Three species of birds vie with each other for food put out on a bird table. Nearest the camera are two blue tits on the left and, to their right, a great tit. Opposite the great tit is a long-tailed tit. Blue tits and great tits belong to the same family because their bodies are alike in shape, although the great tit is slightly bigger. The long-tailed tit belongs to a different family because it has a long tail.

thinner outer branches may be classed as the *genera*, and the terminal twigs may be thought of as the *species*.

Within a genus, each different species has a scientific name of its own. This is little different from our own use of first and surnames, John Smith and Susan Smith both being members of the Smith family. For bird examples, the curlew is *Numenius arquata* and the whimbrel *Numenius phaeopus*; the common gull is *Larus canus* and the herring gull *Larus argentatus*; the common tern is *Sterna hirundo* and the little tern *Sterna albifrons*. It will be seen that while the genus has a capital letter, the species name conventionally does not. As in human names, initials can be used for the forenames (genera) of birds; thus the common gull can be called *L. canus* and the herring gull *L. argentatus*. Sometimes the same species name is given to different birds. For example *major* means 'great', and is given to both the great spotted woodpecker (*Dendrocopos major*) and the great tit (*Parus major*). Hence it is necessary to indicate both the genus and the species name when identifying a bird by its scientific name. The latter is always given in italics to distinguish it clearly from group and vernacular names, which are always in Roman letters.

Species And Subspecies

Broadly speaking, birds of the same *species* are identical with each other apart from the constant differences between male and female and the seasonal plumage changes of both. However, this species constancy may apply only within one geographical area. If one looks at a series of museum specimens that have been collected over the whole width of Europe and Asia, often it will be seen that there are subtle differences between those collected in different regions; this is called *geographical variation*. Those breeding in dry country will tend to be paler, while those breeding in humid regions and in maritime climates will tend to be darker; moreover, body size tends to be larger in cooler regions of altitude or latitude. A striking example of such geographical variation is shown by male yellow wagtails, which have olive crowns in Britain, blue crowns in west Europe, grey crowns in north Europe and black crowns in the Balkans.

Another good example of this is provided by the European carrion crow and hooded crow. The first is completely black, and the second has a grey body while still having black head, wings and tail. These birds inhabit different halves of the continent, but where they meet they interbreed freely and all sorts of intermediates occur. The carrion and hooded crows belong to the same species, *Corvus corone*; but to identify them more fully it is necessary to add a third (subspecies) name: the carrion crow is *Corvus corone corone* (or *C. c. corone*) and the hooded crow is *Corvus corone cornix* (or *C. c. cornix*). The two subspecies probably arose through their ancestral stock being separated into two isolated populations by the ice age. During the thousands of years that they were separated the two populations evolved slightly differently, but they did not change so much that they could not later interbreed. When the ice retreated, the two populations expanded their respective ranges, and where they have met they are still able to interbreed freely.

Above: A greenfinch sings out from a tree. The greenfinch is a member of the finch family, which also includes crossbills and linnets. Finches are characterized by their stout beaks that can split open seeds and nuts with ease.

How, then, does one differentiate between species and subspecies? This is not a question to which there is a simple answer, and there are plenty of cases over which ornithologists still disagree. Broadly speaking, a species comprises a set of individuals which breed among themselves but not with other groups, so that the main characters of each species are preserved. Subspecies, on the other hand, interbreed freely where their ranges meet so that there is usually a transition zone of intermediate birds. The problem area lies in island populations, where one can seldom apply the test of whether they would interbreed with their closest relatives elsewhere if they ceased to be isolated. In such cases one often has to make a 'best guess' based on degrees of difference in plumages, calls and displays; the more these differ, the less chance there is that interbreeding would occur if individuals of the separated populations came into contact. Unfortunately, the interbreeding rule cannot be applied rigidly because even good species will sometimes interbreed (or hybridize, as it is called); this is often seen in captivity, where waterfowl and gamebirds in particular will hybridize freely if mates of their own species are not available.

Subspecies need isolation if they are to develop fully. Islands provide the best examples, but subspeciation can also proceed on continents where 'islands' of habitat occur in the midst of otherwise unsuitable terrain, for example the forested slopes of a mountain. Given long enough isolation, a subspecies can differentiate from its original stock to the point where it is entitled to be ranked as a species in its own right. Thus subspeciation is an essential step in the evolutionary process.

Things To Watch For

Even with good binoculars, it may be hard to get a good view of a bird so that you can study its plumage and readily identify it. The bird may be moving fast, it may be too far away or the light may be too bad. Even worse, you may be able to hear the bird but not be able to catch a glimpse of it. However, as you get to know more and more about birds, you will be able to recognize other features that will enable you to identify them in all kinds of poor conditions.

A general idea of markings may be enough to identify the bird in combination with some other feature, should the silhouette not tell you everything. If the bird is black and white, it is most likely to be either a magpie, lapwing or oystercatcher. A glimpse of a long tail could prove it to be a magpie, a crest to be a lapwing, and a long beak an oystercatcher.

Birds can also be identified by their actions. Many have special ways of flying, of moving on the ground and of living in trees. A large seabird seen to fly continually low over the waves is very likely to be a shearwater, while a medium-sized bird seen hovering beside a motorway is certainly a kestrel. A small bird jerkily running over the ground and wagging a long tail is most likely to be a wagtail, and a small bird seen clinging upside-down to a tree trunk will almost certainly be a nuthatch or treecreeper.

The sound that a bird makes can be a sure way to identify it, should you not be able to see the bird. Almost everyone has heard a cuckoo and recognized its distinctive song, but few people would know a cuckoo on sight. Even if you can see the bird, its song can still help. It is very difficult to tell a chiffchaff from a willow warbler unless you hear the bird sing, for the two birds are virtually identical in appearance. Fortunately, their songs are very different. Experienced birdwatchers can recognize many species of birds just by hearing them sing, and they keep their ears as well as their eyes open. The best way to learn birdsong is to go birdwatching with a person who will be able to tell you which bird is singing.

Left: The silhouette or outline of a flying bird is often enough to tell you the family or order to which it belongs. Crows have rounded wings with spread primary feathers that may give them a 'ragged' appearance. Swifts have very long and narrow pointed wings, often held out stiffly. Pigeons can be recognized by their plump breasts and broad pointed wings. Herons draw their necks back into an S-shape as they fly; by contrast, cranes and storks look similar but thrust their long necks forward.

Left: A nuthatch can instantly be recognized from the way it clings upside-down to the trunk of a tree.

Left: Treecreepers have a characteristic way of climbing up trees, often moving in a spiral around the trunk.

Right: Woodpeckers are renowned for their habit of carving nest holes in tree trunks by chiselling away at the wood with their beaks. This is a green woodpecker.

When and Where to See Birds

Birdwatching is not an activity that has to be confined to a particular time of year or to one particular place. At any time, and in any place, there will be birds to see and conclusions to be made about their behaviour. Birdwatching is always rewarding, and this is why it is such a popular pastime.

Wherever you are, and at whatever time, birds will come to you – or at least will carry on their lives around you. However, although different kinds of birds will come to the same place throughout the different seasons, if you want to study a wide range of birds then you have got to go and look for them. You cannot ever expect to see a gannet, say, in your back garden or a kingfisher on your seaside holiday, to name just two birds that are of great interest. Every habitat has a particular range of birds that varies from season to season. By visiting certain habitats at particular times, you will be able to find a lot of different birds. Of course, nowhere in Britain and Europe will you come across exotic tropical or southern birds such as hummingbirds or penguins. And even the most energetic birdwatcher is unlikely to see more than about 300 different species without travelling far afield. Nevertheless, a wide range of interesting birds is to be found in Britain and continental Europe, and the study of them is worth a great effort.

A Year Of Birds

The kinds of birds that may be seen in a particular habitat at different times of the year vary greatly from one part of Britain and Europe to another. In October, for example, the winter will have already arrived in Arctic regions while it is still late summer in southern Europe, and totally different kinds of birds will be living in the two regions. It is no use therefore to try to list the kinds of birds that may be seen in Europe month by month throughout the year. We can only talk generally about the influence of the seasons on the bird populations.

Almost all birds follow yearly cycles in their lives, and it is convenient to start the year with the spring and the onset of the breeding season. Garden and woodland birds begin singing, if they have not already done so, and perhaps brightening in colour as they start their courtship. Shore birds such as waders and ducks move inland to nest, and migrants such as swifts, swallows and cuckoos arrive to breed. Seabirds fly in from the ocean, many to gather in breeding colonies at cliffs. Birds such as geese and some thrushes move to the north to nest.

Late spring and early summer see the birds raising their young. The parents are active in searching for food, and trails of ducklings and other young birds may be seen. In mid- to late summer, things quieten down as the young become independent and the parents moult. Coastal breeding sites are deserted as the seabirds leave, and

Above: The shallow lakes and marshes of this bird reserve at Slimbridge in England attract ducks, geese and swans of many kinds, especially during the winter. Many birds return there year after year to escape the harsh winter in the far north.

inland migrants begin to gather in preparation for their departure.

Autumn sees the long-distance migrants leaving for southern Asia or Africa, and the northern nesters flying south. The waders and ducks that have nested inland on moors and marshes move back to the coast to feed at mudflats and inshore waters. As winter arrives, birds from the north may be seen roaming for food while resident woodland birds move out into fields and gardens to find food. Though the winter may be hard, the first signs of spring will see the birds preparing to breed again.

Bird Habitats Of Europe

The various habitats that support populations of birds in Europe are shown on the following pages. They are: woods and forests; mountains and moors; fields, hedgerows and farms; lakes, rivers and marshes; sea and coastal cliffs; seashores and estuaries; and towns. A number of birds are illustrated as living in each habitat, and these are common representatives of the typical inhabitants to be found there. Other kinds of birds may be seen in each habitat, either because they have strayed from their usual habitat, or because they move between one habitat and another as the seasons pass. In most habitats, the summer and winter populations of birds are different.

Birds may also be seen in special reserves where they are protected. The reserves are not like zoos where the animals are forced to stay. The birds live there naturally, but are guarded from human interference so that they do not leave. Many rare and unusual birds may be seen in bird reserves. It is necessary to obtain permission or to pay an admission fee to enter most of them.

Birds Of Woods And Forests

Two main kinds of woods and forests are found in Europe — coniferous and deciduous. Coniferous forest consists of stands of tall needle-leaved trees such as pines and firs. These trees do not lose their leaves in winter, and the ground beneath the thick canopy of branches overhead is perpetually cast in shadow and is consequently rather bare. Coniferous trees are adapted to cold climates, and this type of forest is found mainly in the north of Norway and Sweden, across Finland, and towards the summits of high mountain ranges, such as the Alps. However, plantations of coniferous trees may be found in many other places.

Deciduous woods and forests are found in milder climates. Although the great forests of former times no longer cover the land, there are many areas of deciduous woods and forest to be found throughout Europe outside the Arctic and below the coniferous belt on mountain slopes. Deciduous trees are mostly broad-leaved and drop their leaves in winter. This allows light to penetrate to the forest floor, encouraging bushes to grow up.

Below: Several typical birds of coniferous woods and forests.

Goldcrest

Crossbill

Great Grey Owl

Capercaillie

90

Coniferous forest is a rather inhospitable place for birds, especially during the harsh winter. With the exception of the crossbill and capercaillie, few birds can feed from the trees themselves. Insect-eaters such as warblers, tits and woodpeckers may come for the summer. There are also some birds of prey, especially the goshawk, and owls like the great grey owl.

Deciduous woods and forest on the other hand support a wide range of birds, especially during the summer. Seed- and fruit-eaters such as finches, thrushes and pigeons abound, as do insect-eaters like tits and warblers. Tree-living birds like treecreepers, nuthatches and woodpeckers are common, and jays can gather acorns. Birds of prey, such as sparrowhawks, and tawny owls feed on the smaller woodland animals. The thick bushy undergrowth brings in wrens, and provides nesting places for many of the smaller forest birds. Several birds, such as starlings and crows, gather in woods to sleep. However, winter sees the woods and forests comparatively deserted. Many of the summer birds are migrants, and most of the others leave to roam in fields.

Below: Several typical birds of deciduous woods and forests.

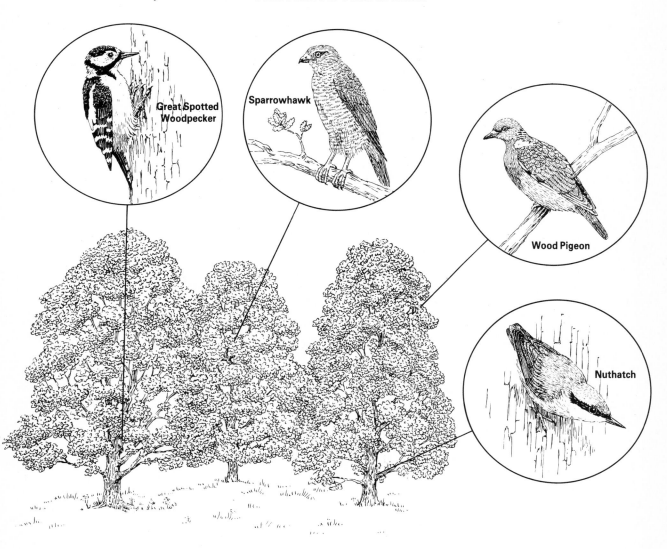

Great Spotted Woodpecker

Sparrowhawk

Wood Pigeon

Nuthatch

Above: Several typical birds of fields and hedgerows.

Birds Of Fields, Hedges And Farms

Throughout Europe, forested land has been cleared of trees and marshland has been drained to make way for farming. The result, from a bird's point of view, is a varied landscape of fields, hedgerows, scattered trees and isolated farm buildings that provide many places to feed and nest. Some take direct advantage of the farmer. Sparrows and rooks descend on fields of crops and grains to feed, and gulls follow ploughs to eat worms and grubs that are exposed as the soil is turned over.

These birds may be seen on fields at all times of the year, and so too may magpies and jackdaws, seeking anything to eat. Lapwings root in the fields during the winter, and hide their nests among the grass in summer. Over them hovers the kestrel, seeking mice and other small animals on the ground below.

In the spring, the bushes and hedgerows provide nesting places for many small birds. Buntings like the yellowhammer may be seen singing there. Dunnocks and warblers like blackcaps are nesting birds of hedgerows, and the long-tailed tit makes its delicate domed nest in a bush or tree. Finches like the goldfinch and linnet may nest on farmland and roam the fields in winter. In the summer, swallows, shrikes and flycatchers hunt for insects on the wing, while in the cornfields, quails skulk among the wheat or other grains.

Several birds make their homes around farm buildings, finding that food and nesting materials are readily available. Barn owls may use straw to nest in barns, and swallows and house martins often make their mud nests on farms. The grain attracts collared doves and pigeons. Pied or white wagtails are a common sight, perching on walls or roofs and running about the farmyard.

The autumn sees some change in the bird population of fields and farms. The insect eaters like swallows, shrikes, flycatchers and warblers depart, and waders like the curlew may come down from the moors to spend the winter. Flocks of lapwings and starlings can be seen roaming the fields in winter, and pheasants and partridges come to root about in the open after hiding away during the breeding season.

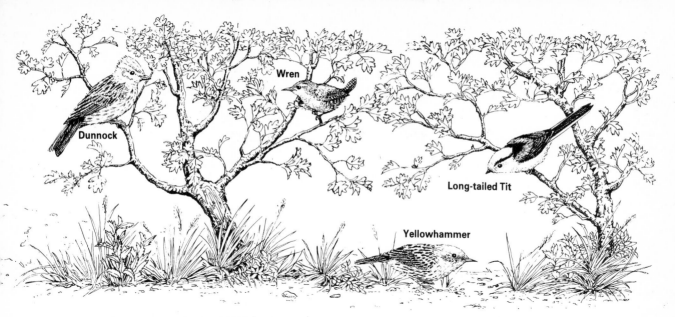

Dunnock

Wren

Long-tailed Tit

Yellowhammer

Left: The skylark makes its nest on the ground, hiding its eggs and young among the grass. Outside the breeding season, skylarks may roam the fields in flocks.

Left: The red–legged partridge is also a ground nester. It conceals its light-coloured eggs by sitting on them, abandoning the nest only if discovery is inevitable. During the winter, partridges can be seen rooting about in fields.

Birds Of Mountains And Moors

Mountain slopes are usually covered with deciduous forest, above which lies a belt of coniferous forest before the tree line is reached. Above this level, only low plants grow, and at the summit there may be nothing but bare rock and howling winds. Even at such altitudes, birds may brave the cold and make their homes. Some, like the ptarmigan and wallcreeper, can scratch a living from the ground by eating plants or insects. Snow buntings or snow finches may also be seen, their white plumage helping to camouflage them against any snow. Eagles may soar high in the air, riding the gusts of wind as they seek prey on the ground below, and choughs and ravens fly to great heights, ready to scavenge anything they may find. Several birds, including the peregrine falcon, use mountain crags and high cliffs for nesting, seeking to avoid the attentions of animals hungry for eggs and young birds.

Moors are high areas of open land, covered with rough grass or other low plants such as heather. There may be a few scattered trees, but the land is too dry and windswept to allow many trees to grow, even if it was once covered with forest. In the Mediterranean region, there are many areas of arid open country where the removal of forests long ago and grazing by domestic animals such as goats has eroded the land so that little can now grow.

These regions, though fairly inhospitable, can support many birds. The little orange-brown wheatears and chats actively seek insects there during the summer. There are several ground-living birds, including the meadow pipit and larks such as the skylark and woodlark, that find insects and seeds to eat on the ground, often all the year round. These little brownish birds are effectively concealed by the low plants and nest among them. Larger birds live on moors and open uplands too. During the summer, plovers and sandpipers including the long-beaked curlew and whimbrel come to nest, but leave for the seashore or fields below in winter where they can continue to root and dig for food. Grouse live among the heather all the year round, foraging for young shoots, seeds and insects.

Right: Several typical birds of mountains and moors.

Below: A golden eagle raises its young on a rock ledge among remote mountains.

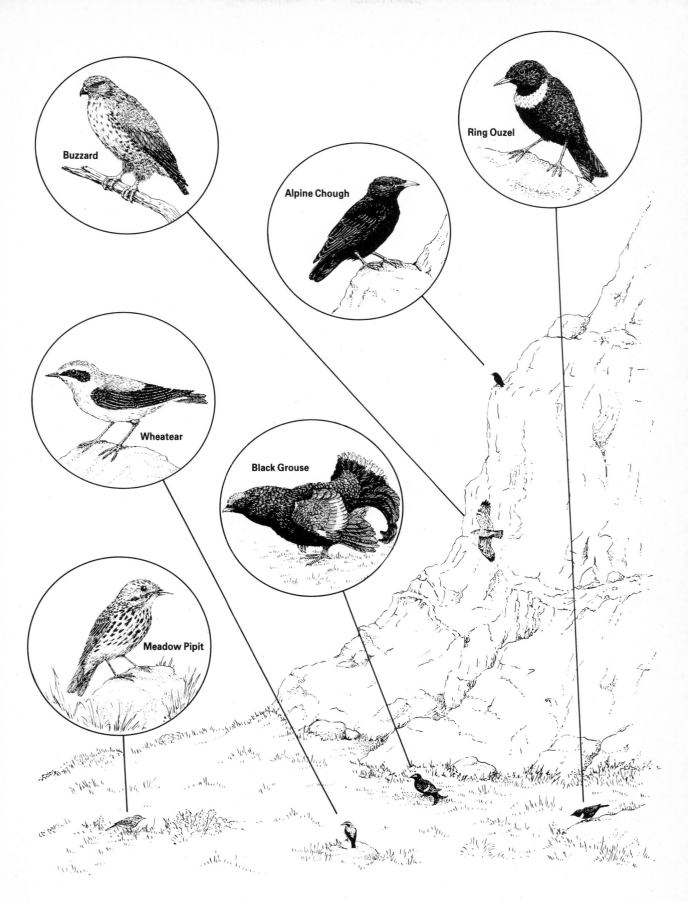

Buzzard

Alpine Chough

Ring Ouzel

Wheatear

Black Grouse

Meadow Pipit

Birds Of Lakes, Rivers And Marshes

Many birds make their home in fresh water. They may swim on the water, feeding on water plants, or they may dive to catch fish or other water creatures. Others wade in shallow water to find food, and some dig in the damp soil at the water's edge. There is a wide variety of watery habitats in Europe that support many different kinds of birds.

Lakes vary greatly in size, from small ones not much bigger than ponds to huge stretches of water like Lake Geneva in Switzerland and Lake Balaton in Hungary. The depth of water gives diving birds an opportunity to seek food. During the summer, ospreys may be seen splashing down into a lake to grab a fish. Divers and grebes may also be seen on lakes in summer, the grebes building floating nests of water plants. Most depart for the seashore in winter, though little grebes and great crested grebes may remain. Watch out for the grebes' courtship dances in spring. Diving ducks such as the tufted duck and pochard are common on lakes, though some go to the coast for the winter. Reservoirs may also attract these birds, and in winter they are a good place to see gulls and ducks which come to roost on the water. The shallow waters at the edges of lakes suit dabbling ducks and swans, which lower their heads or up-end

Below: Several typical birds of marshes, rivers and lakes.

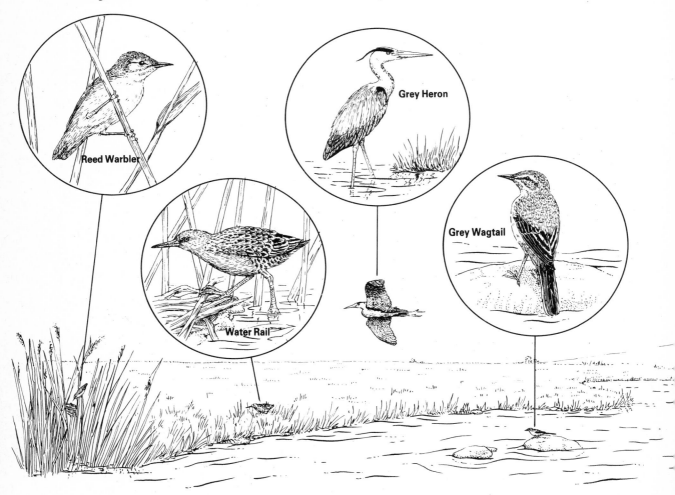

Reed Warbler

Grey Heron

Water Rail

Grey Wagtail

in the water to feed. On the grass at the sides of the lake, various species of geese may graze.

The flowing water of rivers contains all kinds of food for water birds, but many will come only if the current is slow. Some birds are suited to rivers. Dippers fly up and down, and can swim down into the water to feed. They may be seen on rivers all the year round, as can the multicoloured kingfishers, which make lightning dives into the water to catch fish. Grey wagtails are also resident river birds, even though they feed on insects. The yellow wagtail and swallow may be seen hunting for insects over the water in summer.

The shallow water, damp soil and reed beds of marshes and lake shores suit many birds. Long-legged wading birds like herons can stand or walk in the water and lower their heads to catch fish and other water animals. Moorhens and coots swim on the water and nest among the reeds. The reeds may also conceal such timid birds as bitterns, warblers, water rails and bearded tits. Birds such as plovers, sandpipers and snipe dig in damp soil to find food. They come to marshes to nest, and many remain during the winter if the ground does not freeze. Over the reeds throughout the year may fly harriers. These large birds of prey fly slowly to and fro, seeking animals in the reeds and marshy pools.

Tufted Duck

Osprey

Coot

Great Crested Grebe

Birds Of Seas And Cliffs

No seabird can remain out at sea all its life. It has to come ashore once a year to breed. Outside the breeding season, several birds that nest along the coasts of Europe fly out to sea and they may then be seen only from boats. These seabirds include shearwaters, petrels, the gannet, auks such as the razorbill, guillemot and puffin, and the kittiwake (which is a gull). Most of them are to be found out in the Atlantic Ocean and a few in the Mediterranean Sea. This is because cold water contains more oxygen than warm water and consequently cold seas are richer in fish and other marine life than warm seas. The cooler waters of the Atlantic are therefore a richer feeding ground and attract more seabirds.

Most seabirds stay around the continental shelves. Apart from Sabine's gull and the kittiwake, gulls do not fly out of sight of land. Gulls may be seen at the coast all the year round, though many go inland for the winter. Winter is the time to see marine ducks such as the eider and mergansers, which dive for food near the shore. In summer, nesting seabirds fly over the waves seeking food for their young. Terns may be seen diving from the air into the water in many places, for they nest in colonies on beaches. Gannets and auks can be seen around their cliff and island colonies. Cormorants and shags may be seen at any time of year, flying low over the sea or perched on a rock with their wings spread out to dry, for the feathers are not waterproof.

Offshore islands and high cliffs by the sea afford safe nesting places for seabirds, and breeding colonies gather at traditional sites in the spring and summer. Puffins and shearwaters burrow in the ground on islands or at the tops of cliffs. On the cliff ledges gannets, guillemots, razorbills, kittiwakes and fulmars may be seen nesting. The colonies can become very crowded with birds and some, such as kittiwakes, may use window ledges on coastal buildings instead of cliffs. Sea cliffs are further used by birds that also nest on inland cliffs, such as jackdaws, crows, kestrels and peregrine falcons. Sandy cliffs make good places for sand martins to excavate their nesting burrows. These birds do not feed from the sea but may seek food at the shore, catching insect food in flight.

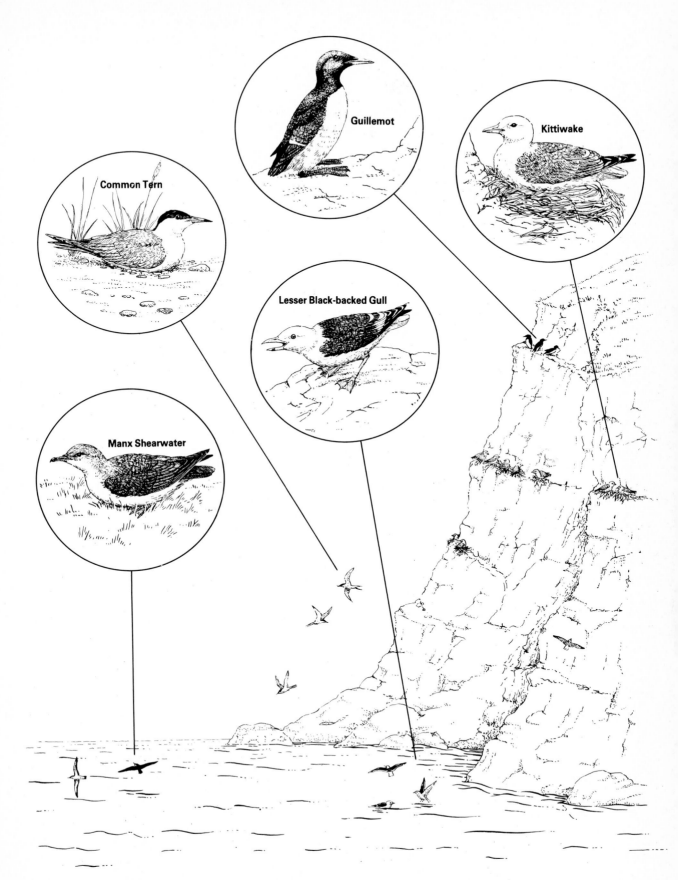

Common Tern

Guillemot

Kittiwake

Lesser Black-backed Gull

Manx Shearwater

Birds Of The Seashore

The seashore may appear to be a barren place where few animals of any kind could survive, but this is not at all the case. At high tide, the bare rocks and deserted stretches of pebbles or sand may be inhospitable but as the tide goes down, a wide range of food is uncovered and many birds take advantage of it. Shellfish such as mussels cling to the rocks, and small creatures shelter beneath the pebbles and among the seaweed. Buried in the sand are more shellfish and worms. With their very small tides, the shores of the Mediterranean Sea do not offer much of a feeding ground for birds. The shores of the Atlantic Ocean and the seas around the British Isles have a wide tidal range, and at low tide great expanses of mud, sand, rocks and pools may be uncovered, each with a range of food that attracts many birds to feed.

Several species are to be found along rocky and stony shores. Oystercatchers can prise open shellfish and feed at beds of mussels and other molluscs. Turnstones root about, looking under pebbles and probing among the seaweed to find insects and other small seashore animals. These birds can be seen at the shore all the year round, while others may be there only for nesting. Terns may lay their speckled eggs among the pebbles, the blotches on the eggs camouflaging them so that they are difficult to spot. Plovers also nest at stony shores.

The openness of sandy beaches attracts few nesting birds, but they are a good place to see birds in winter, as are the mudflats that lie along the shore and estuaries. Plovers and sandpipers may gather there in large flocks during the winter. They probe in the soft mud or sand with their long beaks, while the longer-legged birds like the avocet may wade in the shallows and sift through the mud and water for food. Water birds such as divers, grebes and ducks also gather at these rich feeding grounds in the winter, and geese come to browse on the vegetation that lines the shore. Migration time is particularly good for birdwatching on the seashore. Unusual birds may settle to feed there, and many birds like to follow the coastline as they migrate, coming in to visit at favourable locations on the way.

Right: Oystercatchers gather in large flocks at the seashore to feed on the shellfish exposed as the tide goes down.

Below: Several typical birds of seashores.

Turnstone

Common Sandpiper

Ringed Plover

Curlew

Knot

Bar-tailed Godwit

101

Below: Several typical birds of cities and towns.

Birds Of Towns

Many birds live in cities, towns and villages. They eat food offered by people or consume waste food, and they forage in parks and gardens. Feral pigeons are able to live in city centres, finding the ledges of the buildings little different to the cliffs where they originally lived, and where rock doves, their wild counterparts, are still to be found. Sparrows abound in city centres, but these birds have probably lived alongside man for thousands of years and so have found themselves in cities. Both birds are able to feed from plants on waste ground as well as on bread and other scraps.

Feral Pigeon

Starling

Swift

Blue Tit

House Sparrow

Chaffinch

Kestrels may also be seen in cities, where they hunt sparrows. Starlings may come in their thousands to roost in city centres after a day's feeding in parks and gardens or the countryside surrounding the city.

Urban bird life is interesting because it may vary from one city to another and it may change quickly. Some birds are found in some towns and not in others because their range does not extend that far. White storks may be seen nesting on roofs in central and southern Europe, but not in Italy, France, Britain or Scandinavia. Some cities attract certain birds. For example, you can see a colony of Arctic terns at Reykjavik in Iceland. Changes occur in town bird populations more rapidly than in the countryside. Black kites were once common in the cities of Europe. They fed on garbage, but were driven away by improvements in public health. Ravens were also common, but left as cities expanded and the nesting places disappeared. Gulls were not seen in London until about a century ago, after severe weather had forced them in from the sea; they then began to stay. The invasions of starlings in city centres has only happened in this century. However, sparrows are less common now, because as horses have disappeared from cities, so has a source of food in the droppings from their nosebags.

Parks and gardens support many typically woodland birds, especially the more common tits, thrushes and finches. Safe nesting places abound, and food is available in winter as well as summer. Several species make their nests in walls or on buildings, especially swifts, swallows and house martins, which may be seen in the outer parts of cities and towns. They do not live in city centres, because there are few flying insects to feed them and little mud to help construct a nest.

Below: This pair of white storks have built their nest on top of a chimney. In the parts of Europe where the storks breed, people regard them as lucky and do not stop them from making nests on houses.

Birdwatching Sites In Britain And Europe

The letters *s*, *w* or *m* indicate the best time of year to visit, *s* standing for summer, *w* for winter and *m* for migration time.

AUSTRIA
1 Grossglockner Pass *s*
2 Neusiedler See *s, m, w*

BELGIUM
1 Blankaart *s*
2 Campine *s*
3 Genk *s, m*
4 Hautes-Fagnes National Park *s, m*
5 Yser Estuary *s, m*
6 Zwin *s, w, m*

BRITAIN
1 Cley *s, w, m*
2 Dee Estuary *s, w, m*
3 Farne Islands *s, w, m*
4 Firth of Forth *s, w, m*
5 Minsmere *s, m*
6 North Kent Marshes *s, w, m*
7 Shetland Islands *s*
8 Skokholm and Skomer *s, m*
9 Slimbridge *s, w, m*
10 Speyside *s*

BULGARIA
1 Burgas *s, m*
2 Rila *s*
3 Lake Srebarna *s*

CZECHOSLOVAKIA
1 River Danube *s, m*
2 Lednice *s, m*
3 Mala Fatra *s*
4 Sturovo *s*
5 Tatra National Park *s*
6 Velky and Maly Tisy *s, w, m*
7 Vihorlat *s*

DENMARK
1 Blaavandshuk *w, m*
2 Limfjorden *s, m*
3 Naskov Indrefjord *s, w, m*
4 Ringkobing Fjord *s, w, m*
5 Skagen *s, w, m*
6 Tisso *s, w, m*

FINLAND
1 Aland Islands *s*
2 Enontekio *s*
3 Lake Inari *s*
4 Karigasniemi *s*
5 Oulanka National Park *s*
6 Parikkala *s*

FRANCE
1 Baie d'Aiguillon *s, w, m*
2 Lac du Bourget *s, w*
3 La Brenne *s, w, m*
4 Camargue *s, w, m*
5 Dombes *s, m*
6 Port de Gavarnie *s, m*
7 Landes *s, w, m*
8 Golfe du Morbihan *s, w, m*
9 Ile de l'Olonne *s, m*
10 St Flour *s*
11 St Nazaire *s, w, m*
12 Sept-Iles *s*
13 Sologne *s*
14 Vanoise National Park *s*

GERMANY, WEST
1 Bodensee (L. Constance) *s, w, m*
2 Elbe Estuary *s, w, m*
3 Federsee *s*
4 Heligoland *s, m*
5 Husum *s*
6 Inn Lakes *s, w, m*
7 Kiel Bay *s, m*
8 Kühkopf *s, m*
9 Oberammergau *s*
10 Uthörn *s, w, m*

GREECE
1 Gulf of Arta *s, m*
2 Avas Gorge *s*
3 Corinth *s*
4 Delphi *s*
5 Evros Delta *s, w*
6 Ioannina *s, m*
7 Lake Koronia *s, m*
8 Mesolonghi *s, m*
9 Meteora *s*
10 Nestos Delta *s, m*
11 Porto Lago *s, m*
12 Pyrgos *s*

HOLLAND
1 Biesbosch *s, w, m*
2 Hoge Veluwe and Veluwezoom *s*
3 Naardermeer *s*
4 Oostelijk Flevoland *s, w, m*
5 Texel *s, m*
6 Westzaan *s*
7 Zwanenwater *s, m*

HUNGARY
1 Bakony Hills *s*
2 Csakvar *s*
3 Hortobagy *s*
4 Kisbalaton *s*
5 Ocsa Forest *s*
6 Saser *s*
7 Kecskemet *s, m*
8 Lake Velence *s*

ICELAND
1 Huna Floi *s*
2 Myvatn *s*
3 Snaefellsnes *s*
4 Thingvallavatn *s*
5 Westmann Islands *s*

IRELAND
1 Cape Clear Island *m*
2 Dublin Bay *s, w, m*
3 Lough Erne *s, w*
4 Kerry Islands *s*
5 Lough Neagh *s, w, m*
6 Strangford Lough *s, w, m*
7 Wexford Slobs *s, w, m*

ITALY
1 Abruzzi National Park *s*
2 Capri *m*
3 Gargano *s, w, m*
4 Gran Paradiso National Park *s*
5 Orbetello *s, w, m*
6 Oristano (Sardinia) *s, w, m*
7 Venetian Lagoons *s, m*

NORWAY
1 Börgefjell National Park *s*
2 Dovrefjell *s*
3 Hardanger Vidda *s*
4 Lofoten Isles *s*
5 Runde *s*
6 Utsira *m*
7 Varangerfjord *s*

POLAND
1 Barycz Valley *s, m*
2 Beibrzanski Marshes *s*
3 Bialowieska Forest *s*
4 Bieszczady Mountains *s*
5 Druzno Lake *s, w, m*
6 Goplo Lake *s*
7 Kampinoski National Park *s*
8 Krynica Morska *m*
9 Masurian Lakes *s*
10 Pieniny Mountains *s*
11 Slowinski National Park *s, m*
12 Tatrzanski National Park *s*
13 Wolin Island *s, m*

PORTUGAL
1 Aveiro *s, m*
2 Berlenga Islands *s, m*
3 Elvas *s*
4 Faro *s, m*
5 Sado and Tagus Estuaries *s, w, m*
6 Sines *s, m*

ROMANIA
1 Baneasa *s*
2 Calarasi *s*
3 Danube Delta *s, m*
4 Oltenita *s*
5 Satchinez *s*

SPAIN
1 Andorra *s*
2 Badajoz *s*
3 Coto Donana *s*
4 Ebro Delta *s, w, m*
5 Estartit *s*
6 Gibraltar *s, m*
7 Sierra Guadarrama *s*
8 Majorca *s, m*
9 Sierra Nevada *s*
10 Ordesa National Park *s*
11 Silos *s*

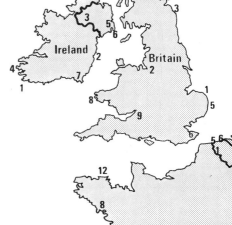

SWEDEN
1 Abisko *s*
2 Annsjon *s, m*
3 Falsterbo *s, m*
4 Getteron *s, m*
5 Gotland *s, m*
6 Hornborgasjon *s, m*
7 Kvismaren *s, w, m*
8 Osten *s, w, m*
9 Oland *s, m*
10 Oset *s, m*
11 Sappisassi *s*
12 Takern *s, m*
SWITZERLAND
1 Col de Bretolet *s, m*
2 Chavornay *s, m*
3 Grindelwald *s*
4 Lac Leman (Lake Geneva) *s, m*
5 Lac de Neuchatel *s, m*
6 Mont Tendre *s*
TURKEY
1 Lake Apolyont *s, m*
2 Bosporus *m*
3 Lake Iznik *s, m*
4 Lake Manyas *s, m*
YUGOSLAVIA
1 Baranja *s*
2 Carska Bara *s, m*
3 Lake Dojransko *s, m*
4 Metkovic *s, w, m*
5 Obedska Bara *s*
6 Plitvice *s*
7 Lake Skadarsko (Scutari) *s, m*
8 Titov Veles *s, m*

How to Watch Birds

Birdwatching is a pastime, hobby or pursuit that can be practised with any degree of enthusiasm, and yet will always be rewarding. At one end of the scale, there are people who enjoy looking at birds from the windows of their home or on their way to and from work or school. They find the activities of the birds entertaining as well as interesting, and like to be able to name the birds they find. These birdwatchers may study the birds they see, perhaps observing the peck order at a bird table or seeking to explain the population changes or bird movements that take place over the year.

This initial interest in birds may well lead to a greater devotion to the subject. The birdwatcher becomes dissatisfied with observing the same birds around the home, and begins to look out for new birds when travelling and on holiday. Often, the collector's instinct begins to take over and the birdwatcher may become obsessed with seeing as many new birds as possible. He or she starts to make special birdwatching expeditions, devoting weekends and even holidays to the new hobby, and often joining other bird enthusiasts. Mere listing of new species may then begin to take second place to serious behaviour study and practical projects such as counting birds and ringing them. Such work is not just of academic value, but may be important in conservation.

But however dedicated a birdwatcher you may be, from the casual observer to the committed professional ornithologist, there are certain 'rules' that enable you to make the most of birdwatching. They are concerned with the kind of equipment you should use, the best ways of using it and how to behave while birdwatching. The rules aim to give you a good view of birds in the wild while disturbing them as little as possible. They also aim to give you the maximum amount of useful information that can be gained from watching birds. By following these rules, which you can get from other birdwatchers as well as by reading about them, you will learn a lot about birds and come to understand them, and you may be able to help them.

Equipment For Birdwatching

Birdwatching must be one of the cheapest hobbies to take up because you do not actually need any equipment at all. A lot can be learned about birds simply by keeping your eyes open, and by remembering what you observe. However, to see birds more easily and to retain as well as interpret the information you gain about them, you need a small amount of inexpensive equipment.

There is not much to be gained from birdwatching if you do not know which birds you are observing. A good field guide that will help you to name the birds you see is essential. A field guide is a book that has illustrations of all the birds you are likely to see in the region where you live. Several good field guides are listed on page 193, and you should choose one that you can understand and use easily. It should fit into a coat pocket so that your hands will be free when you are not consulting it.

Above: A group of birdwatchers scan the seashore from a sea wall. The wall helps to hide the bird-watchers from the birds below, as well as giving them a good view of the shore.

A field guide is not the only kind of book that is useful to a birdwatcher. To understand and learn more about birds, it is a good idea to read general books about birdwatching and the lives of birds. Some may tell you how to make the most of birdwatching, like the second section in this book, and give practical hints and advice. Other books, like the first section of this book, talk about the various ways in which birds live, and they will help you to understand why the birds that you see behave in the ways they do. Then there are books about the different kinds of birds found throughout the world. With these books, you can get to know about all the strange and unusual birds that exist, and you will begin to understand how the birds you know fit into the overall world of birds. And if you are very interested in one particular group of birds, say birds of prey or owls, then there is likely to be a book just about these birds. Most of these books have good photographs or illustrations and are a pleasure to read.

Keen birdwatchers will also want to read bird journals and magazines, which are published by bird societies. These publications give news about birds, as well as special articles on aspects of birds that you would not find in a book. New discoveries about birds are usually published first in such journals.

Binoculars And Telescopes
It is usually difficult to get very close to a wild bird. Unless you are hiding, the bird will become well aware of your presence long before you approach closely. As soon as it feels threatened by you, whether or not you mean any harm, it will fly away. Birds may also

be hard to see close to because they live in remote places that you cannot reach, or because they usually keep to the air. To be sure of getting as good a view of any bird as possible, you will have to carry a pair of binoculars or a telescope.

Binoculars and telescopes can give you a close-up view of a bird that is nearby without you having to approach it and disturb it. They can also give you a view of a distant bird that is large enough for identification and general observation.

Binoculars are easier to use than telescopes, but they do not give such a magnified view. This is not necessarily a disadvantage, because the field of view (how much you can see) gets smaller as the magnification increases. Having a small field of view makes it difficult to locate a bird, and to keep track of it if it is moving. On the other hand, you do want sufficient magnification to show up details of the bird's body and its behaviour. Every pair of binoculars bears a sign such as 8×30 or 10×50. The first number indicates the magnification of the instrument. The bird will appear eight times ($8 \times$) or ten times ($10 \times$) bigger than it appears to the naked eye. The second figure is the diameter of each of the objective lenses (the bigger lenses) in millimetres. The higher this figure, then the wider the field of view and the brighter the image seen. From this, you might think that you should get a pair of binoculars with the highest figures indicated. However, big binoculars are heavy and tiring to hold up to the eyes. Also, if the magnification is too high, the image appears to dance about as your hands shake. In practice, the largest binoculars that can be satisfactorily used for birdwatching are 10×50, and the smallest 7×30. Choose a pair in between these limits that produce the sharpest image for the price you can afford, but do not buy a pair that feels too heavy. When birdwatching, *always* carry the binoculars on a strap around your neck – in case you drop them.

Telescopes give much higher magnifications than binoculars – from about $20 \times$ up to about $60 \times$. They can give a very good view

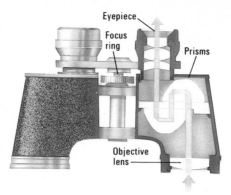

Above: Most binoculars are of the prismatic kind. They contain prisms that reflect the light rays inside the binoculars so that they can be made small and portable. The ring is turned to move the eyepieces in or out and focus the image.

Below: Birdwatchers can use permanent hides at bird reserves to get good views of birds. This hide is at the RSPB's reserve at Minsmere, Suffolk, and has been built near an artificial island especially constructed to attract nesting terns.

of distant birds, but should be fixed to a tripod to prevent the image shaking. Some telescopes have zoom lenses, which are useful for locating birds at low power and then zooming in on them to get a close-up view.

Notes

One further piece of equipment is essential to good birdwatching and that is a notebook. Many birdwatchers make rough notes of the birds they see at the time of observation, and then write up these notes to make a permanent record in a loose-leaf book or filing system. Some people prefer to speak their observations into a portable cassette recorder instead of making rough notes. This has the advantage that the birdwatcher's hands are left free to hold binoculars, though it is still a good idea to carry a notebook in case a sketch of a bird is required.

The purpose of taking notes may be no more than to keep a diary of birdwatching expeditions. It can then be a pleasure to look back at the notes at a later time and recall exciting days spent birdwatching. Note taking may also have a more serious purpose in providing proof of an unusual sighting for a bird society or other bird organization.

If you simply want to list the birds you see, then you can buy special lists of local birds from bird societies. You tick off the birds as you spot them, and can easily add up your score at the end of a year. Some of these lists have extra columns so that you can record the date, weather, habitat and other features of the bird you have spotted, thus making more precise observations.

If you are looking for a new bird that you have never seen before, or if you are making special observations of particular birds, then you should make detailed notes. These should include the date, time, place of observation and weather (including wind direction) at the time; the habitat, the size of the bird and any sound it is making; the identities, numbers and sexes of any other birds in company with the bird; plus a complete description and a drawing of the bird labelling the various parts and their colours, together with any comments on the bird's actions and anything else of interest. At the end of the notes, you should add your conclusion of the bird's identity if you think you have seen a new bird.

Going Birdwatching

Birdwatching is an occupation for which you must dress in the right way. Any wild bird that you meet is going to think that you are an enemy, so it is best to make sure that you are not too visible. This involves camouflage, by dressing in dull or dark green, brown or grey colours that will merge in with the landscape. Wear a hat, because it will help to break up the line of your head. Gloves will help too, and avoid having shiny surfaces on metal objects such as cameras and binoculars. Remember that you will be standing or sitting about for long periods and could get cold, so dress in warm clothes if necessary. Carry a rucksack for your equipment, and include an inflatable cushion if you want to be comfortable. Attention to the right footwear is especially important.

Plan your birdwatching trip carefully. Consult tide tables if you are going to the coast, and aim to be there at low tide. Otherwise, it is often a good idea to start out early. Birds are up with the sun, and you can have a long day ahead of you. Think about companions. Two or three of you can spot more birds than one, and company can make the day more rewarding.

Once you have arrived, search for birds quietly and carefully. Pick out the most likely place to see them and settle down to find something interesting. If possible, make yourself inconspicuous by hiding behind a bush or some other obstruction. Use your binoculars to search for birds. If you look for them with the naked eye and then raise your binoculars when you see something, the bird may have flown before you can get it in view, especially if it is startled by your sudden action.

If you want to get really close to birds, particularly to photograph them, then you may need a hide. This is a portable tent in which you can conceal yourself. A hide is rather large and heavy to carry about, and you can use netting camouflaged with coloured material instead. The nettting is spread over some bushes, or you may be able to drape it over yourself. At bird reserves, permanent hides are available for use by birdwatchers. Remember that birds are not stupid, and will not come near a hide if they think someone is inside it. Several people may have to go in and then some come out, before the bird is likely to accept that it is safe to approach the hide.

All birdwatchers have a responsibility to birds, and must not disturb them unduly, particularly if they are nesting. In any case, it may be against the law to interfere with them. The wishes of other people should also be respected. Take care not to trespass on private land or to damage crops, gates and walls. Do not leave litter and beware of starting fires, for example by throwing down lighted cigarette ends.

Below: A hide constructed to photograph the nest of a skylark. The hide is disguised with hay, and a flashlight is placed beside it.

Photographing Birds

The British were pioneers in bird photography. Men like Cherry and Richard Kearton set out to photograph every British bird at the nest. Although they failed to do this, these brothers developed and perfected the photographic hide after experimenting with such things as sheep and cow skins that resembled living animals.

The modern pioneer is Eric Hosking who used the first 'pylon' hide for photographing species that use tall trees. He also spent several years developing the use of the electronic flashgun and electronic beam photography, a system whereby the bird flies through a beam which triggers a device that sets off the shutter. In fact many of the pictures that we see in bird books today have been taken without the photographer being anywhere near the equipment! Owl photographers are now able to take pictures with sophisticated equipment, but spend the night in bed! This rapid advance in technology has taken place in the space of just over a hundred years, since the first bird photograph was published in 1868.

Since World War II, the quality of colour film has improved dramatically, particularly in the high speed range. Processing too has become much quicker, with some firms offering same day service, whilst others produce home developing kits.

All these recent developments in equipment and film have been responsible for the current boom in bird photography. The 'price war' has also brought prices into the range of everyone's budget.

Those starting bird photography for the first time, and seeking equipment will be confused by the vast range of cameras and lenses available. Opinions will always vary as to the best camera body and lenses to buy. It is important to get a camera body of the single lens reflex type, which will have through-the-lens focusing and metering. Bayonet fitting bodies are best for the quick changing of lenses, and these must be in the 300–400 mm telephoto range for photographing birds. These lenses can be used on a tripod in a hide for birds at the nest or with a pistol-type shoulder support for stalking and flight shots. Before making any purchases it is a good idea to talk to an established bird photographer for advice, as equipment salesmen in shops know very little about bird photography.

An electronic flashgun is a very important piece of equipment when photographing birds at the nest in poorly lit areas. Most of the flashguns now have automatic and manual settings. Some bird photographers prefer the flashgun outside the hide on a separate tripod close to the lens, while others cut a hole in the hide and mount it inside, where it is much easier to adjust the settings. Fairly slow speed films can be used for flash photography, in the 64 to 100 ASA range, but for stalking and flight shots, high speed film in the 200 to 400 ASA range is best in order to 'freeze' the subject.

It is a good idea to get plenty of practice in the garden before attempting anything too ambitious. The winter birds on the nut feeders and bird table make good subjects. Another good place to practise is in the local town park using the wildfowl and pigeons as subjects. The various wildfowl collections are excellent for gaining experience with the telephoto lens and also the flashgun. Most of the collections have excellent public hides.

One of the easiest ways to make a hide is to buy a green camping toilet tent, reduce it in height and add small nylon windows and a lens sleeve. But all sorts of natural materials can be used for hides, such as rocks at the coast or bracken on the hills. A well camouflaged hide will be much better for the birds, and result in superior pictures. All mobile hides should be put up some distance from nests and slowly moved nearer in stages under the guidance of an expert if you happen to be new to this type of photography.

Before photographing any bird at the nest, it would be a good idea to study breeding biology in one of the many books on the subject. Always remember that the welfare of the birds is much more important than the pictures.

In recent years the Protection of Birds Acts have been extended to cover disturbance at the nest by the activities of photographers. First of all, a general permit must be obtained from The Nature Conservancy Council, 20 Belgrave Square, in London. British birds are grouped into various schedules according to how rare they are. Special written permits must be obtained to photograph all species in the first schedule, even if they are breeding on your own land or buildings!

Many people wonder why birdwatchers take up photography. One reason is that it can be very difficult to get a really good set of pictures of house sparrows and starlings! Apart from the challenge, it is also an extremely interesting, healthy outdoor hobby, the results of which can be used for teaching and lecturing to others, particularly in the field of conservation. Good pictures may be used by publishers in magazines and books, but competition in this area is fierce, due to the large number of superb bird photographers in Britain. Photography is also useful when counting birds, especially flocks in flight and seabird colonies.

Recording the Sounds of Birds

In just over seventy years, the art of recording the sounds of birds has been perfected. Ludwig Koch, the pioneer, made the first ever recording of a bird in captive conditions, using an Edison phonograph with a wax cylinder. Now there are hundreds of excellent sound recordists all over Britain with special societies for them to exchange ideas on technique and equipment.

For those taking up sound recording of birds for the first time, the basic requirements are endless patience and a good knowledge of the species to be worked on. Although there are several books on the subject now, it is best to make contact with an experienced recordist before buying any equipment etc. Basic techniques can also be learnt from others.

Choosing equipment is not easy, as the choice is enormous, but there is something on the market to suit everybody's needs, both in quality and price. First of all, decide what type of recording you wish to do and how much you are able to carry!

The small portable battery operated tape recorder can produce excellent results, providing the microphone is of good quality and suitable for windy days. But the problem with these outfits is that they pick up all kinds of extraneous sounds, especially in urban areas.

Those looking for top quality recordings will certainly need a tape recorder, microphone, headphones and, most of all, a parabolic reflector to eliminate unwanted sounds. It is best if the recording machine is portable and fitted with a manual record level and monitoring point, so that the recording can be monitored and the recording level adjusted to prevent distortion. The microphone should be one with directional response pattern. Parabolic reflectors normally come in a range of sizes between 18″ and 40″, but

Below: A birdwatcher records some birdsong on a portable tape recorder, monitoring the sounds on headphones to get the best results.

18″ to 24″ would probably be best for general work. Once the recordings are made, they can be edited to remove unwanted sounds etc. This is where the spool tape machines have the advantage over the cassette type.

Recordists will soon realize that subject material is endless, but it is a good idea to practise first on garden birds, such as the robin with its beautiful winter and summer songs. The tawny owl is another rewarding species for beginners, but if you live near a harbour the arrival of the fishing boat, surrounded by calling gulls, can also be a stimulating sound.

The Purpose Of Birdwatching

You can get great personal satisfaction from listing birds, and photographing and recording them. You may also use your skills as a birdwatcher to help birds and widen our knowledge of them. For example, you may take a particular interest in one species that is common near your home. Intensive study of the behaviour of this bird could well reveal a facet of its life – say, its feeding methods, or its courtship and breeding behaviour or its migration pattern – about which little is generally known.

However, there is usually not a great deal that you can do without help. It is a very good idea to join a local bird club as well as a national bird society, and work with others. You will be able to visit field study centres and bird observatories to widen your knowledge, and you could become a voluntary warden at a bird reserve if you want to be directly involved in the protection of birds. Bird societies organize large projects to discover where birds live and how numerous they are, and you can take part in these. Bird counts are made to find out where birds are concentrated. You may be asked to count the number of birds on a particular lake, to estimate the size of a colony of seabirds at a cliff, or to measure the bird population of a particular wood. The information obtained in this way is not just of interest to birdwatchers. It shows up the effects of pollution on birds, and can give conservationists valuable evidence in their fight to protect birds. It can help wildlife organizations to campaign against industrial development that would threaten birds, and can pinpoint notable concentrations of birds that would justify a reserve status for the site, if this can be negotiated.

You could also take part in atlas projects that map the ranges of birds. You would be given a small square of land and asked to record all the birds to be seen there over a certain period. From the results, accurate and up-to-date maps can be drawn showing the range of every species to be found in the country. These maps show up any changes in bird population.

Migration is studied by ringing birds. Birds are caught and numbered rings are placed around their legs. If the bird is caught later, or found dead, the number, date and location are reported to the ringing organization. In this way, a picture of bird movements can be built up. Ringing recoveries also provide valuable data on how long wild birds live and have already shown how average life spans fall far short of the potential maximum for a species. Ringing is not easy, and it is necessary to be trained by experienced ringers if you want to carry it out.

Birds and the Home

Most of us live in cities and towns, and perhaps do not have the opportunity to watch birds daily as may people who live in villages or on farms. Nevertheless, many kinds of birds do live in cities and towns and, simply by caring for them, you can attract the birds to your home. You can then have the pleasure of watching them in comfort through the windows. The kinds of birds that will come to your home will normally be the common birds of your region. However, keep a sharp lookout at migration time and during severe weather, for uncommon or shy birds may be forced to take advantage of your hospitality.

To bring birds to your home, it helps to have a garden and to live in the outer parts of a city or town or near a park. Few birds are able to live in places where there is no open ground. However, do not be put off if you live in a flat or in the centre of a city. You will be able to put out food for birds on window ledges, and possibly set up a bird table or nest box. Once the birds have found that you will help them, they will keep on coming to visit you.

Feeding Birds

You will find that birds will come to your home as soon as you put out food for them, especially in winter when natural food is likely to be scarce. If you want to see as many different birds as possible, then you will have to give them a wide range of food. Also, the food should be placed in various positions around your home, as birds like to feed in different ways. Nuts and seeds make a nutritious food for birds. Peanuts and birdseed can be bought at pet shops, often in net bags that can be hung up outside a window or from a washing line or a branch. Alternatively, nuts can be placed in wire-mesh baskets or other kinds of feeders. However, avoid feeders made of a metal spiral that look like a spring. Birds can get their feet caught in

Above: A great spotted woodpecker hangs upside-down on a net bag containing pieces of fat. Its eye looks grey because the eyelid is closed. Woodpeckers normally feed in trees, gripping the bark and seeking insects and spiders as well as seeds and nuts. Their agility and wide range of tastes in food enable them to survive at bird tables when severe weather makes food hard to find. However, they are not common visitors to bird tables.

Left: The house sparrow is man's constant companion, and can be found in villages, cities and towns in most parts of the world. In the East, it is replaced by its near relative, the tree sparrow. It is possible that the sparrows spread throughout Europe, Africa and Asia in company with man, immediately occupying any settlements that sprang up. The house sparrow was introduced to North and South America, Australia and New Zealand, and has thrived there. This is a male house sparrow.

Above: A house sparrow and a blackbird meet at a bird table. Being the bigger of the two birds, the blackbird is higher in the peck order and takes the food first, threatening the smaller bird if necessary.

the spiral and may die. Tits like to clamber about to get food, and will perch on bags and baskets of nuts. So too will greenfinches and sparrows. Thread unshelled peanuts on a string and watch these birds peck through the shells to get at the nuts. Half a coconut suspended upside-down provides another challenge that tits can easily meet. Other birds are not so agile, and prefer to feed on the ground or a flat surface such as a ledge or bird table. Nuts and seeds put out in these places will attract finches such as chaffinches and thrushes such as blackbirds. Do be careful not to put food out on the ground or at a low level if cats are about. Also, do not put out salted nuts or desiccated coconut, and do not feed nuts to birds in summer. The birds may give the nuts to their young, which cannot digest them. Scraps and waste food from the kitchen will help birds. Bacon rinds and pieces of fat or suet can be placed in mesh baskets, hung up or put out on the ground or a bird table. Bread or stale cake can be put out either crumbled up or in slices. Rotting apples make a good bait to attract fruit eaters such as thrushes.

Many birds like to eat insects, but this is a food that most of us would find difficult to provide. A good substitute may be worms, either mealworms bought from a pet shop or chopped-up earthworms. Place them in a small dish. Worms make a good food in summer when nuts are forbidden. However, it is not really necessary to feed birds in summer, as natural food should then be abundant.

Birds may come to depend on food put out for them by people, especially in winter. Once you start feeding birds, you should continue to do so throughout the winter. If you stop suddenly, the birds that you have been feeding may be unable to find food elsewhere and could die of starvation.

Bird Tables And Baths

If you have the room, it is a good idea to make a bird table to feed birds. This is basically a wooden tray either mounted on a post or hung from a branch. Place it high enough to make it safe from cats, and put a guard of some kind around the post to prevent cats climbing up to the table. A roof over the table helps to keep rain off the food. Place the table outside a window so that you can easily observe the birds feeding. However, do not put it too close or the birds will fly away when there is any movement inside the house. Always keep the table clean by washing it and removing old uneaten food. This will stop infection spreading among the birds who come to feed at the table.

Birds need to drink as well as eat, and you will help them by placing a small dish of water in one corner of the bird table. Alternatively, you could build a bird bath if there is enough room in the garden. Birds will come not only to drink but also to bath in the water. A simple bath can be made by filling an upside-down dustbin lid with water. Place a brick, a stone or an upturned flower pot in the middle to make an 'island' where the drinking or bathing bird can stand. A more elaborate bird bath can be made by digging a shallow hole and lining it with plastic sheeting to make it hold water. Make an island of stones in the middle, and have a sloping edge so that birds can drink at the side. If you are not good with your hands or do not want to make your own bird table or bird bath, you can buy them from a pet shop.

Above: A great tit enters a nest box to feed its brood of hungry youngsters.

Below: An artificial nestbox especially made for house martins. It is fixed below the eaves of a house.

116

Nest Boxes

Birds are not so dependent on people to provide food for them during the summer as they are during the winter. The groups of birds that gather at bird tables in the winter, endlessly trying to beat their neighbours to the next morsel of food, are not a common sight in summer. However, we can still provide for birds at this time of year by giving them somewhere to nest and raise their young in safety. You can put up nest boxes in trees, fix them to the walls of your house or a shed, or even stick one on the top of a pole. While the boxes may not always attract breeding birds, there is a good chance that birds which are seeking somewhere to raise their young will come to nest every year.

Nest boxes can be made from wood or bought from pet shops. There are several different designs, depending on the kinds of birds that are to use them. A box with a hole in the front will attract hole-nesting birds, especially tits. The hole must be the right size to prevent larger birds such as sparrows and starlings taking over. Special nest boxes for house martins can be bought from pet shops and fixed under the eaves of a roof. Boxes with an open front attract robins and blackbirds, and large boxes may bring in tawny owls or kestrels. In the countries of Europe where white storks breed, people build platforms on their roofs or put up cartwheels on high poles to attract the storks, which are said to bring good luck, though most people probably go to such trouble to attract one of Europe's most interesting and striking birds to adorn their houses rather than to seek good fortune.

Nest boxes should be made of thick, strong wood, and must be waterproof. A sloping, hinged roof will keep off the rain, and allow for the box to be opened in order to inspect the nest and young. Do not make a perch on the front of the box; it may help a marauding cat or squirrel to raid the nest inside. Place nest boxes high up to avoid cats, and possibly vandals, but not so high that you cannot inspect them. Two metres is about the right height. Open-fronted boxes should be placed among foliage for protection, but should not be so completely hidden that the parent birds could not get to the nest. Place the boxes out of the sun and wind. Put up new boxes in the autumn so that the birds have time to get used to them before nesting, and do not have many boxes close together. Birds take territories and spread themselves out when nesting, and if the boxes are too close to each other, then some of them are likely to remain unoccupied.

Putting some moss or straw into a nest box will help to attract birds to nest in it, and you can also aid the birds by leaving net bags of nesting materials, such as straw, feathers, cotton wool and pieces of cotton or wool near the box. With any luck, late spring or early summer will see a brood of baby birds in the box. You can inspect them from time to time, say every two or three days. Do not look in on them more often, and do not frighten away the parent bird from the nest box – it may not return. Wait until the parent bird has left the nest to find food for its young. When the young have been raised and have left the nest, clean out the box and put some moss or straw in it. You may attract a bird to raise a second brood right away, but in any case it will be ready for use next year.

150

250 Side 200

200 Side 250

200 Front

212 Roof

112 Base

450 mm Back

Above: The basic plan for a nestbox suitable for tits, tree sparrows and nuthatches. The nestbox should be positioned high up on a trunk or wall where predators cannot reach it easily. Full instructions for this and other nestboxes can be found in the booklet 'Nestboxes', published by the British Trust for Ornithology, RSPB Sales Department, The Lodge, Sandy, Bedfordshire SG19 2DL.

Bird Gardening

As well as feeding birds in winter and providing nest boxes for them in summer, you can 'improve' your home to attract birds to it. Your house and garden may not be very rich in natural places to nest, nor harbour the kinds of plants that birds use for food and as a source of insects to eat. By altering your immediate surroundings, you can provide birds with an environment that is much more like their natural habitat.

Many birds like to nest in hedges, bushes and trees. If your garden has none of these, then planting them will be the first step in attracting birds to nest there naturally. If the garden is well planted, then it may help to prune hedges, bushes and trees to provide better nesting sites. Aim to have plenty of forks in the branches so that the birds can build secure nests. You may find that this attracts such pretty birds as goldfinches and bullfinches.

Hole-nesting birds can also be brought in to nest. Making holes in tree trunks could attract woodpeckers or nuthatches, and enlarging cracks and crannies in walls could provide nesting places for tits and wagtails. Growing a creeper on a wall could attract flycatchers and robins to nest. A shed or garage provides several opportunities for nesting birds. Swallows and blackbirds like to make their nests inside buildings. Leave them a space to get in and out, and provide shelves for nesting if necessary. Think twice about clearing away garden things such as bundles of sticks or flowerpots – they may be just the place that a wren or a robin may want to make a nest, however old or useless they may appear.

Below: A fieldfare feasts on some rotten apples. Fieldfares belong to the thrush family, and have general purpose beaks that enable them to consume worms and insects as well as fruit and berries.

Outside in the garden, much can be done to provide more natural food for birds. Those to be found around the home are mostly woodland birds, and a garden with a patch of lawn surrounded by bushes and trees is very like the edge of a wood where it gives way to fields. Your garden may not be big enough to arrange in this way, but if neighbouring gardens have trees or lawns, then two or three gardens together may make up a very natural habitat for birds to live in.

A lawn provides a feeding ground for such birds as starlings and thrushes that peck for worms and ants. Flower beds are generally not of great value to birds, though sunflowers produce masses of seeds for seed-eaters in the autumn. A hedge is a very good source of insects and berries all the year round, as well as providing good nesting places for small birds. Gardeners spend much time removing weeds from the garden, but these may be useful food plants for birds. A rough patch of teazels, nettles, ragwort, cow parsley and thistles could bring in finches. Bushes and trees that bear berries are particularly valuable to birds, and they are often attractive to look at as well. A good bird garden would include such plants as hawthorn, cotoneaster, elder, ivy, rowan or mountain ash, berberis, yew, holly and honeysuckle. Fruit and nut trees are also worth planting or encouraging. They provide a useful crop for us, while harbouring insects for birds. Bullfinches are attracted to the buds of fruit trees in spring, and bird-loving gardeners are often torn between admiring these beautiful birds and saving their fruit crop in any way they possibly can.

Below: A bird table laden with scraps and baskets of nuts will help many small birds to survive the winter. Here, great tits and blue tits cluster round the food.

Part Three

Identifying Birds

Left : The vivid markings of this bird mark it out immediately as a male chaffinch.

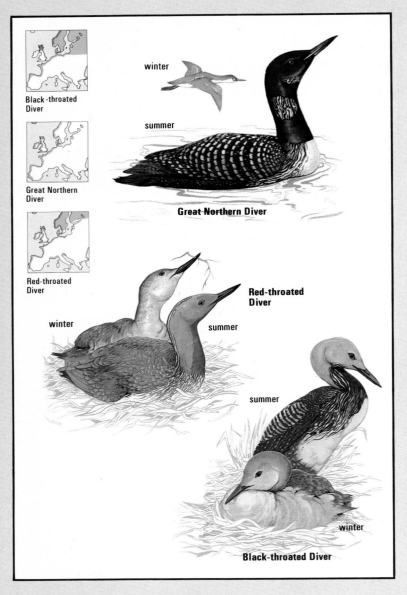

Black-throated
Diver

Great Northern
Diver

Red-throated
Diver

winter

summer

Great Northern Diver

winter

summer

**Red-throated
Diver**

summer

winter

Black-throated Diver

DIVERS

Order Gaviiformes Family Gaviidae

Divers are really at home underwater, where they catch fish and crustaceans. They either dive suddenly from the surface or sink slowly into the water. On land, divers walk clumsily and they normally come ashore only to breed. In winter, all divers become grey-brown above and white below. They can then only be told apart by their size, bill shape and the colours of their backs.

Black-throated Diver *Gavia arctica* 63 cm 25 in. Breeds at remote lakes or lochs, usually on rocky islands. Seen at coasts in autumn and winter, often in small flocks.
Great Northern Diver *Gavia immer* 76 cm 30 in. Breeds on lakes in Iceland. Found at coast at other times.
Red-throated Diver *Gavia stellata* 56 cm 22 in. Breeds at coast and lakes, flying daily to the sea to feed. May be seen on reservoirs and lakes as well as at coast during autumn and winter.

WHAT TO LOOK FOR

Black-throated Diver Intermediate bill. Summer: black throat patch; dark spotted back. Winter: blackish back.

Great Northern Diver Heavy bill. Summer: all-black head; chequered back. Winter: grey-brown back.

Red-throated Diver Thin upturned bill. Summer: red throat patch; plain grey back. Winter: grey-brown back speckled with white.

GREBES

Order Podicipediformes
Family Podicipitidae

Grebes are elegant water birds with colourful breeding plumage in spring and summer. The boldly patterned heads and necks, with their ear tufts and frills, clearly mark them out from other birds. In winter, grebes lose their colour and adornments, becoming grey-brown above and white below. Then they look like divers, but are smaller and have wedge-shaped heads.

Great Crested
Grebe

summer

winter

Great Crested Grebe

Grebes feed by diving for fish and other water animals. Although agile in the water, they are not good fliers and may escape danger by partly submerging themselves until only the head remains above water.

Grebes build nests of water plants among reeds at the edges of lakes and rivers, and lay about four eggs. The eggs may be covered with vegetation. Before building the nest, the birds perform extraordinary courtship dances in which they rush to and fro over the water and freeze in absurd postures. The chicks are often carried on the parents' backs, even during dives.

Grebes spread to the coast and open water in autumn and winter.

Great Crested Grebe *Podiceps cristatus* 46 cm 18 in. Found on inland waters in summer and winter; also at coast in winter. Once hunted for its plumage, it came near to extinction in Britain in 1800s. Recovery mainly due to protection, though building of reservoirs has enabled it to expand.
Red–necked Grebe *Podiceps grisgena* 43 cm 17 in. Found on inland waters in summer; usually at coast in winter.
Slavonian Grebe or **Horned Grebe** *Podiceps auritus* 36 cm 14 in. Found on inland waters in summer and at estuaries in winter.
Black–necked Grebe *Podiceps nigricollis* 30 cm 12 in. Often seen in small flocks on inland waters in summer and at estuaries and inland in winter.
Little Grebe or **Dabchick** *Tachybaptus ruficollis* 25 cm 10 in. Found on inland waters in summer and winter; also at coast in winter.

A pair of red-necked grebes in summer plumage. The nest floats among reeds at the edge of a lake. A chick nestles between the wings of the parent bird on the nest.

winter

Slavonian Grebe

Red-necked Grebe

winter

summer

winter

summer

Little Grebe

Black-necked Grebe

summer

winter

| Red-necked Grebe | Slavonian Grebe | Black-necked Grebe | Little Grebe |

WHAT TO LOOK FOR

Great Crested Grebe Long white neck and pink bill. Summer: large ear tufts and frill.

Red-necked Grebe Medium-sized neck and black and yellow bill. Summer: red neck and pale grey cheeks but no frill.

Slavonian Grebe Blue-grey bill. Summer: golden ear tufts and chestnut neck. Winter: white cheeks.

Black-necked Grebe Slightly upturned bill. Summer: black neck and chestnut ear tufts. Winter: dusky neck and cheeks.

Little Grebe Duck-like shape with almost no tail. Summer: rust-coloured neck.

Leach's Petrel

Great Shearwater

Sooty Shearwater

Cory's Shearwater

Storm Petrel

Manx Shearwater

light phase

Fulmar

dark phase

Fulmar

Cory's Shearwater

Great Shearwater

Sooty Shearwater

Storm Petrel

Leach's Petrel

Manx Shearwater

FULMARS, PETRELS AND SHEARWATERS
Order Procellariiformes

The fulmar and shearwaters (family Procellariidae) and petrels (family Hydrobatidae) are all ocean birds that normally come ashore only to breed. They may then be seen in colonies on coastal cliffs and islands. Some shearwaters are southern birds that visit European waters when migrating.

Fulmar *Fulmarus glacialis* 46 cm 18 in. Often follows ships, but may come ashore and occupy buildings. Nests in colonies on cliffs. Parents protect the young by ejecting a foul-smelling oily liquid at intruders. There are two colour phases.

Cory's Shearwater *Calonectris diomedea* 46 cm 18 in. Breeds on Mediterranean islands and ventures into Atlantic in autumn. Does not follow ships.

Manx Shearwater *Puffinus puffinus* 36 cm 14 in. Breeds in colonies in burrows on islands and cliff-tops. Does not follow ships. Commonest European shearwater.

Great Shearwater *Puffinus gravis* 46 cm 18 in. Breeds in south Atlantic in winter and visits open north Atlantic in summer and autumn. Sometimes seen offshore.

Sooty Shearwater *Puffinus griseus* 41 cm 16 in. Breeds in south Atlantic in winter and visits north Atlantic in summer and autumn. May be seen offshore.

Storm Petrel *Hydrobates pelagicus* 15 cm 6 in. Nests in crevices in rocks or stone walls on islands. Can be seen following ships, flitting over the waves summer and autumn. May be seen offshore.

Leach's Petrel *Oceanodroma leucorhoa* 20 cm 8 in. Breeds in burrows on islands. Flight is more erratic than storm petrel, and does not follow ships or patter over waves.

WHAT TO LOOK FOR

Fulmar Thick neck; stubby bill; light grey with white head and underparts (light phase) or smoky grey all over (dark phase).

Cory's Shearwater Light brown head; yellow bill.

Manx Shearwater Dark upperparts and white underparts; small size.

Great Shearwater Black cap and white throat; white at base of tail.

Sooty Shearwater Dark all over; narrow wings.

Storm Petrel Square tail; flitting and pattering flight.

Leach's Petrel Shallow fork in tail, erratic flight.

GANNETS, PELICANS AND CORMORANTS

Order Pelecaniformes

Gannets (family Sulidae), pelicans (family Pelecanidae) and cormorants (family Phalacrocoracidae) are the largest European sea birds. Although they all have webbed feet, they are not habitual swimmers. They all have different and interesting methods of fishing.

Gannet *Sula bassana* 91 cm 36 in. Breeds in summer in vast colonies on cliffs of rocky islands. Winters at sea, but may be seen offshore. May follow ships. Makes spectacular dive into the water to catch fish.

White Pelican *Pelecanus onocrotalus* 168 cm 65 in. Breeds in swamps and marshes in eastern Mediterranean. May also be seen at coast in winter. Uses pouch beneath bill as net to catch fish. Rare.

Dalmatian Pelican *Pelecanus crispus* 168 cm 65 in. Same habitat and behaviour as white pelican and inhabits same areas. Rare.

Cormorant *Phalacrocorax carbo* 91 cm 36 in. Found at seashores and on inland waters. Flies low over water but settles on surface before diving for fish. Often perches with wings outspread, probably to dry them. Atlantic form is found in Britain, Norway and Iceland and breeds on rocky cliffs. Continental form is found on mainland Europe and nests in trees and bushes.

Shag *Phalacrocorax aristotelis* 76 cm 30 in. Identical to cormorant in behaviour, but smaller in size and rarely seen inland. Breeds on rocky cliffs at coast. Rare inland at any season.

Pygmy Cormorant *Phalacrocorax pygmaeus* 48 cm 19 in. Usually found on inland waters. Nests in trees and bushes.

WHAT TO LOOK FOR

Gannet White body with pointed tail; black wingtips; yellow head with blue eye-ring.

White Pelican Underside of wings white at front, dark at rear; flesh-coloured feet.

Dalmatian Pelican Underside of wings all white except for dark wingtips; grey feet.

Cormorant Atlantic form: all black with white chin. Continental form: black with white head and neck in summer.

Shag Green-black; yellow base of bill.

Pygmy Cormorant Breeding: dark spotted plumage; rust-coloured head. Non-breeding: unspotted plumage, white throat, rust-coloured breast.

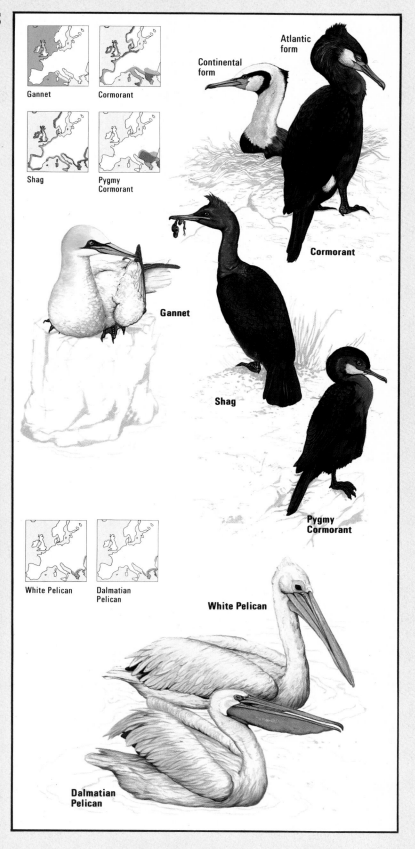

Gannet

Cormorant

Shag

Pygmy Cormorant

White Pelican

Dalmatian Pelican

Atlantic form

Continental form

Cormorant

Gannet

Shag

Pygmy Cormorant

White Pelican

Dalmatian Pelican

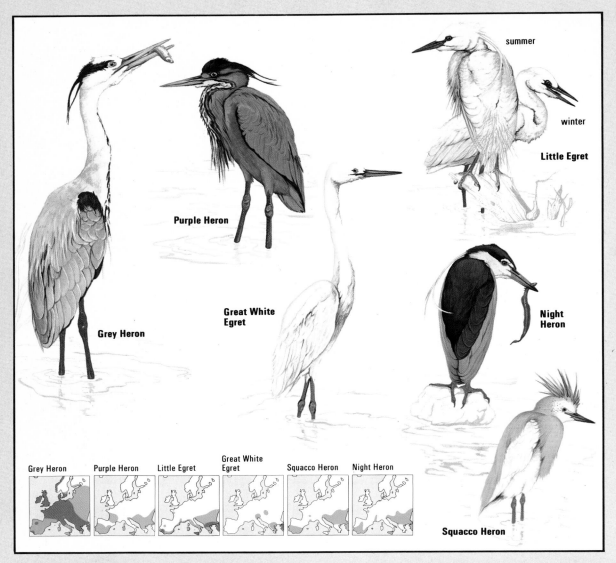

Purple Heron

Little Egret

summer

winter

Grey Heron

Great White Egret

Night Heron

Squacco Heron

Grey Heron	Purple Heron	Little Egret	Great White Egret	Squacco Heron	Night Heron

HERONS AND ALLIES
Order Ciconiiformes

These birds are elegant long-legged waders. They feed mainly in shallow water, lowering their long necks and bills to catch aquatic animals. Some herons spread their wings while fishing, perhaps to cut out the reflection of the sky. Herons and bitterns (family Ardeidae) and storks (family Ciconiidae) all have straight bills. They can easily be identified in flight because herons and bitterns draw back their heads whereas storks fly with necks outstretched. Ibises, spoonbills and flamingos have bills of unusual shapes.

Grey Heron *Ardea cinerea* 91 cm 36 in. The most common and largest European heron. Found on inland waters and at seashore, where it stands motionless in or near water then suddenly darts head down after prey. Also perches in trees, where it usually nests in colonies.

Purple Heron *Ardea purpurea* 79 cm 31 in. Found in swamps and marshes, where it breeds in colonies among reed-beds and bushes.

Little Egret *Egretta garzetta* 58 cm 23 in. May be found at shallow water of any kind. Usually nests near water. In summer develops hanging plumes, for which it was once hunted.

Great White Egret *Egretta alba* 89 cm 35 in. Found at shallow water; nests in reed-beds. Resembles little egret but is much larger and less common.

Squacco Heron *Ardeola ralloides* 46 cm 18 in. Found in marshes and swamps and at small stretches of water, where it nests among reeds or in bushes or trees. It is like a bittern in shape but is much less shy.

Night Heron *Nycticorax nycticorax* 61 cm 24 in. Usually seen feeding at dusk in pools and marshes, or roosting in bushes and trees during the day.

WHAT TO LOOK FOR

Grey Heron Large size; black crest; pale grey and white; black wing edges.

Purple Heron Long S-shaped chestnut neck with black stripe; reddish underparts.

Little Egret Yellow feet; long white crest (summer only).

Great White Egret Black feet; no summer crest.

Squacco Heron Thick neck and stocky shape; buff body with white wings, but looks white in flight.

Night Heron Stocky with rather short legs; black back, white breast; black cap.

Little Bittern *Ixobrychus minutus* 36 cm 14 in. Hides away and nests among dense reeds and thickets near water. May escape detection by freezing stockstill.

Bittern *Botaurus stellaris* 76 cm 30 in. Same habitat and behaviour as little bittern, but much larger size. Freezes with bill pointing upwards. Foghorn-like booming call may be heard at a great distance.

White Stork *Ciconia ciconia* 102 cm 40 in. Found in marshes, farmland and open country. Nests on buildings, often on special platforms, or in trees near farms and villages. Walks slowly over ground.

Black Stork *Ciconia nigra* 96 cm 38 in. Frequents marshes and pools among forests, where it nests in trees. Uncommon.

Spoonbill *Platalea leucorodia* 86 cm 34 in. Found in reedy marshes, shallow lakes and estuaries. Nests in colonies among reeds or in bushes or trees. The odd spoon-shaped bill is used to sift small animals from the water. Uncommon.

Glossy Ibis *Plegadis falcinellus* 56 cm 22 in. Inhabits marshes and mudflats; nests in groups in reeds, bushes or trees, often with herons and egrets. The glossy play of colour can only be seen at close range; from a distance the plumage appears black. Uncommon.

Greater Flamingo *Phoenicopterus ruber* 125 cm 50 in. Found in flocks only in the nature reserves at the Camargue region in southern France, where it breeds, and at the Coto de Doñana in southern Spain, where breeding is rare. Single birds seen in the wild have probably escaped from collections. Wades in shallow water, dipping its bill to strain tiny creatures from the water, and nests on mudflats or on heaps of mud in water.

WHAT TO LOOK FOR

Little Bittern Small size; black wings with buff patch, black back (male) or brown back (female).

Bittern Large stocky shape; in freezing posture has upward-pointing bill; booming call.

White Stork White neck and upperparts; red bill and legs.

Black Stork Black neck and upperparts.

Spoonbill Long black spoon-shaped bill (pink in young bird).

Glossy Ibis Long down-curving bill.

Greater Flamingo Large bent bill; very long neck and legs; pink and black wings (in flight).

Bittern

Spoonbill

Little Bittern

Greater Flamingo

Black Stork

White Stork

Glossy Ibis

Glossy Ibis

Greater Flamingo

White Stork   Black Stork   Little Bittern   Bittern   Spoonbill

WATERFOWL OR WILDFOWL

Order Anseriformes
Family Anatidae

This group of birds consists of ducks, geese and swans. They are all water birds, and use their webbed feet to swim strongly. The young are born with feathers and can walk and swim soon after hatching. Many species can also be seen on lakes in parks.

DUCKS

Ducks are usually smaller in size and have shorter necks than geese and swans. In addition, the two sexes have different plumage, although in late summer the drakes (males) moult and for a time resemble the ducks (females). Ducks nest on the ground or in holes. There are three main groups of ducks. *Surface-feeding* or *dabbling ducks* live in shallow water, where they feed on water plants by dabbling or up-ending. They leap into the air to get airborne, and have a brightly coloured patch of glossy wing feathers called a *speculum*. The colour of the speculum is important in identifying the drably coloured females. *Diving ducks* dive from the surface for water plants and animals, and so prefer deeper water than do dabbling ducks. Their legs are set farther back so that they can swim underwater, and they run along the surface to take wing. The third group of ducks, the *sawbills*, are also divers.

WHAT TO LOOK FOR

Mallard Male: dark green head; chestnut breast. Female: blue-purple speculum.

Teal Male: brown and green head. Female: small size; green speculum.

Garganey Male: white stripe on head. Female: blue-grey forewing; indistinct speculum.

Gadwall Male: grey body with black rear; brown wing panel; black and white speculum. Female: white belly; black and white speculum.

Mallard *Anas platyrhynchos* 58 cm 23 in. Dabbling duck. A very common duck, found on all kinds of inland waters and at coasts and estuaries. Often seen in flocks. Most domestic ducks, though different in colour, are descended from wild mallards.

Teal *Anas crecca* 36 cm 14 in. Dabbling duck. Smallest European duck.

Prefers secluded inland waters in summer; spreads to open waters and coast in winter.

Gadwall *Anas strepera* 51 cm 20 in. Dabbling duck. Prefers inland waters.

Garganey *Anas querquedula* 38 cm 15 in. Dabbling duck. Prefers inland waters, seldom seen on coast.

A male mandarin duck. This species is usually seen in parks.

Wigeon *Anas penelope* 46 cm 18 in. Dabbling duck. Prefers inland waters in summer; spreads to coast in winter, when it may be seen in flocks. May graze on land.
Pintail *Anas acuta* 63 cm 25 in. Dabbling duck. Prefers inland waters in summer, but coasts in winter. Breeds on moors, marshes etc.

Shoveler *Anas clypeata* 51 cm 20 in. Dabbling duck. Usually found on ponds and in marshes. The odd-shaped bill, unlike that of all other ducks, is used to strain tiny plants and animals from the water.
Mandarin Duck *Aix galericulata* 46 cm 18 in. Dabbling duck. Introduced from China and seen mainly on

park lakes. Nests in tree holes. Escaped birds live in the wild, preferring ponds surrounded by trees.

129

Red-crested Pochard

Scaup

Tufted Duck

Pochard

Ferruginous Duck

male

female

male

female

male

female

female

male

female

male

Red-creasted Pochard

Scaup

Tufted Duck

Pochard

Ferruginous Duck

Red-crested Pochard *Netta rufina* 56 cm 22 in. Diving duck. Prefers inland waters. Uncommon.

Scaup *Aythya marila* 46 cm 18 in. Diving duck. Breeds inland, but otherwise seen at coast and estuaries.

Tufted Duck *Aythya fuligula* 43 cm 17 in. Diving duck. Often seen on lakes and ponds; also at seashore and estuaries in winter.

Pochard *Aythya ferina* 46 cm 18 in. Diving duck. Breeds among reeds, otherwise seen mainly on lakes and at estuaries.

Ferruginous Duck *Aythya nyroca* 41 cm 16 in. Diving duck. Breeds among reeds on inland waters; winters at open inland waters, rarely at coast.

WHAT TO LOOK FOR

Wigeon Male: chestnut head with light crown; white forewing. Female: black and green speculum; white belly.

Pintail Large but slim build. Male: long pointed tail; white neck stripe. Female: long tail; long neck.

Shoveler Spoon-shaped bill. Male: green head, white breast and chestnut flanks. Female: blue forewing with dark green speculum.

Mandarin Duck Male: orange sidewhiskers; orange 'fins' on wings. Female: white eye-ring and stripe; white chin; spotted underparts.

Red-crested Pochard Male: chestnut head with red bill; long white wingbar; white flanks. Female: brown plumage with light cheeks and long white wingbar.

Scaup Male: as tufted duck, but no crest and with grey back. Female: as tufted duck, but no crest and with larger white face patch.

Tufted Duck Male: drooping crest; dark head and neck, black back and tail with white belly. Female: small crest; small white patch at base of bill; white wingbar.

Pochard Male: dark chestnut head and neck with pale grey back; black breast. Female: brown head with light stripe through eye; blue band on bill; grey wing band.

Ferruginous Duck Male: rich brown head, neck and breast; white eye; white patch under tail; bold white wingbar. Female: as male, but dull brown and brown eye; white patch under tail and white wingbar.

Goldeneye *Bucephala clangula* 46 cm 18 in. Diving duck. Nests in tree holes and burrows near fresh water; winters on lakes, rivers and coastal waters. Drakes raise bill in courting display in early spring. Wings whistle in flight.

Long–tailed Duck *Clangula hyemalis* 51 cm 20 in (female 41 cm 16 in). Diving duck. Breeds in the Arctic; winters on coastal waters.

Velvet Scoter *Melanitta fusca* 56 cm 22 in. Diving duck. Usually breeds on inland waters; winters at coast and on large lakes.

Common Scoter *Melanitta nigra* 51 cm 20 in. Breeds on islands as well as inland; winters mainly at coast.

WHAT TO LOOK FOR

Goldeneye Male: round white patch before eye. Female: brown head with white collar.

Long-tailed Duck Male: long pointed tail; dark head and neck with white face patch (summer) or white head and neck with dark neck patch (winter). Female: white face and belly with dark back, shoulders and wings.

Velvet Scoter Male: all black except for white patch below eye and white wingbar. Female: two light patches on each side of head; white wingbar.

Common Scoter Male: all black except for orange patch on bill; black knob above bill. Female: dark cap; light cheek.

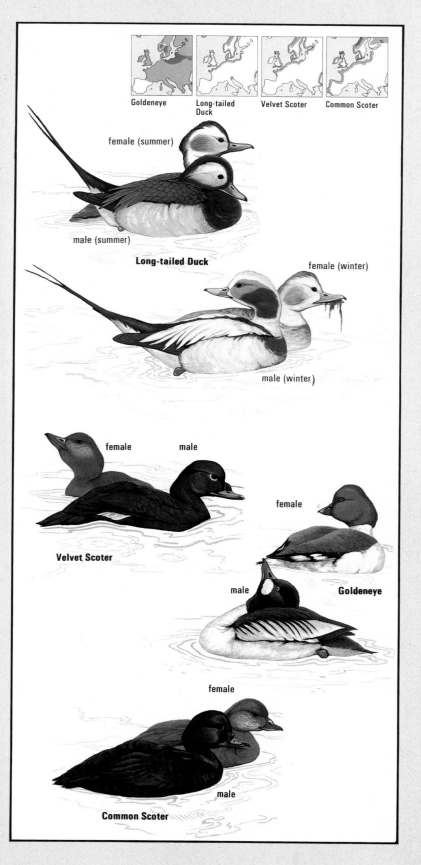

Goldeneye Long-tailed Duck Velvet Scoter Common Scoter

female (summer)

male (summer)

Long-tailed Duck

female (winter)

male (winter)

female male

Velvet Scoter

female

Goldeneye

male

female

male

Common Scoter

White-headed Duck

Smew

White-headed
Duck

Red-breasted
Merganser

Smew

Shelduck

Eider

Goosander

male female

Eider

female

male

Red-breasted Merganser

male

female

Shelduck

female male

Goosander

Eider *Somateria mollissima* 61 cm 24 in. Diving duck. Most marine of all ducks, seldom found inland. Breeds at seashore, lining nest with soft breast feathers known as eider down.

White-headed Duck *Oxyura leucocephala* 46 cm 18 in. Diving duck. Confined to inland waters. Often points tail upwards when swimming. Uncommon. Very similar Ruddy Duck *Oxyura jamaicensis* has been introduced into Britain.

Red-breasted Merganser *Mergus serrator* 56 cm 22 in. Sawbill (see page 24). Breeds near fresh or salt water, hiding nest among rocks or vegetation. Mainly found at coasts in winter.

Goosander *Mergus merganser* 66 cm 26 in. Sawbill. Nests in tree cavities and burrows near fresh water. Usually remains inland in winter.

Smew *Mergus albellus* 41 cm 16 in. Sawbill (but duck-like appearance). Nests in holes in trees near inland waters. Also found at coast in winter.

Shelduck *Tadorna tadorna* 61 cm 24 in. Large goose-like duck. Nests in hollow trees and burrows or among bushes. Winters mainly at coasts, often on mudflats. Sexes almost identical.

WHAT TO LOOK FOR

Eider Male: white back and black belly. Female: brown plumage closely barred with black.

White-headed Duck Male: white head; blue bill (in summer). Female: light cheek with dark line.

Red-breasted Merganser Male: green-black head with double crest, white collar and chestnut breast band. Female: chestnut head with double crest.

Goosander Male: dark green head with long thin red bill, pinkish-white breast and flanks. Female: as female red-breasted merganser, but with single crest and striking white throat.

Smew Male: white with black markings, especially patch around eye. Female: white head and throat with chestnut cap and nape.

Shelduck Male: green-black head and white body with broad chestnut band; red knob over bill. Female: as male but no red knob.

Bean Goose

dark-bellied form

light-bellied form

Brent Goose

Pink-footed Goose

Greenland race

Main race

Lesser White-fronted Goose

White-fronted Goose

Eastern race

Western race

Greylag Goose

Greylag Goose

White-fronted Goose

Pink-footed Goose

Lesser White-fronted Goose

Brent Goose

Bean Goose

GEESE

Geese are between ducks and swans in size. They graze mainly on land, and the legs are set forward so that they can walk easily. The sexes are alike. There are two groups of geese. Geese of the genus *Anser* are grey–brown and those of the genus *Branta* are black and white.

Greylag Goose *Anser anser* 84 cm 33 in. Very common goose. Breeds on moors, marshes, reedy lakes, and offshore islands. Winters in fields, inland and coastal marshes and at estuaries. There are two subspecies, or races. The western race (*A.a. anser*) is found in Iceland, Britain and western Europe; the eastern race (*A.a. rubrirostris*) inhabits eastern Europe. All domestic geese are descended from the greylag goose.

White–fronted Goose *Anser albifrons* 71 cm 28 in. Found in same habitat as greylag goose in winter, but breeds in far north. There are two subspecies. The Greenland race (*A.a. flavirostris*) migrates from Greenland to winter in Ireland and western Scotland. The main, or typical, race (*A.a. albifrons*) breeds in northern Russia and winters in the rest of Britain and mainland Europe.
Lesser White–fronted Goose *Anser erythropus* 61 cm 24 in. Similar habitat and appearance to white-fronted goose, but smaller size.
Bean Goose *Anser fabalis* 76 cm 30 in. Breeds in northern woods and tundra; winters inland in fields near water.
Pink–footed Goose *Anser brachyrhynchus* 68 cm 27 in. Breeds in Arctic; similar winter habitat to bean goose.
Brent Goose *Branta bernicla* 58 cm 23 in. Winter visitor to coasts and estuaries. Feeds mainly on eel grasses in water, and feeding times depend on tides. There are two subspecies. The light-bellied form (*B.b. hrota*) breeds in Greenland and Spitsbergen, and the dark-bellied form (*B.b. bernicla*) in northern Russia.

WHAT TO LOOK FOR

Greylag Goose Pink feet and legs with head and neck no darker than body; orange bill (western race) or pink bill (eastern race).

White-fronted Goose White patch at base of bill; irregular black bars on belly; pink bill (main race) or yellow or orange bill (Greenland race).

Lesser White-fronted Goose As main race of white-fronted goose, except yellow eye-ring and larger white patch.

Bean Goose Orange-yellow feet and legs; dark head and neck; black and orange-yellow bill.

Pink-footed Goose As bean goose, but pink feet and legs and pink and black bill.

Brent Goose Black head and neck with small white neck mark.

133

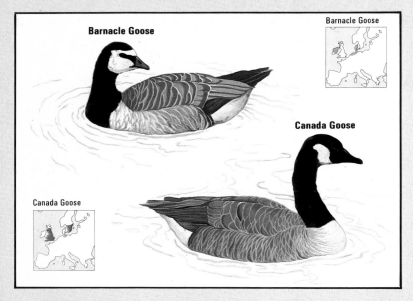

Barnacle Goose *Branta leucopsis* 63 cm 25 in. Winter visitor from Arctic to salt marshes and estuaries and surrounding fields. The odd name comes from a medieval belief that the birds hatch from goose barnacles instead of eggs.

Canada Goose *Branta canadensis* 97 cm 38 in. Largest European goose. Introduced from North America to parks. Escaped birds now breed in Britain and Sweden, and may straggle to western Europe for the winter. Wild birds nest on islands in lakes and graze in marshes and fields by lakes and rivers.

WHAT TO LOOK FOR

Barnacle Goose White face, black neck and breast.

Canada Goose Long black neck, black head with white throat, light breast.

SWANS

Swans are the largest waterfowl and immediately recognised by their long elegant necks, which they lower into the water or to the ground to pull up plants. The sexes are alike. The black swan seen in parks has been introduced from Australia. The birds should be approached with caution, especially when breeding.
Juveniles of all European species are brown, with indistinct bill patterns.

Mute Swan *Cygnus olor* 152 cm 60 in. Very common. Often found in tame state on park lakes and village ponds and along rivers. Usually nests at banks of rivers and lakes; winters on open waters and at coast.

Whooper Swan *Cygnus cygnus* 152 cm 60 in. Nests in swamps and by lakes in far north; winters along coasts and on lakes and rivers. Its name refers to whooping sound of call.

Bewick's Swan *Cygnus bewickii* 122 cm 48 in. Winter visitors from Arctic. Similar habitat to whooper swan, though prefers larger areas of water in more open country.

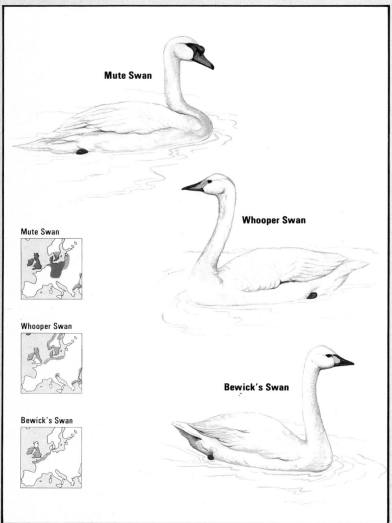

WHAT TO LOOK FOR

Mute Swan Orange bill with black knob; neck usually curved.

Whooper Swan Large size; yellow bill with black tip; neck usually straight.

Bewick's Swan Small size; black bill with yellow base; neck usually straight.

BIRDS OF PREY

Order Falconiformes

The birds of prey hunt other animals. Usually they catch live prey on the ground, in the air or in water, but sometimes they eat dead animals. Other birds, such as owls and crows, also feed in these ways, but the birds of prey are different in that they all have sharp claws to grip their victims and hooked beaks to tear them to pieces. Also, unlike most owls, birds of prey hunt by day and not by night.

VULTURES, EAGLES, BUZZARDS, HAWKS, KITES AND HARRIERS

Family Accipitridae

Most of these birds of prey soar through the air, keeping a sharp lookout for prey below and then dropping on an unsuspecting victim. However, vultures land on the ground to feed on carrion (dead animals) and on refuse. Eagles mainly seek live prey as they soar. Buzzards and kites also soar and look rather like small eagles, though buzzards may also be seen perching and kites can be told by their long forked tails. Hawks and harriers fly near the ground, hawks dashing rapidly through the air and harriers gliding gently.

Egyptian Vulture *Neophron percnopterus* 63 cm 25 in. Usually seen in mountains, but comes to rubbish dumps in villages. In Africa, it is well known for its habit of dropping stones on ostrich eggs to break them open.

Griffon Vulture *Gyps fulvus* 100 cm 39 in. Usually found in mountains. Unlike eagles, has head and tail that appear very small in flight.

Black Vulture *Aegypius monachus* 102 cm 40 in. Usually found in mountains and plains, but rare. If all three vultures arrive at a carcass together, the black vulture feeds first, then the griffon vulture and finally the Egyptian vulture.

Lammergeyer or **Bearded Vulture** *Gypaetus barbatus* 110 cm 43 in. Found in mountains; does not join other vultures to feed. Known for unusual habit of dropping bones from the air to rocks to break them open.

Black Vulture

Griffon Vulture

Egyptian Vulture

Lammergeyer

Egyptian Vulture

Griffon Vulture

Black Vulture

Lammergeyer

Bonelli's Eagle

light form

Booted Eagle

dark form

Short-toed Eagle

dark form

light form

Golden Eagle

Spanish form

Imperial Eagle

Honey Buzzard

Golden Eagle

Bonelli's Eagle

Imperial Eagle   Booted Eagle   Short-toed Eagle   Honey Buzzard

WHAT TO LOOK FOR

Golden Eagle   Dark brown all over with golden feathers on head.

Imperial Eagle   White shoulders; white wing patches (Spanish form only).

Bonelli's Eagle   White underparts; wings dark above or white with dark band beneath.

Booted Eagle   Small size like buzzard but long narrow tail.

Short-toed Eagle   White underparts with white underwings and often dark breast and head.

Honey Buzzard   Like buzzard, but longer tail with black bands.

Golden Eagle *Aquila chrysaetos* 84 cm 33 in. Usually seen soaring above mountain slopes, though may hunt near the ground. May also be found at coasts and in woods and fields. Nests in trees or on rock ledges.
Imperial Eagle *Aquila heliaca* 81 cm 32 in. Found in low-lying forests, woods, plains and marshes. Nests in tall trees.
Bonelli's Eagle *Hieraaetus fasciatus* 71 cm 28 in. Usually found in mountains, but may also be seen in more open country in winter. Dashes rapidly through the air, hunting for small mammals and birds. Nests in trees and on rock ledges.
Booted Eagle *Hieraaetus pennatus* 51 cm 20 in. Usually found in forests or woods, hunting in clearings. Nests in trees. Plumage varies from light to

dark, but light birds are more common than dark birds.
Short–toed Eagle *Circaetus gallicus* 66 cm 26 in. Found in mountains and gorges, plains and woods and at coasts. Often hovers, seeking snakes, lizards and frogs. Nests in trees. Head plumage may be light or dark, dark being more common.
Honey Buzzard *Pernis apivorus* 53 cm 21 in. Usually found in clearings and at edges of forests and woods. Gets its name from its habit of feeding at the nests of bees and wasps, though for grubs and not for honey. Nests in trees. Colour varies from cream to dark brown.

Buzzard

light form

dark form

Rough-legged Buzzard

Goshawk

Montagu's Harrier

male

female

female

male

Sparrowhawk

| Buzzard | Rough-legged Buzzard | Sparrowhawk | Goshawk | Montagu's Harrier |

A female Montagu's harrier arriving at her nest.

WHAT TO LOOK FOR

Buzzard Like small golden eagle but broad rounded tail.

Rough-legged Buzzard Dark belly; white tail with black band at tip.

Sparrowhawk Broad rounded wings with long tail; closely barred underparts.

Goshawk Both sexes similar to sparrowhawk but larger size.

Montagu's Harrier Male: as male hen harrier but black wingbar, grey rump and streaky underside. Female: very similar to female hen harrier.

Buzzard *Buteo buteo* 53 cm · 21 in. Found in woods, fields and plains, at coasts and on mountain slopes and hillsides. Often soars, but hunts near the ground. Nests in trees and on rock ledges. Plumage varies from cream to dark brown.

Rough–legged Buzzard *Buteo lagopus* 56 cm 22 in. Found in winter on moors and in marshes and fields, in summer among mountains. Nests on cliff ledges or on ground in Arctic. Often hovers before swooping on small mammals; also hunts birds.

Sparrowhawk *Accipiter nisus* 33 cm 13 in. Usually seen in forests and woods, but also among scattered trees and bushes. Dashes through trees and hops over hedges, hunting small birds. Female is much larger than male. Nests in trees and bushes.

Goshawk *Accipiter gentilis* 53 cm 21 in. Usually seen in woods and forests, dashing through trees in pursuit of birds. Nests mainly in fir trees. Resembles female sparrowhawk, but much bigger. Female is larger than male.

Montagu's Harrier *Circus pygargus* 43 cm 17 in. Found in same places and has similar flight and nesting habits to hen harrier.

Red Kite

Black Kite

White-tailed Eagle

White-tailed Eagle

Black Kite

Red Kite

female

Marsh Harrier

male

female

male

Hen Harrier

Marsh Harrier

Hen Harrier

Red Kite *Milvus milvus* 63 cm 25 in. Usually found in woods, but also among scattered trees. Nests in trees.

Black Kite *Milvus migrans* 53 cm 21 in. Usually seen near lakes and rivers surrounded by trees. In southern Europe, also found in more open country and seeking refuse in towns and villages. Nests in trees.

White-tailed Eagle or **Sea Eagle** *Haliaeetus albicilla* 81 cm 32 in. Found at coasts and remote lakes. Takes fish from surface of water or plunges; also hunts mammals and birds. Nests in trees and on rock ledges.

Marsh Harrier *Circus aeruginosus* 51 cm 20 in. Usually seen flying low over swamps and marshes and nearby fields. Nests in reed-beds.

Hen Harrier *Circus cyaneus* 46 cm 18 in. Hunts while flying low over moors, heaths, fields, pasture, marshes and swamps. Makes its nest on the ground.

WHAT TO LOOK FOR

Red Kite Like buzzard, but reddish colour and deeply forked tail.

Black Kite As red kite, but dark plumage and shallow forked tail.

White-tailed Eagle White tail with brown body.

Marsh Harrier Male: grey wing patch and tail. Female: pale crown and throat.

Hen Harrier Male: grey with white rump and underside. Female: streaky brown with white rump (very like Montagu's harrier).

Osprey Dark above and white below, with white head crossed by dark line.

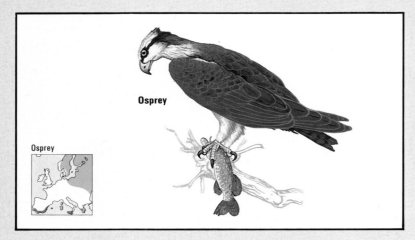

Osprey

Osprey

OSPREYS

Family Pandionidae

The osprey differs slightly from all other birds of prey and is in a family by itself.

Osprey *Pandion haliaetus* 56 cm 22 in. Found on lakes and rivers and at coast, where it hunts fish by soaring or hovering high over the water and then plunging in feet-first. Carries fish back to perch near water.

FALCONS
Family Falconidae

Falcons are generally smaller than other birds of prey, and have long, pointed wings and long tails. They are ferocious hunters, diving on or chasing their prey at great speed. Falconers train falcons to hunt and bring their prey back to them.

Hobby *Falco subbuteo* 33 cm 13 in. Lives in light woodland and among scattered trees, streaking through the air in pursuit of small birds such as larks, swallows and swifts, as well as flying insects. Nests in trees.

Peregrine Falcon *Falco peregrinus* 43 cm 17 in. Found among cliffs and crags, on which it nests, and also at flat coasts and marshes in winter; sometimes seen in forests and towns. Hunts by diving steeply at great speed, wings drawn back, mainly after birds, especially pigeons. Has become rare, suffering badly from effects of pesticides and raids by egg collectors.

Gyrfalcon *Falco rusticolus* 53 cm 21 in. Found in mountains and at coasts and forest edges. Nests on cliff ledges. Hunts like peregrine falcon but is not so fast in flight.

Lanner Falcon *Falco biarmicus* 43 cm 17 in. Found in mountains and rocky open country and at shores. Nests in rocks and trees. Flight similar to peregrine falcon, but preys on smaller birds.

Merlin *Falco columbarius* 30 cm 12 in. Found in open country, on hills and moors in summer and also at coast in winter. Nests on ground or in trees. Darts through the air close to the ground, chasing small birds. May be seen hovering and perching.

Lesser Kestrel *Falco naumanni* 30 cm 12 in. Found in open and rocky country and marshes, and often in fields around towns and villages. Nests on cliffs and buildings. Resembles kestrel, but does not hover so often.

Kestrel *Falco tinnunculus* 33 cm 13 in. Very common bird of prey. Found in all kinds of places, including cities and towns; often spotted alongside motorways. Usually seen hovering near ground, flapping wings quickly, and then diving down in pursuit of rodents and insects.

Hobby

Peregrine Falcon

Lanner Falcon

Hobby

Peregrine Falcon

Gyrfalcon

Lanner Falcon

Gyrfalcon

male

female

Merlin

Merlin

Lesser Kestrel

Kestrel

female

male

Lesser Kestrel

Kestrel

male (winter)

female (winter)

Willow Grouse

female (summer)

male (summer)

female

Red Grouse

male

Ptarmigan

female (summer)

female (winter)

male (winter)

autumn

male (summer)

male

female

Black Grouse

Willow Grouse   Red Grouse   Ptarmigan   Black Grouse

GAME BIRDS OR FOWLS

Order Galliformes

These birds are plump in shape, rather like chickens. They rarely fly very far or high and prefer to run or hide from danger, only taking to the air at the last moment. They spend most of their time on the ground rooting for seeds and insects, and they also nest on the ground. They are called game birds because most of them are hunted for sport, although hunting is forbidden when the birds are nesting and raising their young.

GROUSE

Family Tetraonidae

These birds live in cold places, and their legs and sometimes their feet are covered with feathers for warmth.

Willow Grouse *Lagopus lagopus* 38 cm 15 in. Found on moors, often living among heather and scattered bushes. Plumage changes from white in winter to brown and white in summer, helping to hide bird among winter snow and summer plants.
Red Grouse *Lagopus lagopus scoticus* 38 cm 15 in. A variety of willow grouse found only in the British Isles. No colour change takes place because snow does not always fall in winter. Lives among heather on moors, but also found in fields in winter.
Ptarmigan *Lagopus mutus* 36 cm 14 in. Found on high mountain slopes, usually above tree level. Plumage changes from brown and white in summer to grey and white in autumn and pure white in winter. In this way, it always matches its surroundings and cannot easily be spotted by an eagle or a fox.
Black Grouse *Lyrurus tetrix* Male 53 cm 21 in; female 41 cm 16 in. Found on moors, in woods, among scattered trees and in fields. In spring, groups gather at courting grounds and the males display themselves before the females, spreading their wings and raising their white tail feathers in a fan.

Capercaillie *Tetrao urogallus* Male 86 cm 34 in; female 61 cm 24 in. Lives among fir trees on hills and mountains. Male raises tail in a fan when courting female.

Hazelhen or **Hazel Grouse** *Tetrastes bonasia* 36 cm 14 in. Lives in woods, usually hiding among bushes and thickets, but takes to the air when disturbed.

WHAT TO LOOK FOR

Willow Grouse Male: in summer, red-brown body with white wings and belly; in winter, pure white with black tail (but exactly like female ptarmigan). Female: in summer, as male, but body less red and more barred; in winter, as male.

Red Grouse Male: red-brown body with dark wings and tail edges. Female: as male, but body less red and more barred.

Ptarmigan Male: as willow grouse, but greyer body in summer and autumn, and black face patch in winter. Female: very like female willow grouse, but usually found at higher altitudes.

Black Grouse Male: glossy black with lyre-shaped tail. Female: grey-brown with slightly forked tail.

Capercaillie Male: grey with broad fan-shaped tail; brownish wings. Female: as female black grouse, but with fan-shaped tail and reddish breast patch.

Hazelhen Male: black throat and grey tail with black band. Female: as male but whitish throat.

---

male

Capercaillie

female

female

male

Capercaillie   Hazelhen

Hazelhen

PARTRIDGES AND PHEASANTS

Family Phasianidae

Unlike grouse, these birds have bare legs and feet and are not found in cold places. Brightly coloured pheasants from other parts of the world are seen in parks. Some now live in the wild. Pheasants make their nests on the ground and produce large numbers of young birds. Partridges too nest on the ground and are difficult to see. They are not good fliers and do not migrate. Quails are small shy birds prized as a delicacy.

The spectacular colouring of its crest gives the golden pheasant its name. It is a native of central Asia and China, like the ring-necked pheasant, which has a characteristic white ring around its throat, and the beautiful Lady Amherst's pheasant, with its orange back and long black and white tail. These exotic birds have both been introduced into Britain, where they now breed in the wild.

141

Rock Partridge *Alectoris graeca* 33 cm 13 in. Found on rocky ground and among trees, usually high up. Looks very like red-legged partridge, but lives in different countries.

Red–legged Partridge *Alectoris rufa* 34 cm 13½ in. Found on moors, and in fields and low treeless hills, often in dry and stony places. Looks like rock partridge, but lives in different countries.

Partridge *Perdix perdix* 30 cm 12 in. Seen mainly in fields, but also on moors and heaths and in marshes, sand dunes and low treeless hills.

Quail *Coturnix coturnix* 18 cm 7 in. The smallest European game bird, and the only one that migrates. Hides among grass and crops. May be seen in bevies (small flocks) during migration, but is usually a solitary bird.

Pheasant *Phasianus colchicus* Male 84 cm 33 in; female 58 cm 23 in. Often seen in fields, especially in winter; also in woods and marshes. Pattern of male varies; for example some have white neck-ring while others do not. Introduced from Asia, probably in ancient times. Most pheasants are semi-domesticated, being protected during the breeding season by gamekeepers to raise numbers for hunting later. Some are truly wild.

Rock Partridge

Red-legged Partridge

Partridge

male   female

Pheasant

male

female

Quail

female   male

Rock Partridge   Red-legged Partridge   Partridge   Quail   Pheasant

CRANES, RAILS AND BUSTARDS

Order Gruiformes

All these birds have long legs and many of them wade in shallow water. Cranes (family Gruidae) are tall, elegant birds living on dry land and in marshes, whereas rails, crakes, gallinules, moorhens and coots (family Rallidae) are mainly water birds, small to medium in size and chunky in shape. Bustards (family Otididae) are land birds, medium to large in size with long thick necks.

Crane *Grus grus* 114 cm 45 in. Nests on the ground in swamps and among reeds; in winter moves to rivers, fields and plains. Told from storks and herons by bushy tail. Flies with neck outstretched, migrating in long lines or V-formations. In spring, cranes perform crazy leaping dances before nesting.

Water Rail *Rallus aquaticus* 28 cm 11 in. Usually hides among reeds in marshes and ponds, and nests on concealed platform of reeds built above water. Likely to come into the open during cold weather.

Spotted Crake *Porzana porzana* 23 cm 9 in. Location and behaviour similar to water rail, but even more shy.

Baillon's Crake *Porzana pusilla* 18 cm 7 in. Same location and behaviour as water rail, and similar appearance but much smaller. Very shy.

Little Crake *Porzana parva* 19 cm 7½ in. Same location and behaviour as water rail but much smaller; male is very like Baillon's crake in appearance. Very shy.

Corncrake or **Land Rail** *Crex crex* 25 cm 10 in. Hides away and nests among long grass and crops in meadows and fields. Mowing machines and other changes in agriculture have caused a drop in numbers.

WHAT TO LOOK FOR

Crane Red crown and white cheek stripe; bushy drooping tail.

Water Rail Long red beak.

Spotted Crake Dark brown spotted and streaky plumage.

Baillon's Crake Grey underside with bars on flanks; flesh-coloured legs.

Little Crake Male: as Baillon's crake, but no bars on flanks and green legs. Female: as male, but buff underside.

Corncrake Buff plumage with reddish wing patches.

Crane · Water Rail · Spotted Crake · Baillon's Crake · Little Crake · Corncrake

Crane

Corncrake

Water Rail

Spotted Crake

Baillon's Crake

female

male

Little Crake

Courtship display of male Great Bustard

Little Bustard

female   male

Great Bustard

male

female

Great Bustard   Little Bustard

Purple Gallinule

Moorhen

Coot

Purple Gallinule

Moorhen

Coot

Purple Gallinule *Porphyrio porphyrio* 48 cm 19 in. Lives and nests among reed-beds in swamps and lakes.
Moorhen *Gallinula chloropus* 33 cm 13 in. Lives on ponds, lakes and streams, bobbing its head up and down as it swims to and fro and sometimes diving for food. Often seen in parks. Nests in reeds, bushes and trees, usually near the water. Often feeds on grassy banks and in nearby fields.
Coot *Fulica atra* 38 cm 15 in. Found on lakes, reservoirs and rivers, and in parks. Also at coast in winter. Prefers larger stretches of water than does moorhen, and dives more often. Usually seen in groups, with the birds always quarrelling. Nests in reeds and plants at water's edge.

Great Bustard *Otis tarda* Male 102 cm 40 in; female 76 cm 30 in. Lives on plains and in fields, where it also nests. May be seen walking through grass with head upright, but is very shy. Males court females by bending themselves into contortions to display fans of white feathers. Hunting in past reduced numbers and is now rare.
Little Bustard *Otis tetrax* 43 cm 17 in. Same location and behaviour as great bustard. Hides by crouching flat when danger approaches. In winter, male looks like female.

WHAT TO LOOK FOR

Purple Gallinule Large red beak and long red legs and toes; purple-blue plumage.

Moorhen Black body with red bill and shield above bill.

Coot Black body with white bill and shield.

Great Bustard Large size; grey head and neck; moustache of long white bristles (male only).

Little Bustard Male: black and white pattern on neck (summer only). Female and male in winter: streaky brown head and neck.

WADERS, GULLS AND AUKS

Order Charadriiformes

This is a huge group of many different kinds of birds, but they all spend at least part of their lives in or near water. Waders (mainly plovers and sandpipers) live at the seashore and in marshes. They have long legs so that they can walk in shallow water.

OYSTERCATCHERS

Family Haematopodidae

Oystercatcher *Haematopus ostralegus* 43 cm 17 in. The only European member of its family. Seen at seashore, prising shellfish open with its chisel-like beak. Also probes for food in mud. May also be found inland on moors and by lakes and rivers.

PLOVERS

Family Charadriidae

Plovers can be told from almost all other waders by their short beaks. They probe for worms, grubs and shellfish.

Lapwing, Peewit or **Green Plover** *Vanellus vanellus* 30 cm 12 in. Very common plover. Found in fields and marshes and on moors; also at coast in winter. Usually in large flocks.
Ringed Plover *Charadrius hiaticula* 19 cm 7½ in. Usually found on sandy and stony beaches, sometimes inland.
Little Ringed Plover *Charadrius dubius* 15 cm 6 in. Lives on sandy or stony shores of lakes and rivers, and in old gravel pits.
Kentish Plover *Charadrius alexandrinus* 15 cm 6 in. Found at seashore, on sandy or stony beaches.
Grey Plover *Pluvialis squatarola* 28 cm 11 in. Found on mudflats and sandy beaches.

WHAT TO LOOK FOR

Oystercatcher Black and white plumage with long orange beak.

Lapwing Black and white plumage with crest; glossy dark-green back.

Ringed Plover Black breast band and yellow legs; white wingbar in flight.

Little Ringed Plover As ringed plover but no wingbar and legs often pink.

Kentish Plover As ringed plover, but breast band incomplete and black legs.

Grey Plover Summer: black below and silver-grey above. Winter: white below and grey above.

Oystercatcher

Lapwing

Little Ringed Plover

Ringed Plover

Grey Plover

winter   summer

Kentish Plover

Lapwing   Ringed Plover   Little Ringed Plover   Kentish Plover   Grey Plover

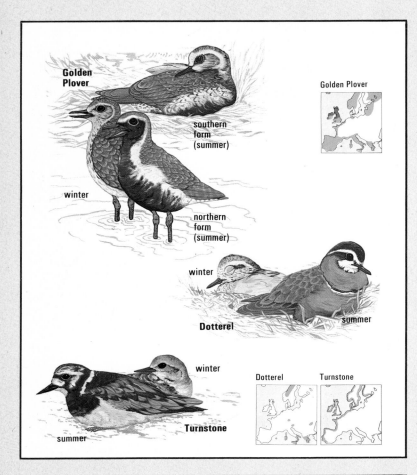

Golden Plover *Pluvialis apricaria* 28 cm 11 in. Nests on moors in summer. In winter, also found in fields and at seashore, usually with lapwings.
Dotterel *Eudromias morinellus* 23 cm 9 in. Nests on barren high ground. In winter, found in fields and at seashores.
Turnstone *Arenaria interpres* 23 cm 9 in. Found at coast, usually on rocky and stony shores. Gets name from its habit of turning over stones, shells and seaweed when looking for food.

SANDPIPERS

Family Scolopacidae

These are wading birds with long bills. Most also have long legs. They may be found inland at damp places as well as at the seashore, and they usually nest on the ground. Flocks of several different kinds of sandpipers can often be seen feeding together at the shore, poking their bills into the water, mud or sand to find shellfish and worms. The different kinds of birds have bills of various lengths, so that they probe at different depths and live on different kinds of food.

Snipe *Gallinago gallinago* 27 cm 10½ in. Hides away in marshes, bogs and damp meadows. Flies away with zigzag flight when disturbed. Often dives from sky, making a drumming noise with its tail.
Great Snipe *Gallinago media* 28 cm 11 in. Hides away in marshes or reedy river banks, especially when nesting. At other times, may also be found in fields and on heaths. Usually flies off in straight line when disturbed.
Jack Snipe *Lymnocryptes minimus* 19 cm 7½ in. Found in same places as snipe and behaves in same way, except that when disturbed it flies off with a more direct flight. Its call sounds rather like a distant galloping horse.

Woodcock

Curlew

Whimbrel

Black-tailed Godwit

Bar-tailed Godwit

Woodcock

Curlew

Whimbrel

Bar-tailed Godwit

winter

summer

winter

summer

Black-tailed Godwit

WHAT TO LOOK FOR

Snipe   Long straight beak with dark stripes along head. Also zigzag flight.

Great Snipe   As snipe, but white sides to tail and straight flight pattern.

Jack Snipe   As snipe but shorter bill and pointed tail.

Woodcock   Long beak with dark stripes across head. Stout shape.

Curlew   Very long down-curving bill and plain head.

Whimbrel   As curlew, but shorter bill and striped head.

Black-tailed Godwit   Summer: long bill (very slightly upturned) with chestnut breast and white tail with black band at end. Winter: as summer but grey breast. Broad white wing stripe.

Bar-tailed Godwit   As black-tailed godwit, but upturned bill and barred tail and no wing bar.

Woodcock *Scolopax rusticola* 36 cm 14 in. Hides away among damp woodland. Most likely to be seen at dawn or dusk flying through the trees or in circles above the trees.
Curlew *Numenius arquata* 56 cm 22 in. Nests on moors and in marshes, damp meadows and sand dunes. In winter, also seen on mudflats at seashore.
Whimbrel *Numenius phaeopus* 41 cm 16 in. Found in same places as curlew, and looks like a small curlew, but told apart by its head pattern.
Black–tailed Godwit *Limosa limosa* 41 cm 16 in. Nests in damp meadows and on boggy land. In winter, also seen on mudflats and in marshes.
Bar–tailed Godwit *Limosa lapponica* 38 cm 15 in. Nests in marshes in Arctic and migrates to spend winter at seashore.

147

A greenshank at its nest.

Green Sandpiper

Redshank

Greenshank

Wood Sandpiper

summer

winter

Spotted Redshank

Common Sandpiper

Green Sandpiper	Wood Sandpiper	Common Sandpiper	Redshank	Spotted Redshank	Greenshank

Green Sandpiper *Tringa ochropus* 23 cm 9 in. Nests in swamps in woodland. Winters in marshes and on lakes and rivers, seldom at coast.

Wood Sandpiper *Tringa glareola* 20 cm 8 in. Found in northern forests and in Arctic, where it nests on ground near water and in old nests in trees.

Common Sandpiper *Tringa hypoleucos* 20 cm 8 in. Nests beside streams,

rivers and lakes, usually in hills. In winter, also seen at seashore. Bobs its tail and nods its head as it wades.

Redshank *Tringa totanus* 28 cm 11 in. Nests among grass in meadows and inland and coastal marshes and on moors and heaths. In winter, usually found at seashore.

Spotted Redshank *Tringa erythropus* 30 cm 12 in. Nests in far north and

migrates to spend winter at seashore and in marshes.

Greenshank *Tringa nebularia* 30 cm 12 in. Nests on ground on moors or in forests, usually near water.

Knot *Calidris canutus* 25 cm 10 in. A winter visitor from the Arctic. Seen at mudflats along seashores, often in flocks. Birds in summer plumage may be seen in spring and autumn.

Purple Sandpiper *Calidris maritima* 20 cm 8 in. Found at rocky shores and harbours in winter. Nests among low plants in far north. Back has purple gloss, but this can be seen only in bright light.

Little Stint *Calidris minuta* 13 cm 5 in. Nests in Arctic and winters in Africa. During migration in spring and autumn may be seen throughout Europe on mudflats at coasts and inland on reservoirs, lakes and sewage farms.

Temminck's Stint *Calidris temminckii* 14 cm 5½ in. Nests among low plants in far north, and winters in Africa. During migration in spring and autumn may be seen throughout Europe (though unlikely in British Isles), mainly in marshes.

Dunlin *Calidris alpina* 18 cm 7 in. Nests on moors and in marshes; spends winter in flocks on mudflats at or near coast and also inland. Flies in tight groups known as 'wader smoke' from the way the birds twist and turn through the air.

Curlew Sandpiper *Calidris ferruginea* 19 cm 7½ in. Nests in Arctic and winters to south of Europe. During migration in spring and autumn may be seen throughout Europe at mud-flats and in marshes.

WHAT TO LOOK FOR

Green Sandpiper White rump with dark legs, no wingbar. Not green.

Wood Sandpiper White rump with pale legs, no wingbar.

Common Sandpiper Dark rump, white wingbar seen in flight; bobs tail.

Redshank White rump with long red legs; white band at back of wing in flight.

Spotted Redshank Summer: black with red legs, no wingband. Winter: pale grey with red legs, no wingband.

Greenshank White rump with greenish legs; no wingband.

Knot Summer: reddish underparts. Winter: stout body, short neck, pale tail.

Purple Sandpiper Summer: speckled plumage with yellow legs. Winter: dark head and breast, yellow legs.

Little Stint Small size, black legs. Autumn: light V-shaped pattern on back.

Temminck's Stint As little stint, but pale legs and no V-pattern on back.

Dunlin Summer: black patch on underside. Winter: dark above and pale below with down-curving beak.

Curlew Sandpiper Summer: down-curving beak with reddish body. Winter: as winter dunlin but white rump.

149

Sanderling

winter

summer

Sanderling

Male displaying
in summer

Sanderling

Ruff

Ruff

male (winter)

female

Sanderling *Calidris alba* 20 cm 8 in.
Seen in winter at sandy beaches,
racing about as if chasing the waves.
Migrates to Arctic to breed.
Ruff *Philomachus pugnax* Male: 30 cm
12 in; female: 23 cm 9 in. Nests on
moors and in marshes and meadows;
also found beside rivers and lakes
in winter. In late spring and early
summer, the males attract the females
by raising a beautiful ruff of feathers
around the neck. The colour of the
ruff varies greatly. The female is also
known as a reeve. Has recently recol-
onized Britain after earlier extinction
as a breeding species.

WHAT TO LOOK FOR

Sanderling Summer: reddish
plumage with white belly. Winter:
almost white with black spot at front
of wing.
Ruff Male: ruff (spring and summer)
brown heavily mottled black
(autumn). Female: as autumn male,
but smaller.
Avocet Long up-turned bill; black
and white back.
Black-winged Stilt Long straight bill;
black back and white underside; long
pink legs.
Red-necked Phalarope Female: red
neck and white throat (summer); dark
eye-patch and thin bill (winter). Male:
as female but less bright in summer.
Stone Curlew Large yellow eyes and
white wingbar on ground; double
white wingbar in flight.
Pratincole Light throat patch;
reddish-brown under wings.
Great Skua Fan-shaped tail without
long protruding feathers.
Arctic Skua Fan-shaped tail with long
protruding central feathers.

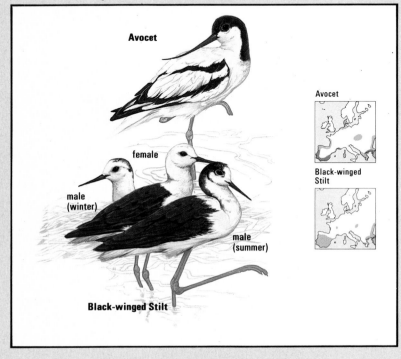

Avocet

female

male
(winter)

Avocet

Black-winged
Stilt

male
(summer)

Black-winged Stilt

AVOCETS AND STILTS

Family Recurvirostridae

These birds are the most elegant
wading birds. They pick their
way through the shallow water on
stilt–like legs, snapping up
insects from the air or lowering
their long thin beaks into the
water.

Avocet *Recurvirostra avosetta* 43 cm
17 in. Nests in marshes at or near
coast; spends winter at estuaries.
Best seen at bird reserves. Beak
curves upwards so that the end skims
surface of water.
Black–winged Stilt *Himantopus
himantopus* 38 cm 15 in. Found in
marshes and lagoons, often wading
deeply in large stretches of water.

PHALAROPES

Family Phalaropodidae

Red–necked Phalarope *Phalaropus lobatus* 18 cm 7 in. Nests in marshes and beside lakes; spends winter out to sea. Often swims, unlike other waders, floating high in the water and sometimes spinning in circles to stir up small animals from the bottom. Phalaropes are unusual birds. The females court the males, and the males build the nest, sit on the eggs and raise the young.

THICK-KNEES

Family Burhinidae

Stone Curlew *Burhinus oedicnemus* 41 cm 16 in. Gets its name because it is often found in stony and rocky places, and because its call (usually heard after dark) is like that of a curlew. Also found in open treeless country. Runs with its head down when disturbed. Thick-knees got their strange name because their 'knees' (which are in fact their heels) appear to be swollen.

PRATINCOLES

Family Glareolidae

Pratincole *Glareola pratincola* 25 cm 10 in. Found on dried mudflats and grassy plains, and at open spaces in marshes. Pratincoles fly and look like large swallows, but also run about the ground. They often stand on tiptoe and stretch their necks, as if trying to see something.

SKUAS

Family Stercorariidae

Skuas are sea birds, as are gulls, terns and auks. They are also pirates of the skies, for they often chase other sea birds and make them drop a fish they have just captured or even half eaten! The skua then swoops down to catch its stolen meal before it hits the water below.

Great Skua *Stercorarius skua* 58 cm 23 in. Nests among grass or heather on moors, and spends winter out to sea. May be seen at coast on migration in spring and autumn.
Arctic Skua *Stercorarius parasiticus* 46 cm 18 in. Lives in similar places to great skua. The neck, breast and underparts may be light, dark or any shade between.

male (summer)

winter

Red-necked Phalarope

female (summer)

Red-necked Phalarope

Stone Curlew   Pratincole

Stone Curlew

Pratincole

Great Skua diving

Great Skua

dark form

light form

Great Skua

Arctic Skua

Arctic Skua

151

Great Black-backed Gull

Herring Gull

Scandinavian form

British form

Lesser Black-backed Gull

Common Gull

Glaucous Gull

A flock of gulls. These birds often follow ploughs to pick up worms and grubs as the soil is turned over. The gulls are helpful to farmers because they devour pests in this way.

Great Black-backed Gull

Lesser Black-backed Gull

Herring Gull

Common Gull

Glaucous Gull

GULLS AND TERNS

Family Laridae

These two kinds of sea birds are easy to tell apart. Gulls have broad wings and fan-shaped tails, and their beaks are usually heavy with a hooked tip. They can be seen in flocks at the seashore and at harbours, constantly making mewing cries as they wheel to and fro in the air. To feed, they settle on the water and seize some floating waste or dip their heads under the water to catch a fish. They also follow ships, but not out of sight of land. Gulls also fly inland, especially in winter. They nest in colonies on the ground and on cliffs. Young gulls look brown and white until they are as much as four years old. Terns have slender wings and forked tails, and sharp beaks that often point downwards during flight.

Great Black–backed Gull *Larus marinus* 68 cm 27 in. Usually seen at rocky coasts and offshore islands; may be seen inland, especially in winter. Often feeds on eggs and young of other sea birds.
Lesser Black–backed Gull *Larus fuscus* 53 cm 21 in. Often seen at seashore and harbours and also inland. The British form (*Larus fuscus graellsii*) has a lighter back than the Scandinavian form (*Larus fuscus fuscus*), which looks like a small great black-backed gull.

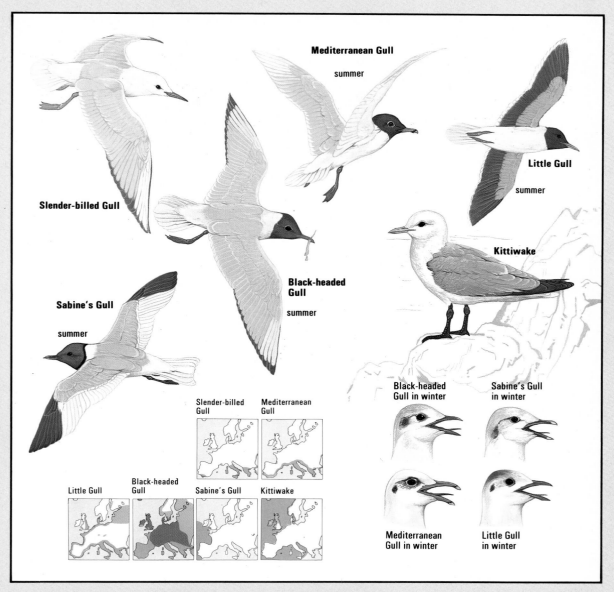

Mediterranean Gull

summer

Slender-billed Gull

Little Gull

summer

Sabine's Gull

summer

Black-headed Gull

summer

Kittiwake

Slender-billed Gull   Mediterranean Gull

Little Gull   Black-headed Gull   Sabine's Gull   Kittiwake

Black-headed Gull in winter   **Sabine's Gull in winter**

Mediterranean Gull in winter   **Little Gull in winter**

Herring Gull *Larus argentatus* 56 cm 22 in. A very common gull, seen both at the coast and inland.

Common Gull *Larus canus* 41 cm 16 in. Found at coast and inland. In spite of its name, it is not the most numerous gull.

Glaucous Gull *Larus hyperboreus* 71 cm 28 in. Nests in Iceland and in Arctic; seen at coasts and harbours in winter, rarely inland. Preys on eggs and small birds.

Slender-billed Gull *Larus genei* 43 cm 17 in. Nests in marshes and by lagoons and rivers, but is otherwise found at coasts and river mouths. Long bill is pointed down in flight.

Mediterranean Gull *Larus melanocephalus* 38 cm 15 in. Nests in marshes and by lakes and lagoons, otherwise seen at seashore and harbours and also inland.

Little Gull *Larus minutus* 28 cm 11 in. Gets its name because it is noticeably smaller than other gulls. Nests in marshes and swamps, but seen at coast and inland at other times. Catches insects in flight.

Black-headed Gull *Larus ridibundus* 38 cm 15 in. A very common gull, often seen inland. Nests in marshes, on moors, and by lakes and rivers. At other times found at coasts and harbours, and in fields and towns. Eats anything, including fish, worms, flying insects and even garbage. Badly named, as other gulls have black heads and the head is dark brown but goes white in winter!

Sabine's Gull *Larus sabini* 33 cm 13 in. Nests in Arctic, and spends winter out to sea but may be seen at coast. Only European gull with noticeably forked tail.

Kittiwake *Rissa tridactyla* 41 cm 16 in. Nests in colonies on cliff ledges and also on buildings in coastal towns. Usually spends winter far out to sea.

WHAT TO LOOK FOR

Slender-billed Gull As black-headed gull but white head throughout year and long thin bill.

Mediterranean Gull As black-headed gull but black head in summer, and no black on wings.

Little Gull Like small black-headed gull but black head in summer, no black on wingtips and dark beneath wings.

Black-headed Gull Dark-brown head (summer only); white patch on front of wings and black edge on back of wings.

Sabine's Gull As black-headed gull, but dark-grey head in summer, black wingtips and forked tail.

Kittiwake Solid black wingtips and black legs.

Roseate Tern

Little Tern

Sandwich Tern

Common Tern

Arctic Tern

Black Tern

Whiskered Tern

Black Tern

Whiskered Tern

Common Tern

Arctic Tern

Roseate Tern

Little Tern

Sandwich Tern

Black Tern *Chlidonias niger* 24 cm 9½ in. Builds floating nest on lakes and marsh pools; may be seen at coast during migration in spring and autumn. Chases insects in air; rarely dives into water.

Whiskered Tern *Chlidonias hybrida* 24 cm 9½ in. Found in same places as black tern, but often dives for food.

Common Tern *Sterna hirundo* 36 cm 14 in. Nests on beaches, among sand dunes, in coastal swamps, on offshore islands and by lakes. Often seen flying along seashore and diving for fish.

Arctic Tern *Sterna paradisaea* 36 cm 14 in. Found in same kinds of places as common tern, but less likely inland. May migrate as far south as the Antarctic to spend the winter.

Roseate Tern *Sterna dougallii* 38 cm 15 in. Nests on rocky islands and beaches, sometimes with common terns and arctic terns; seldom found inland.

Little Tern *Sterna albifrons* 24 cm 9½ in. Nests mainly on sandy and stony beaches, but sometimes at places inland.

Sandwich Tern *Sterna sandvicensis* 41 cm 16 in. Nests in colonies on sandy and stony beaches and also on offshore islands. Rarely found inland. Named after Sandwich in Kent, where a famous colony once existed.

WHAT TO LOOK FOR

Black Tern Black head and body, grey wings and tail.

Whiskered Tern Grey belly, white cheeks.

Common Tern Orange bill, black tip.

Arctic Tern All-red bill short legs; greyer breast than Common Tern.

Roseate Tern All-black bill, sometimes with red base; very long tail. Distinctive barking call note. Pink flush to breast in Spring.

Little Tern Yellow bill with black tip white forehead. The smallest European tern.

Sandwich Tern Black bill with yellow tip; slight crest.

NOTE: the descriptions and illustrations on these pages are of birds in summer plumage. Terns may also be seen in winter plumage, when they all have white foreheads and dark bills, and are very difficult to tell apart. In addition, the black tern and whiskered tern become white beneath.

154

The beak of the puffin has saw-tooth edges so that it can hold several fish in its beak at once.

summer

winter

Puffin

Guillemot

summer

winter

summer

winter

Black Guillemot

Razorbill

summer

summer

winter

summer

winter

Little Auk

Black Guillemot

Razorbill

Little Auk

Puffin

Guillemot

AUKS

Family Alcidae

Auks look and behave very much like penguins. They dive for fish and chase them underwater, using their wings like oars and their feet like a rudder. On land, they sit up and waddle about. Also like penguins, they spend most of the year at sea and only come ashore to breed. However, unlike penguins, they can fly well – although the great auk, which is now extinct, could not. It was a very easy target for hunters, and the last pair of birds was killed in 1844. The great auk was a large bird as big as a goose.

Razorbill *Alca torda* 41 cm 16 in. Breeds in colonies on cliff ledges at coast, often with guillemots. Spends winter out to sea, although storms may force it back to shore.

Little Auk *Plautus alle* 20 cm 8 in. Nests in Arctic and spends winter in northern seas, but may be driven ashore by storms.

Puffin *Fratercula arctica* 30 cm 12 in. Nests in colonies in burrows in steep slopes by sea. May run down slope to get into the air. Can hold several fish at once in its parrot-like beak. Spends winter far out to sea and seldom blown ashore.

Black Guillemot *Cepphus grylle* 33 cm 13 in. Nests in holes and crevices on rocky shores and sea cliffs, but not in large colonies. Stays near shore in winter.

Guillemot *Uria aalge* 41 cm 16 in. Breeds in large colonies on cliff ledges at coast and on offshore islands. The guillemot's egg is laid on bare rock and is pear-shaped, so that it rolls in a circle and not over the edge if knocked. Spends winter out to sea, but may be driven ashore by gales.

WHAT TO LOOK FOR

Razorbill   Broad dark bill with white marks.

Little Auk   Small size and short bill.

Puffin   Triangular beak (bright red and yellow in summer).

Black Guillemot   Summer: black body with white wing patch. Winter: mottled grey back with white wing patch.

Guillemot   Slender pointed bill.

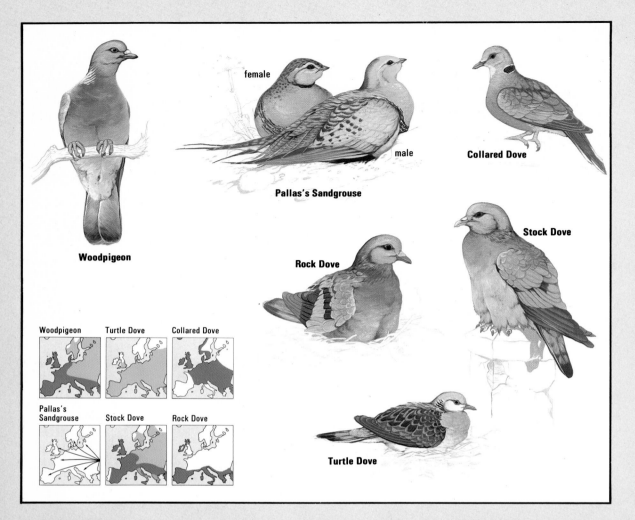

female

male

Pallas's Sandgrouse

Woodpigeon

Collared Dove

Stock Dove

Rock Dove

Turtle Dove

Woodpigeon   Turtle Dove   Collared Dove

Pallas's
Sandgrouse   Stock Dove   Rock Dove

PIGEONS AND DOVES

Order Columbiformes

These birds have plump bodies, small heads and short legs. They can all fly very fast, and people raise pigeons for racing. There are two families, sandgrouse (family Pteroclidae) and pigeons and doves (family Columbidae).

Pallas's Sandgrouse *Syrrhaptes paradoxus* 38 cm 15 in. Nests in central Asia, and sometimes migrates to Europe. Likely to be seen at sandy shores and in fields after the harvesting season.
Stock Dove *Columba oenas* 33 cm 13 in. Found in woods and on farmland; may also be seen in parks and at cliffs and sand dunes along coast. Often found in the company of woodpigeons.

Rock Dove *Columba livia* 33 cm 13 in. Lives at rocky coasts and on mountains, and nests in caves and on cliff ledges. The pigeons that can be seen in city squares and parks, as well as the pigeons that people raise for racing, are all descended from the wild rock dove. Some of these pigeons still look like their wild ancestor, but many now have different plumage. The pigeons are interbreeding with the rock doves, and the wild birds are slowly disappearing.

Because the wild birds are naturally at home on cliffs, pigeons can live and nest on the ledges of buildings. They have long been a companion of man, carrying messages for him as well as providing him with a source of food.
Woodpigeon *Columba palumbus* 41 cm 16 in. Found in woods and on farmland, and also in parks and gardens. Often seen in flocks containing stock doves and domestic pigeons.
Turtle Dove *Streptopelia turtur* 28 cm 11 in. Found in spring and summer in light woods and among scattered trees and bushes; also on farmland and in parks and gardens.

Collared Dove *Streptopelia decaocto* 30 cm 12 in. Usually found in towns or close to houses and farms. Nests on buildings or in trees nearby.

WHAT TO LOOK FOR

Pallas's Sandgrouse   Dark patch on belly, long pointed tail.

Stock Dove   Grey rump, no obvious neck mark or wing marks.

Rock Dove   White rump, no neck mark, two black wing stripes.

Woodpigeon   Grey rump, white neck mark, white wingbar.

Turtle Dove   Black tail with white edges; white neck patch with black stripes.

Collared Dove   Black stripe edged with white at back of neck.

CUCKOOS

Order Cuculiformes Family Cuculidae

Cuckoos are famous for laying their eggs in the nests of other birds and leaving the other birds to bring up the young cuckoos. Both of the cuckoos found in Europe breed in this way.

Cuckoo *Cuculus canorus* 33 cm 13 in. Found in woodland, open ground with scattered trees and bushes, and on moors. Only the male makes 'cuckoo' call; female has babbling call. The female cuckoo lays several eggs, one each in the nests of other birds. Small birds are chosen, such as meadow pipits and robins, but each female cuckoo always uses nests of the same species. When it hatches, the young cuckoo pushes out any other eggs and nestlings, but its adopted parents continue to feed it, driven by instinct.
Great Spotted Cuckoo *Clamator glandarius* 41 cm 16 in. Found in woods and among scattered trees. Does not call 'cuckoo'. Usually lays its eggs in the nests of crows, particularly magpies.

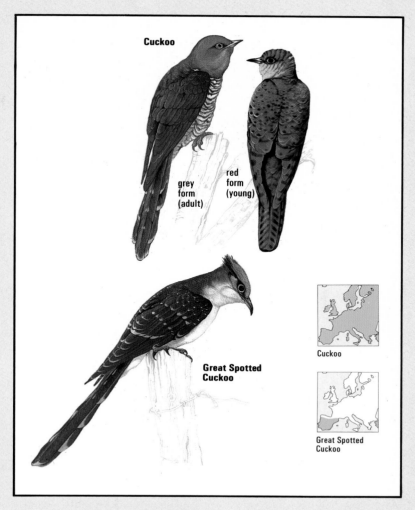

Cuckoo

grey form (adult)

red form (young)

Great Spotted Cuckoo

Cuckoo

Great Spotted Cuckoo

WHAT TO LOOK FOR

Cuckoo Grey head and breast with bars on white underside; but female sometimes red-brown with bars all over body.

Great Spotted Cuckoo White spots on wings, grey crest, long white-edged tail.

OWLS

Order Strigiformes

Owls are not often seen because they usually come out only at night to hunt mice and other small animals. Owls have large eyes set in front of their heads to help them spot their prey in the dark. They also fly without a sound.

Barn Owl *Tyto alba* 36 cm 14 in. Found on farmland and in marshes but also occupies unused buildings, such as barns and church towers, and ruins. Most likely to be seen at dusk. Two forms occur, a white-breasted form (*Tyto alba alba*) in south and west Europe, and a buff-breasted form (*Tyto alba guttata*) in north and east Europe.
Scops Owl *Otus scops* 19 cm 7½ in. Found among trees, often near buildings, as well as in ruins. Rarely seen in daytime. Like other owls, has ear tufts that are not ears but merely tufts of head feathers.

dark-breasted form

Barn Owl

Scops Owl

light-breasted form

Barn Owl

Scops Owl

Pygmy Owl

Tawny Owl

brown form

grey form

Short-eared Owl

Little Owl

Snowy Owl

Snowy Owl

Little Owl

Short-eared Owl

Pygmy Owl

Eagle Owl

Tawny Owl

Long-eared Owl

Long-eared Owl

Eagle Owl

Eagle Owl *Bubo bubo* 68 cm 27 in. Largest European owl. Lives in forests, among mountain crags and gorges, and on dry plains. Active at dawn and dusk, when it hunts animals as large as hares. Rare.

Snowy Owl *Nyctea scandiaca* 61 cm 24 in. Lives and nests in Arctic, Norway and Iceland, but sometimes spreads to northern Europe for the winter. May then be seen on moors, in marshes and at lake shores and coast. Hunts by day, but white plumage may conceal it against snow.

Pygmy Owl *Glaucidium passerinum* 18 cm 7 in. Usually seen in fir forests. Active day and night, chasing small birds through air. Flicks tail up and down when perching. Smallest European owl.

Little Owl *Athene noctua* 23 cm 9 in. Found among scattered trees, in fields and on open ground, often near buildings. May be seen in daytime, bobbing and turning its head as it perches on a post or branch.

Tawny Owl *Strix aluco* 38 cm 15 in. A very common owl. Lives in woods and also in parks and gardens. Usually hunts by night, but may be seen sleeping in tree during daytime, when it is sometimes bothered by small birds. Colour varies from brown to grey.

Long-eared Owl *Asio otus* 36 cm 14 in. Sleeps in woods, especially in fir trees, by day and comes out to hunt, often over open ground, at dusk. May be seen sleeping in groups in winter.

Short-eared Owl *Asio flammeus* 38 cm 15 in. Seen hunting over moors, marshes and open ground during daytime and at dusk. Ear tufts are very short, often invisible.

WHAT TO LOOK FOR

Barn Owl Heart-shaped face; brown back with white or buff unstreaked breast (may look all white at dusk.)

Scops Owl Small, with short ear tufts.

Eagle Owl Huge, with long ear tufts.

Snowy Owl White plumage, large yellow eyes.

Little Owl Small, with flattened head, no ear tufts.

Tawny Owl Streaky plumage with black eyes; stocky shape and no ear tufts.

Long-eared Owl Slender shape and long ear tufts.

Short-eared Owl Similar to tawny owl but yellow eyes and lighter plumage.

Pygmy Owl Very small, with round head, no ear tufts; flicks tail when sitting on perch.

NIGHTJARS

Order Caprimulgiformes
Family Caprimulgidae

Nightjar *Caprimulgus europaeus*
28 cm 11 in. Lives in woods, among
bracken in clearings and on hillsides,
on moors and in sand dunes. Unless
disturbed, it is very difficult to spot.
Sleeps during the day and hunts for
insects at night. Lays eggs on the
ground.

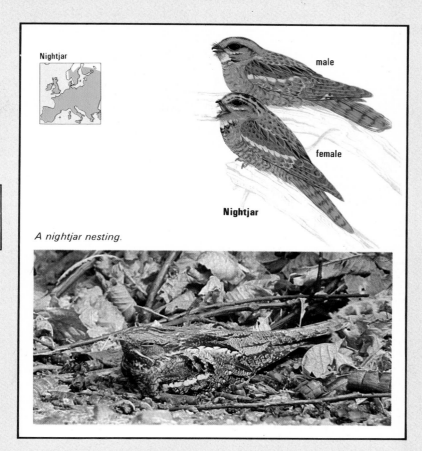

WHAT TO LOOK FOR
Nightjar Plumage pattern looks like dead leaves from above; fine bars below.

A nightjar nesting.

SWIFTS

Order Apodiformes Family Apodidae

Swifts are masters of the air and
are usually seen in flocks,
wheeling high in the sky at great
speed. They may spend weeks in
the air without coming down, as
they catch flying insects for food
and can sleep in flight. Swifts
have weak feet and if they land on
the ground, they cannot walk and
find it hard to get back into the
air. Instead, they usually cling to
vertical surfaces and simply fall
off them to become airborne.

Swift *Apus apus* 16 cm 6½ in. Nests
in holes in trees, crevices in cliffs, and
under the eaves of buildings. Often to
be seen at dusk, dashing around
rooftops in noisy flocks. May be seen
with swallows (page 165), but can
easily be recognized by dark underparts and shallow forked tail.
Alpine Swift *Apus melba* 20 cm
8 in. Found in mountains, at cliffs and
around buildings. Nests in crevices.
Has very long wings, unlike similar
sand martin (picture, page 165).

WHAT TO LOOK FOR
Swift Dark body; shallow forked tail. **Alpine Swift** White belly and throat with dark breast band; very long wings.

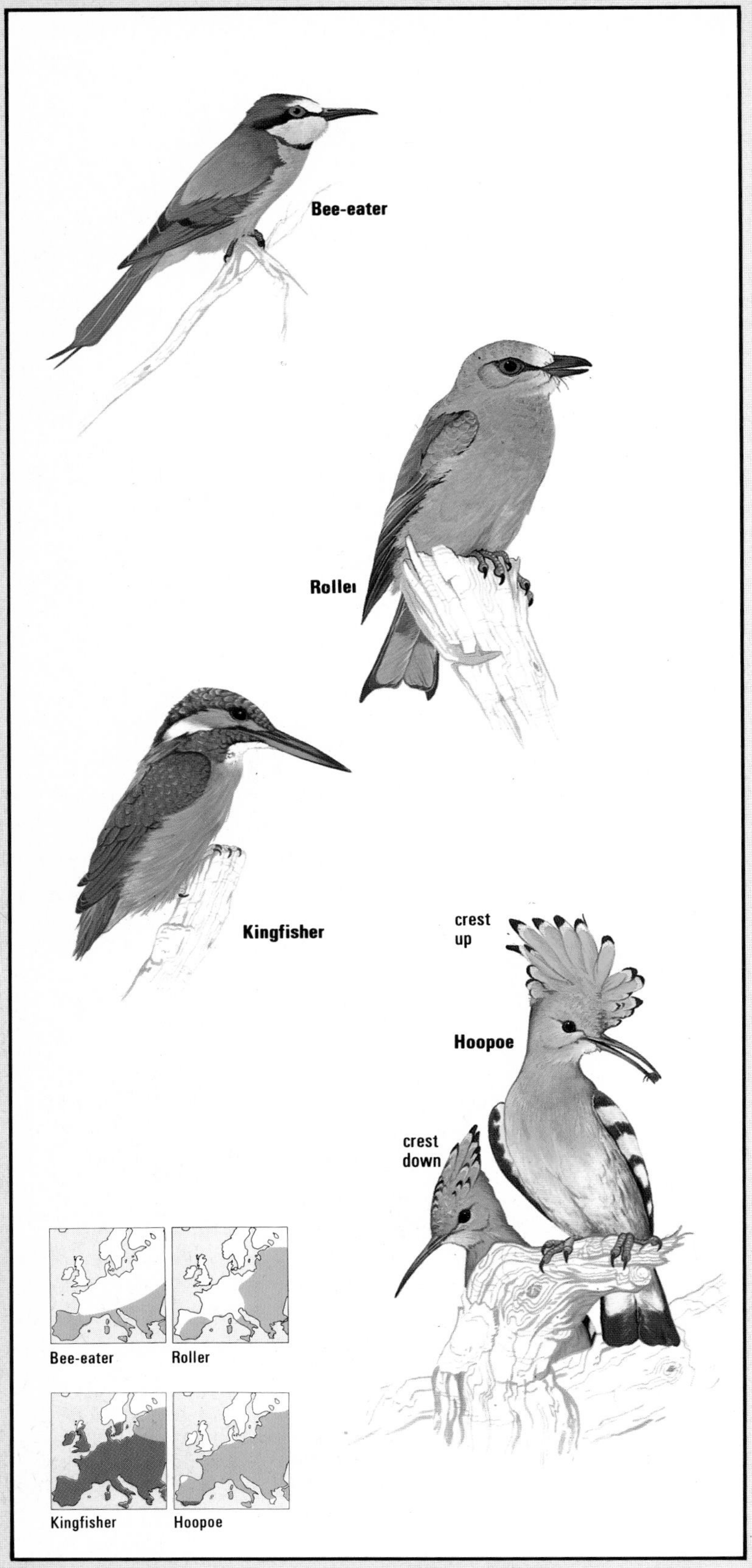

KINGFISHERS AND RELATED BIRDS

Order Coraciiformes

Any birds in this mixed group are worth a special effort to see, for they are the most colourful and spectacular birds to be seen in Europe. None is like any other and they all belong to different families. The kingfisher belongs to the family Alcedinidae, and the bee-eater to the family Meropidae. The roller is a member of the family Coraciidae, and the hoopoe of the family Upupidae.

Kingfisher *Alcedo atthis* 16 cm 6½ in. Seen by rivers and lakes, perching on a branch beside the water or darting down to plunge for a fish. May also be seen at coast in winter.

Bee-eater *Merops apiaster* 28 cm 11 in. Found in open country among scattered trees and bushes, often perching on bushes or telegraph wires. Nests in hole dug in bank of river or pit, or in burrow dug in the ground. Chases flying insects, especially bees and wasps.

Roller *Coracias garrulus* 30 cm 12 in. Found in open country with scattered trees and in woods. Nests in hole in tree or bank. Often seen perching and then swooping down to catch insects and other small animals. Gets its name from the way it rolls over in flight to attract a mate during the spring courtship.

Hoopoe *Upupa epops* 28 cm 11 in. Seen among scattered trees and in woods; sometimes in parks and gardens. Nests in hole in tree or wall. Often seen perching, usually with its crest down. Named after its call.
Several recent nesting records from Britain (not mapped).

Bee-eater

Roller

Kingfisher

crest up

Hoopoe

crest down

Bee-eater

Roller

Kingfisher

Hoopoe

WHAT TO LOOK FOR

Kingfisher Blue-green back and orange underparts.

Bee-eater Yellow throat and blue-green breast.

Roller Blue-green with chestnut back.

Hoopoe Black-and-white striped wings; large black-tipped crest.

WOODPECKERS
Order Piciformes Family Picidae

Woodpeckers are often heard before being seen. Their sharp beaks make a loud rat-a-tat as they chisel into the bark of a tree in search of insects. They also dig out holes for nesting. Woodpeckers grip the trunk or branch with sharp claws and thrust their tails stiffly against the bark to prop themselves up and give a powerful blow with the beak. In the spring, they make a drumming noise by clattering their beaks on a piece of wood; this is part of their courtship.

Green Woodpecker *Picus viridis* 30 cm 12 in. Found in woods and forests, usually of broad-leaved trees, and in open country with scattered trees. Also seen on ground, feeding at anthills. It is a large woodpecker, with dull-green upperparts, a crimson crown and a yellow rump. The sides of the head are black. Seldom drums.
Grey–headed Woodpecker *Picus canus* 25 cm 10 in. Found in same places as green woodpecker. Often drums in spring, unlike green woodpecker.
Three–toed Woodpecker *Picoides tridactylus* 23 cm 9 in. Lives in forests on mountains and in far north.
Black Woodpecker *Dryocopus martius* 46 cm 18 in. Lives in woods and forests, often in mountains. Largest European woodpecker, with black plumage. Slightly crested crimson crown (male), but female has crimson patch on the back of the head.

WHAT TO LOOK FOR

Green Woodpecker Greenish back and yellow rump; large red crown. Thick black (female) or red (male) moustache.

Grey-headed Woodpecker Grey head with thin moustache; male only has red forehead.

Three-toed Woodpecker White back, black cheeks and striped flanks. Yellow crown (male only).

Black Woodpecker Black body with red crown.

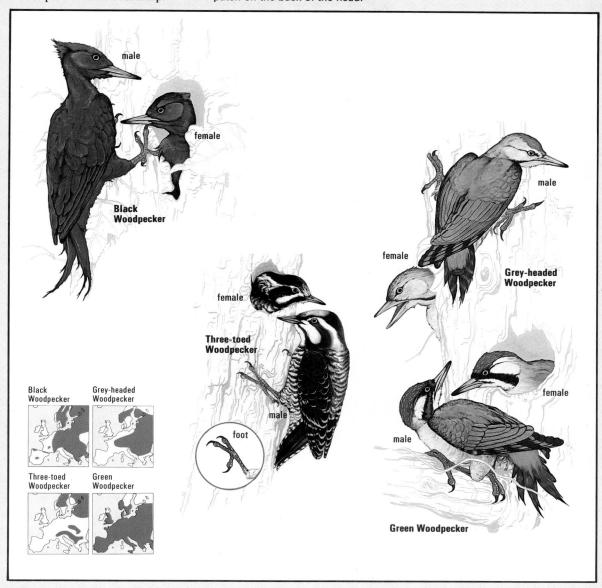

male
female
Black Woodpecker

Grey-headed Woodpecker
male
female

Three-toed Woodpecker
female
male
foot

Green Woodpecker
male
female

Black Woodpecker
Grey-headed Woodpecker
Three-toed Woodpecker
Green Woodpecker

Wryneck *Jynx torquilla* 16 cm 6½ in. Lives in light woodland, and in open country with scattered trees, bushes and hedges, orchards, parks and gardens. Does not look like a woodpecker and does not chisel into bark. Often feeds on ground and nests in existing holes, including nest-boxes. Gets its name from the way it can turn its head round.

Syrian Woodpecker *Dendrocopos syriacus* 23 cm 9 in. Found in woods and forests, and also around villages and farms. Similar to Great Spotted Woodpecker, but tail shows less white.

Great Spotted Woodpecker *Dendrocopos major* 23 cm 9 in. Found in woods and forests of all kinds, and also in parks and gardens. Comes to bird tables, being able to hang upside-down to feed as tits do. Also likes to wedge nuts into cracks in bark and hammer them open with bill. Known for its habit of drumming very rapidly on dead branches. The most common and widespread European woodpecker.

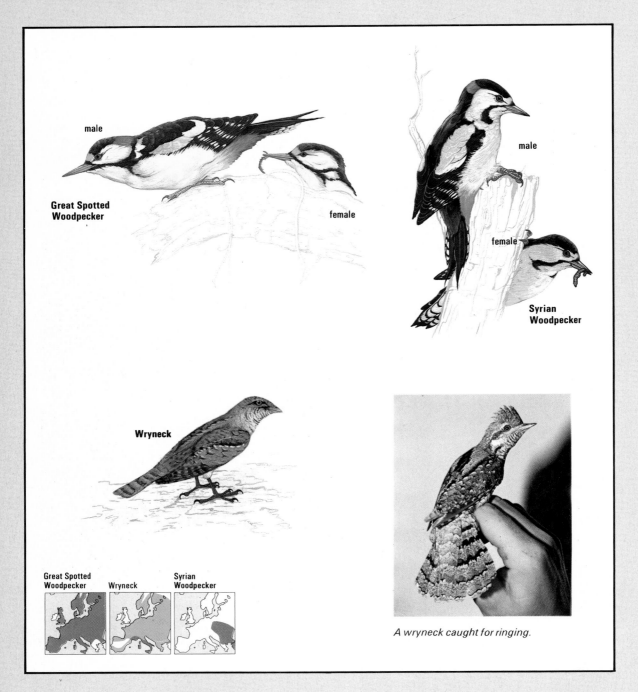

Great Spotted Woodpecker — male, female

Syrian Woodpecker — male, female

Wryneck

Great Spotted Woodpecker   Wryneck   Syrian Woodpecker

A wryneck caught for ringing.

Lesser Spotted Woodpecker
Dendrocopos minor 15 cm 6 in. Lives in same places as middle spotted woodpecker, but may also be found in parks and orchards. Smallest European woodpecker.

White–backed Woodpecker *Dendrocopos leucotos* 25 cm 10 in. Found in woods and forests, though not often among fir trees

Middle Spotted Woodpecker *Dendrocopos medius* 20 cm 8 in. Lives in woods and forests, though seldom among fir trees. Usually stays high up in trees.

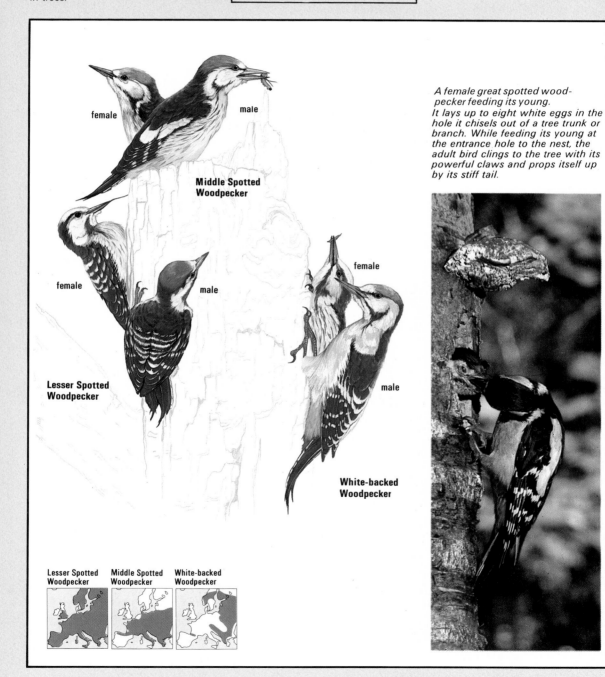

A female great spotted wood-pecker feeding its young.
It lays up to eight white eggs in the hole it chisels out of a tree trunk or branch. While feeding its young at the entrance hole to the nest, the adult bird clings to the tree with its powerful claws and props itself up by its stiff tail.

female · male

Middle Spotted Woodpecker

female · male

Lesser Spotted Woodpecker

female · male

White-backed Woodpecker

Lesser Spotted Woodpecker · Middle Spotted Woodpecker · White-backed Woodpecker

Calandra Lark

Shore Lark

Woodlark

Crested Lark

Skylark

Short-toed Lark

Calandra Lark

Short-toed Lark

Crested Lark

Woodlark

Skylark

Shore Lark

WHAT TO LOOK FOR

Calandra Lark   Black neck patch and large beak.

Short-toed Lark   Pale unstreaked underside.

Crested Lark   Large crest (Note: in southern Spain, almost identical Thekla lark – *Galerida theklae* – may be seen).

Woodlark   Black and white mark at front of wing; all-brown tail; slight crest.

Skylark   White edges to tail; slight crest.

Shore Lark   Horns on head (male only); black and yellow face pattern.

PERCHING BIRDS AND SONGBIRDS
Order Passeriformes

These birds make up the biggest group of birds – more than half of all birds. They are to be found everywhere. None is very large, and most are fairly small. Their feet have three toes in front and a long one behind, which enables them to perch easily – although, of course, other birds can perch too. Many, but by no means all, can sing well and, in a few cases, the song must be heard to be sure of the bird's identity.

LARKS
Family Alaudidae

These birds are most often seen in the air, singing strongly. They make their nests on the ground where, being dull-coloured, they are difficult to spot. However, they may sometimes be seen running along the ground. Some larks look rather like buntings (pages 190-191), but have thin beaks whereas buntings have stout beaks.

Calandra Lark *Melanocorypha calandra* 19 cm 7½ in. Found on stony ground and plains and in fields.
Short–toed Lark *Calandrella cinerea* 14 cm 5½ in. Lives on dry, bare sandy or stony ground, dried mudflats and plains and in fields.
Crested Lark *Galerida cristata* 16 cm 6½ in. Found on stony and sandy ground and in fields; also seen on waste land in towns and villages and beside roads.
Woodlark *Lullula arborea* 15 cm 6 in. Found in fields and open country, often among scattered trees and bushes, and at woodland edges. Often flies in circle while singing; also sings while perched.
Skylark *Alauda arvensis* 18 cm 7 in. Found in all kinds of open country – moors, marshes, fields and sand dunes. Rises straight up into air and may hover while singing.
Shore Lark *Eremophila alpestris* 16 cm 6½ in. Nests on rocky ground in far north or high in mountains. Spends winter at beaches, and in marshes and fields along coast.

SWALLOWS AND MARTINS

Family Hirundinidae

Swallows and martins fly very fast, often near the ground, twisting and turning in the air as they chase flying insects. Swifts (page 159) are similar, but have longer wings that they hold out stiffly as they fly. Unlike swifts, which cannot perch, flocks of swallows and martins often perch on telegraph wires, especially when they are about to migrate.

Swallow *Hirundo rustica* 19 cm 7½ in. Builds an open nest of mud and straw on beams and ledges in farm buildings and sheds. Hunts for insects in nearby fields, often swooping low in flight over water.

Red–rumped Swallow *Hirundo daurica* 18 cm 7 in. Usually found in rocky country and at coast. Builds mud nest with long narrow entrance on walls of caves, cliffs or rocks, under bridges, or on buildings.

Crag Martin *Hirundo rupestris* 14 cm 5½ in. Lives in mountains and on sea cliffs. Builds cup-shaped mud nest on rock face or cave wall, and sometimes on buildings.

House Martin *Delichon urbica* 13 cm 5 in. Often seen in towns and villages, but also lives in open country. Builds mud nest with tiny entrance hole beneath eaves of buildings, under bridges, and also on rock faces and cliffs.

Sand Martin *Riparia riparia* 13 cm 5 in. Lives in open country, especially near ponds, lakes and rivers. Nests in colonies in holes dug in banks of rivers, cuttings and pits, and also in cliffs.

WHAT TO LOOK FOR

Swallow Deeply forked tail, red throat, deep blue back.

Red-rumped Swallow As swallow but without red throat and with buff (not red) rump.

Crag Martin Brown back and underside completely pale buff.

House Martin Deep blue back with white rump, underside completely white.

Sand Martin As crag martin but brown breast band.

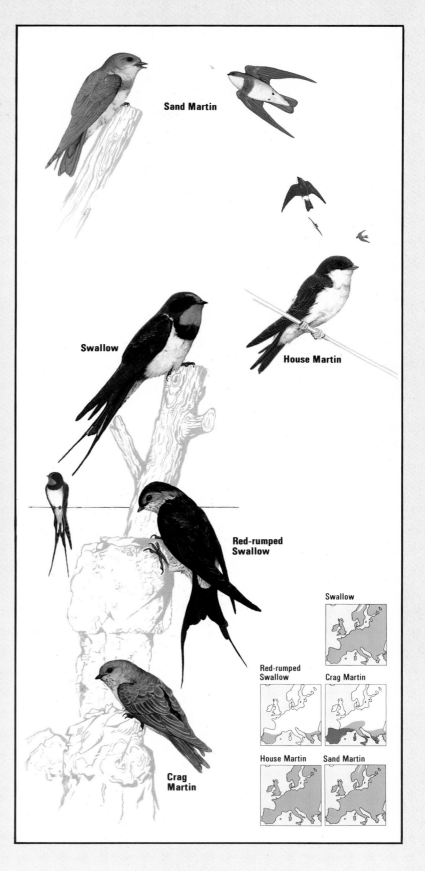

Sand Martin

Swallow

House Martin

Red-rumped Swallow

Crag Martin

Swallow

Red-rumped Swallow

Crag Martin

House Martin

Sand Martin

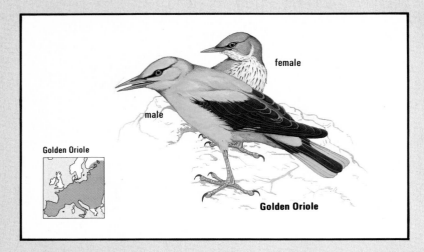

ORIOLES
Family Oriolidae

Most orioles are brightly coloured birds of tropical forests. Only one species is found as far north as Europe.

Golden Oriole *Oriolus oriolus* 24 cm 9½ in. Found in woods and orchards, and among trees in parks. Usually hides among leaves in tops of trees. Has recently colonized England (not mapped).

CROWS
Family Corvidae

Crows are the largest perching birds and they are among the cleverest of all birds. They search boldly for all kinds of food, and will avoid traps and ignore scarecrows that farmers put out to stop them robbing crops. They may also store food for the winter, and open snails by dropping them on to a stone.

Raven *Corvus corax* 63 cm 25 in. Lives on sea cliffs and crags, in woods and open country, especially in hills and mountains and usually far from towns and villages. Builds huge nest on rock ledge or in tree. Often makes acrobatic display in the air, especially in spring. Hunts animals such as rabbits, hedgehogs and rats, but usually eats dead animals. The largest all-black bird found in Europe.

Carrion Crow *Corvus corone corone* 46 cm 18 in. Found on moors, at coasts and in fields, parks and gardens. Often seen alone or in pairs, and pairs nest alone in trees or on cliffs. Usually simply called crow rather than carrion crow.

WHAT TO LOOK FOR

Golden Oriole Male: bright yellow with black wings. Female: head and body green above and streaky white below.

Raven Huge; all-black body with massive black beak and wedge-shaped tail.

Carrion Crow Medium size; all-black body with heavy black beak.

A rookery. Rooks build their untidy nests high in the tree tops for safety. They build their nests in such large colonies because they are sociable birds. Jackdaws and owls may sometimes take over nests that have been abandoned by rooks.

Rook

Hooded Crow

Jackdaw

Magpie

Jackdaw Rook Hooded Crow Magpie

Hooded Crow *Corvus corone cornix* 46 cm 18 in. Found in same places and lives in same way as carrion crow. Belongs to same species as carrion crow, and interbreeds with it in places where their ranges overlap, producing birds intermediate in appearance between them.

Rook *Corvus frugilegus* 46 cm 18 in. Found in fields surrounded by lines of trees or small woods, in which it nests in colonies called rookeries. Also at seashore and open ground in winter. Usually seen in groups.

Jackdaw *Corvus monedula* 33 cm 13 in. Found in fields and open country

and at rocky coasts, nesting in holes in trees and rocks. Also seen on farms, and in towns and villages, where it nests in old buildings. Usually seen in flocks, walking jerkily or flying acrobatically.

Magpie *Pica pica* 46 cm 18 in. Found in fields and open country with scattered trees and bushes, in which it builds a large dome-shaped nest. Often seen in town parks and gardens. May steal bright objects, and store them in its nest. It has a characteristic pattern of flight, in which it intermittently glides and then rapidly flaps its wings.

WHAT TO LOOK FOR

Magpie Black and white body with very long tail.

Hooded Crow Like carrion crow but grey back and belly.

Rook Like carrion crow, but grey patch at base of beak (making beak look large).

Jackdaw Black body but back of head and neck is grey.

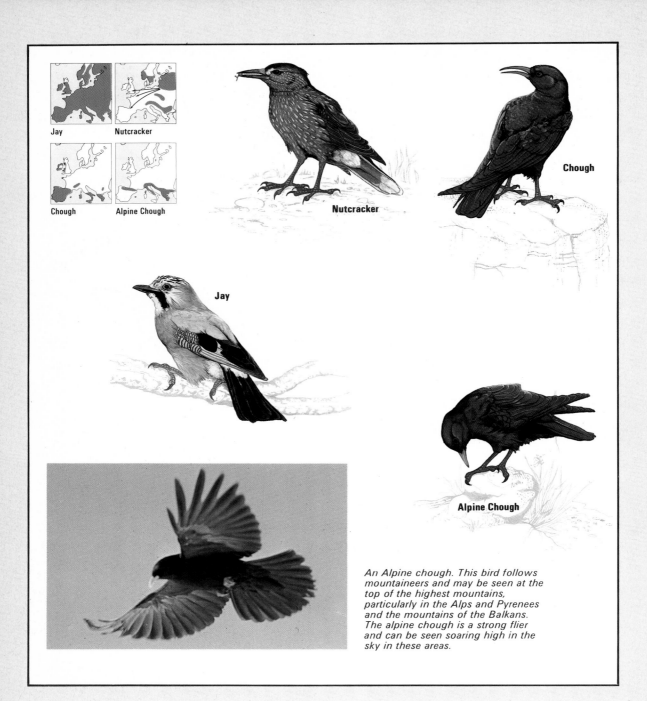

Jay

Nutcracker

Chough

Alpine Chough

Nutcracker

Chough

Jay

Alpine Chough

An Alpine chough. This bird follows
mountaineers and may be seen at the
top of the highest mountains,
particularly in the Alps and Pyrenees
and the mountains of the Balkans.
The alpine chough is a strong flier
and can be seen soaring high in the
sky in these areas.

Nutcracker *Nucifraga caryocatactes*
33 cm 13 in. Lives in mountain forests,
usually among conifer trees. Feeds
mainly on nuts, which it may store in
the autumn and find months later,
even under snow.
Jay *Garrulus glandarius* 36 cm 14 in.
Found in woods and orchards, and
sometimes in town parks and gardens.
Fond of acorns, which it stores for the
winter by burying them in the ground.
Can hold as many as six acorns in its
mouth. It is a very lively and active
bird and often flicks its tail.

Chough *Pyrrhocorax pyrrhocorax*
38 cm 15 in. Lives in mountains and
on cliffs by sea; may also be found in
quarries. Nests on ledges and in caves
and crevices. Often performs aero-
batics in flight.
Alpine Chough *Pyrrhocorax graculus*
38 cm 15 in. Lives on high mountains,
right up to the snowy summits. Alpine
choughs have even been seen near the
top of Mount Everest, higher than any
other bird. Comes down to mountain
villages in winter to feed on any scraps
it can find.

WHAT TO LOOK FOR

Nutcracker Brown body with white
spots; white under tail.

Jay Blue and white patch on wing;
white rump.

Chough Black body with red legs and
red curved beak.

Alpine Chough As chough, but yellow
beak.

Great Tit · Blue Tit · Coal Tit · Crested Tit · Marsh Tit · Siberian Tit · Sombre Tit · Willow Tit

Coal Tit · Sombre Tit · Willow Tit · Siberian Tit · Blue Tit · Crested Tit · Marsh Tit · Great Tit

TITS

Family Paridae

Tits are mainly woodland birds, but several kinds are frequent visitors to gardens. They can easily be told apart from other common woodland and garden birds as they have chunky rounded bodies. In woods, they flit through the branches and hang from twigs to get at insects, buds and seeds; they nest in holes in trees, laying at least four or five eggs and sometimes as many as twenty. Tits can easily be attracted to a garden; they are bold birds and show little fear of man. Their agility enables them to feed easily at bird tables and to take food hung from a branch or a gutter. Being hole nesters, they also come readily to nest boxes.

Great Tit *Parus major* 14 cm 5½ in. Very often seen in woods, parks and gardens. Often pecks through milk bottle tops to reach the cream.
Blue Tit *Parus caeruleus* 11 cm 4½ in. Very often seen in woods, parks and gardens. Like great tit, it often opens milk bottles. Blue tits also tear strips from wallpaper, books and newspapers, an activity thought to be an extension of their habit of tearing bark from trees to find insects.
Coal Tit *Parus ater* 11 cm 4½ in. Common in woods, especially pine woods. Less often seen in gardens than great tit or blue tit.
Crested Tit *Parus cristatus* 11 cm 4½ in. Usually found in woods, especially among coniferous trees. Rarely seen in gardens.
Marsh Tit *Parus palustris* 11 cm 4½ in. Common in woods and often found in gardens. In spite of its name, it does not usually frequent marshes. Nests in natural holes in walls or trees.
Willow Tit *Parus montanus* 11 cm 4½ in. Common in woods, usually in damp places. Excavates nesting hole in rotten wood.

Sombre Tit *Parus lugubris* 14 cm 5½ in. Found in woods and rocky country. Less bold than other tits, and usually lives alone.
Siberian Tit *Parus cinctus* 13 cm 5 in. Found in woods. Has untidy plumage, unlike other tits.

WHAT TO LOOK FOR

Great Tit   Yellow breast with black central stripe.

Blue Tit   Blue cap, wings and tail.

Coal Tit   White patch at back of head.

Crested Tit   Speckled crest on head.

Marsh Tit   Black crown without white nape of coal tit.

Willow Tit   As marsh tit, but light wing patch.

Sombre Tit   As marsh tit, but large black patch on throat.

Siberian Tit   Brown crown, black throat.

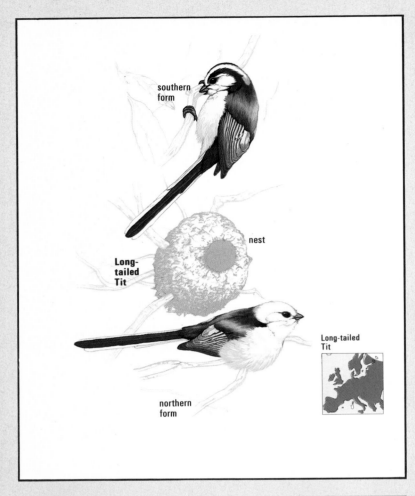

southern form

nest

Long-tailed Tit

Long-tailed Tit

northern form

LONG-TAILED TITS

Family Aegithalidae

Several families of birds are called tits, which is simply an old word meaning little. If it were not for their tails, which take up more than half their length, long-tailed tits would be among the world's tiniest birds. Only one species is found in Europe.

Long-tailed Tit *Aegithalos caudatus* 14 cm 5½ in. Found among bushes, thickets and hedges in woods, farmland and sometimes parks and gardens. Builds delicate globe-shaped nest with tiny entrance hole. The parent bird has to fold its long tail over its back when it is inside the nest.

NUTHATCHES AND WALLCREEPERS

Family Sittidae

Nuthatches are very agile tree birds, and are to be seen clambering up or running headfirst down trunks and along branches, picking insects from the bark.
Wallcreepers climb over rock faces as well as walls, looking more like treecreepers than nuthatches. They also flutter through the air like butterflies.

Nuthatch *Sitta europaea* 14 cm 5½ in. Lives in woods, parks and gardens; may visit bird tables. Nests in hole in tree, often plastering up entrance hole with mud. Two colour forms occur: birds with a white underside in northern Europe (*Sitta europaea europaea*), and birds with a buff underside elsewhere (*Sitta europaea caesia*). In Yugoslavia, Greece and Turkey, the very similar rock nuthatch (*Sitta neumayer*) may be seen climbing rock faces.
Wallcreeper *Tichodroma muraria* 16 cm 6½ in. Lives on mountain slopes, among gorges and cliffs; descends to valleys and foothills in winter, when it may be seen on buildings. Nests in rock cavities.

summer

winter

Wallcreeper

Nuthatch

Wallcreeper   Nuthatch

WHAT TO LOOK FOR

Long-tailed Tit   Very small black and white body with very long tail.

Nuthatch   Blue-grey back, short tail.

Wallcreeper   Crimson wing patch.

TREECREEPERS

Family Certhiidae

These birds are named after the way they creep up tree trunks, seeking insects in the bark. They nest in holes and crevices in trees and behind ivy.

Treecreeper *Certhia familiaris* 13 cm 5 in. Found in woods, parks and gardens. Often seen with tits in winter. **Short-toed Treecreeper** *Certhia brachydactyla* 13 cm 5 in. Lives in same places as treecreeper. In central and southern Europe, this species is usually found at low altitude, whereas the treecreeper often prefers the mountains here.

WRENS

Family Troglodytidae

All but one of the members of the wren family live in America. They are all very small birds.

Wren *Troglodytes troglodytes* 10 cm 4 in. Lives among low plants almost anywhere, from mountains, coasts and moors to woods, fields, parks and gardens. Often seen scurrying about in a flower bed or along the bottom of a hedge or wall, seeking insects among the litter on the ground. Nests in hedges and bushes and in holes in walls and trees.

DIPPERS

Family Cinclidae

Dippers are unusual perching birds because they are water birds. They can swim and dive, and may even walk along the bottom of a stream to look for small freshwater animals. They are called dippers not because they are continually taking a dip, but because they bob their heads up and down as they perch on an overhanging branch or rock. Only one species lives in Europe.

Dipper *Cinclus cinclus* 18 cm 7 in. Lives by streams in mountains; may also be found by water at lower levels and at seashore in winter. Builds nest in river banks, under bridges or behind waterfalls.

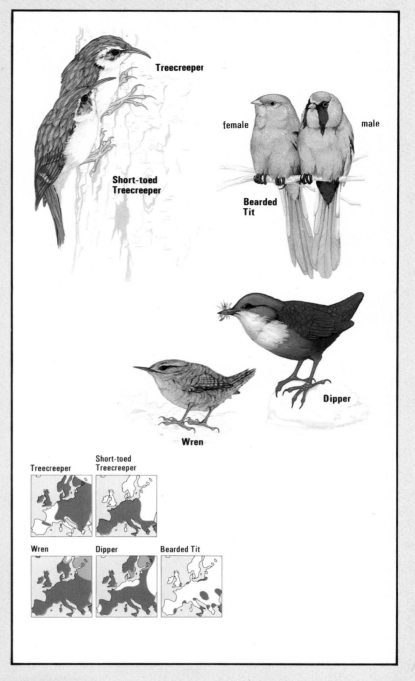

BABBLERS

Family Timaliidae

Babblers get their name from their constant chatter. Only one species is found in Europe.

Bearded Tit or **Reedling** *Panurus biarmicus* 16 cm 6½ in. Lives among reeds; seen in flocks during winter. Gets its name from the large moustache marking of the male bird.

WHAT TO LOOK FOR

Wren Small size, upturned tail.

Dipper Dark with white breast.

Bearded Tit Tawny body with very long tail; black moustache mark (male only).

Treecreeper Curved beak; streaky brown back and all-white underside.

Short-toed Treecreeper Very similar to treecreeper, but may have buff flanks.

THRUSHES

Family Turdidae

This large family of birds contains several birds that are well known as visitors to gardens. They feed mainly on fruits, berries and insects, but are often to be seen looking for worms. Thrushes have beautiful songs, which they seem to perform just for the pleasure of singing.

Mistle Thrush *Turdus viscivorus* 28 cm 11 in. Found in woods, farmland, parks and gardens; also on moors in winter. Nests in trees.

Fieldfare *Turdus pilaris* 25 cm 10 in. Found in woods and, in northern Europe, in parks and gardens. Nests in trees or on buildings. In winter spreads in flocks to fields and open country with hedges and scattered trees.

Song Thrush *Turdus philomelos* 23 cm 9 in. Often seen in woods and orchards, among scattered bushes and hedges, and in parks and gardens. May be seen on lawns cocking its head to one side, as if listening but in fact looking for a worm. Drops snails on to a stone (called an anvil) to break open their shells. Nests in trees, bushes and hedges, and also on buildings.

Redwing *Turdus iliacus* 20 cm 8 in. Found in woods and, in northern Europe, in parks and gardens. In fields and open country in winter. Nests in trees and on the ground.

Song Thrush   Redwing   Mistle Thrush   Fieldfare

Fieldfare

Song Thrush

Mistle Thrush

Redwing

Ring Ouzel *Turdus torquatus* 24 cm 9½ in. Lives on moors and mountain slopes, often where there are scattered trees and bushes. Nests among low plants or on rock ledges or walls.

Blackbird *Turdus merula* 25 cm 10 in. Very often seen in woods, orchards, hedges, parks and gardens; also in fields in winter. Nests in trees, bushes or hedges, on the ground or on buildings. Some blackbirds are albino birds that have white patches or may even be entirely white.

Rock Thrush *Monticola saxatilis* 19 cm 7½ in. Lives and nests on rocky ground and among trees high in mountains in western Europe, but lower down in eastern Europe.

Blue Rock Thrush *Monticola solitarius* 20 cm 8 in. Lives on rocky and stony ground from the seashore up to mountain tops. May be seen in towns in southern Europe. Nests in holes in rocks or cliffs or on buildings.

WHAT TO LOOK FOR

Ring Ouzel   Male: black with white breast band. Female: brown.

Blackbird   Male: all black with bright yellow beak. Female: dark brown all over.

Rock Thrush   Male: blue head, orange breast and tail, white band across back. Female: mottled brown with chestnut tail.

Blue Rock Thrush   Male: blue body with dark wings and tail. Female: as female rock thrush but dark brown tail.

Blackbird nestlings. The white one is an albino.

173

Wheatear *Oenanthe oenanthe* 15 cm 6 in. Lives in open country, from high moors and grassy hillsides down to coasts. Nests in holes in ground or in walls and rocks.

Black-eared Wheatear *Oenanthe hispanica* 14 cm 6 in. Found in rocky and sandy places, often among scattered trees and bushes. Nests in holes in walls and rocks. The male may have either a white or black throat.

Black Wheatear *Oenanthe leucura* 18 cm 7 in. Lives in rocky mountains and at sea cliffs. Nests in holes in rocks, often hiding entrance with pile of stones.

Stonechat *Saxicola torquata* 13 cm 5 in. Found on moors, on headlands at coast and on rough ground with bushes, especially gorse. Often seen perching, flicking its tail up and down. The nest is hidden in a bush or among grass.

Whinchat *Saxicola rubetra* 13 cm 5 in. Lives in similar places to stonechat, but also likes grassy areas and fields. Behaves in same way as stonechat.

Redstart *Phoenicurus phoenicurus* 14 cm 5½ in. Found in woods and among scattered trees; also in parks and gardens. Constantly flicks its tail up and down. Nests in holes in trees and walls.

WHAT TO LOOK FOR

Wheatear   Male in summer: black patch over eye with grey crown, grey back and rump. Female and male in autumn: white stripe over eye and grey-brown back with white rump.

Black-eared Wheatear   Male: black patch over eye with white to chestnut crown, buff back and white rump; black patch may extend to throat. Female: as female wheatear but dark cheek patch and darker wings.

Black Wheatear   Male: black body. Female: dark chocolate brown body. Both have white rump.

Stonechat   Male: black head (brownish in winter) with chestnut breast. Female: as male but much paler.

Whinchat   Male: dark cheeks with white stripe over eye; white at base of tail. Female: as male but paler.

Redstart   Male: black throat with orange breast; reddish tail. Female: buff breast and reddish tail.

Black Redstart *Phoenicurus ochruros* 14 cm 5½ in. Found on rocky ground and cliffs; also in towns, especially around factories. Constantly flicks its tail. Nests in holes in rocks and walls, and on buildings.

Nightingale *Luscinia megarhynchos* 16 cm 6½ in. Hides away among undergrowth in woods, and in thickets and hedges, sometimes around gardens. Nest concealed near ground. Very difficult to spot, but musical song can often be heard, especially at night (though other thrushes may also sing at night).

Thrush Nightingale *Luscinia luscinia* 16 cm 6½ in. Lives, nests and sings in the same way as nightingale. However, the two species are found together only in a narrow band across eastern Europe.

Bluethroat *Luscinia svecica* 14 cm 5½ in. Hides away among thickets and hedges, often close to water. Nest concealed near ground. There are two colour forms: the white-spotted bluethroat (*Luscinia svecica cyanecula*) of central and southern Europe, in which the blue throat patch of the male has a white centre; and the red-spotted bluethroat (*Luscinia svecica svecica*) of northern Europe, in which it has a red centre. The blue is obscured during the winter.

Robin *Erithacus rubecula* 14 cm 5½ in. Very often seen in woods, hedges, parks and gardens, hopping over the ground. Nests in holes in trees and walls. In Britain, robins are bold birds and often come to bird tables, but elsewhere in Europe they are shy. Robins are usually seen alone, or at most in pairs during spring and summer. They are so aggressive towards each other that they will even mistake their own reflection for another bird and attack it.

WHAT TO LOOK FOR

Black Redstart Male: black with reddish tail. Female: as female redstart but darker and greyer.

Nightingale Brown back and chestnut tail with plain breast.

Thrush Nightingale Grey-brown back and partly chestnut tail with lightly speckled breast.

Bluethroat Male: blue throat with red or white patch in centre. Female: dark breast band and orange patches on tail.

Robin Orange-red face and breast.

Nightingale

Thrush Nightingale

female

male, white-spotted form

Bluethroat

male, red-spotted form

female

male

Robin

Black Redstart

Black Redstart Nightingale Thrush Nightingale Bluethroat Robin

175

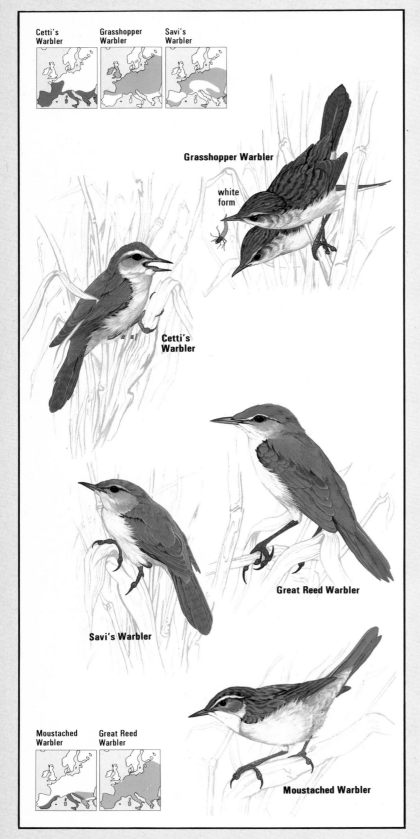

Cetti's Warbler | Grasshopper Warbler | Savi's Warbler

Grasshopper Warbler

white form

Cetti's Warbler

Savi's Warbler

Great Reed Warbler

Moustached Warbler | Great Reed Warbler

Moustached Warbler

WARBLERS

Family Sylviidae

Warblers are small birds that flit about among trees, bushes and reeds, restlessly searching for insects to eat. They are named after their warbling songs, which vary widely from one species to another. The birds are often shy and difficult to spot. Most have dull colours with no very obvious marks to give away their identity. Recognizing the song of a warbler is therefore helpful in making sure of its identity.

Cetti's Warbler *Cettia cetti* 14 cm 5½ in. Hides away and nests among dense thickets and reed-beds beside streams and in swamps. Flicks tail.

Grasshopper Warbler *Locustella naevia* 13 cm 5 in. Hides away and nests among dense undergrowth, long grass and reeds in marshes, and in more open country with scattered trees and bushes. Named after the grasshopper-like whirring sound of its song. The underparts may be white or yellowish.

Savi's Warbler *Locustella luscinioides* 14 cm 5½ in. Lives and nests among reeds and bushes in marshes and swamps. May be seen singing while perched on the tip of a reed or top of a bush.

Moustached Warbler *Acrocephalus melanopogon* 13 cm 5 in. Lives and nests among reeds and small bushes in swamps and beside streams. Bobs its tail up and down, unlike similar sedge warbler and aquatic warbler.

Great Reed Warbler *Acrocephalus arundinaceus* 19 cm 7½ in. Found among reeds beside lakes and rivers. Builds nest around reed stems. Sings from tops of reeds and may be seen on perch in the open. Largest European warbler.

WHAT TO LOOK FOR

Cetti's Warbler Unstreaked red-brown back. Song: repeated 'chewee' in bursts.

Grasshopper Warbler Streaked back with faint eye-stripe. Song: high whirring sound held for long time.

Savi's Warbler Plumage like reed warbler but white chin. Song: like grasshopper warbler's, but lower and held for short time.

Moustached Warbler Dark streaked back; dark cap with vivid eye-stripe. Song: sweet warble with 'tu-tu-tu' sounds.

Great Reed Warbler Large; unstreaked brown back with eye-stripe. Song: loud and strident with harsh sounds.

176

Reed Warbler *Acrocephalus scirpaceus* 13 cm 5 in. Lives and nests among reeds and low bushes beside water and sometimes in fields. Perches on reed to sing, and suspends nest among reeds.

Marsh Warbler *Acrocephalus palustris* 13 cm 5 in. Lives and nests among low bushes in thickets and swamps and beside ditches and streams; also in cornfields. Sings from low visible perch. Very like reed warbler, but unlikely to be found in reeds.

Sedge Warbler *Acrocephalus schoenobaenus* 13 cm 5 in. Lives and nests among reeds, low bushes and hedges, usually near water; also among crops. Sings from perch at top of reed, and also during short flights.

Melodious Warbler *Hippolais polyglotta* 13 cm 5 in. Lives in woods and among bushes along rivers, also in parks and gardens. Nests in bushes and hedges. Very similar to icterine warbler in plumage, but the two species are found together only in a narrow band across the centre of Europe.

Icterine Warbler *Hippolais icterina* 13 cm 5 in. Lives and nests in same places as melodious warbler, but less likely found near water.

Olivaceous Warbler *Hippolais pallida* 13 cm 5 in. Lives and nests in trees, bushes and hedges in light woods, fields, orchards, parks and gardens. Similar to garden warbler, but the two species are usually found in different parts of Europe.

WHAT TO LOOK FOR

Marsh Warbler   Like reed warbler, but olive-brown back and pink legs. Song: varied and musical with trills.

Sedge Warbler   Like moustached warbler, but paler. Song: varied mixture of sweet and harsh sounds.

Melodious Warbler   Green-grey with yellow underside; brown legs. Song: rapid and varied, but musical.

Icterine Warbler   Like melodious warbler, but blue-grey legs. Song: repeated notes, both sweet and harsh.

Olivaceous Warbler   Grey-brown above and white below with buffish eye-stripe. Song: like sedge warbler's.

Reed Warbler   Like great reed warbler, but smaller and with faint eye-stripe. Song: monotonous mixture of sweet and harsh sounds.

Melodious Warbler

Icterine Warbler

Olivaceous Warbler

Olivaceous Warbler

Icterine Warbler

Melodious Warbler

Sedge Warbler

Marsh Warbler

Reed Warbler

Reed Warbler   Sedge Warbler   Marsh Warbler

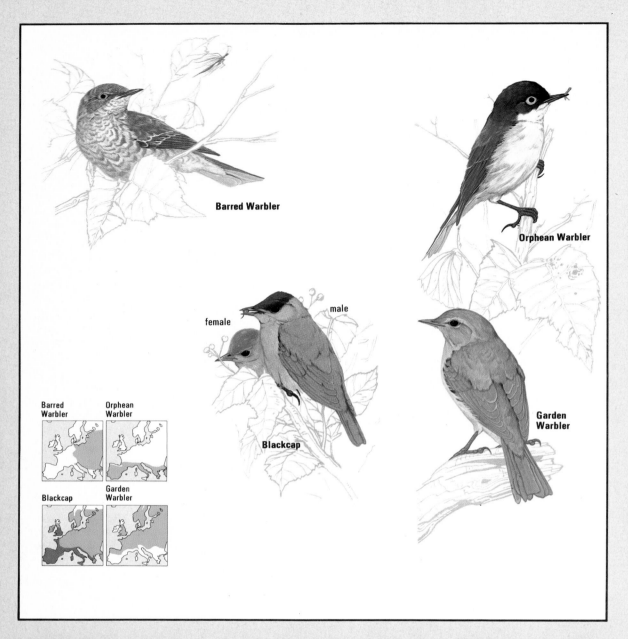

Barred Warbler

Orphean Warbler

female   male

Blackcap

Garden Warbler

Barred Warbler   Orphean Warbler

Blackcap   Garden Warbler

Barred Warbler *Sylvia nisoria* 15 cm 6 in. Lives and nests in bushes and hedges in woods and fields. Usually shy, but may be seen and heard singing in flight.
Orphean Warbler *Sylvia hortensis* 15 cm 6 in. Lives and nests in bushes and trees in woods and orchards.
Garden Warbler *Sylvia borin* 14 cm 5½ in. Hides away and nests among undergrowth in woods and among thickets, hedges and bushes, often in parks and gardens. The plainest of all European birds; has no special markings at all.
Blackcap *Sylvia atricapilla* 14 cm 5½ in. Lives and nests among undergrowth, bushes and hedges in woods, parks and gardens. Usually shy, but may come to bird tables in winter. Only the

male has a black cap, a glossy black crown down to eye level. The sides of the head and the underparts are ash grey. The female has a red-brown cap and browner underparts. The Blackcap can be distinguished from the Orphean and Sardinian Warblers by the sharply-defined cap and the lack of white in the tail. It has a rich, warbling call.

WHAT TO LOOK FOR

Barred Warbler   Bars on underside. Song: musical, but in short bursts interrupted by chatter.

Orphean Warbler   Black cap extending below straw-coloured eye. Song: warble of repeated phrases.

Garden Warbler   Light brown above and grey-white beneath, with no obvious markings at all. Song: musical and liquid, soft but held for long time.

Blackcap   Male: black cap. Female: brown cap. Song: varied warble held for short time.

Aquatic Warbler *Acrocephalus paludicola* 13 cm 5 in. Lives and nests among reeds and low bushes beside open stretches of water. Usually shy, but may be seen and heard singing in flight.

Whitethroat *Sylvia communis* 14 cm 5½ in. Lives and nests among low bushes, hedges and brambles around woods and in fields, also in gardens. Very active, darting in and out of cover and making short flights, singing in the air.

Lesser Whitethroat *Sylvia curruca* 13 cm 5 in. Hides away and nests among bushes and trees in woods, parks and gardens.

Sardinian Warbler *Sylvia melanocephala* 14 cm 5½ in. Lives and nests in low bushes and thickets and in woods and open country; also in parks and gardens. May be seen and heard singing on perch and in flight.

Subalpine Warbler *Sylvia cantillans* 13 cm 5 in. Hides away and nests in bushes and thickets among scattered trees, in clearings in woods, and on river banks. May be seen and heard singing in flight.

WHAT TO LOOK FOR

Aquatic Warbler   Like sedge warbler, but buff stripe through crown. Song : like sedge warbler's.

Whitethroat   White throat with plain grey (male) or brown (female) head; red-brown wings. Song : short bursts of chatter.

Lesser Whitethroat   Like whitethroat, but dark patch around eye and grey-brown wings. Song : fast rattle-like sound, often preceded by a short warble.

Sardinian Warbler   Black (male) or brown (female) cap extending below red eye ; grey flanks. Song : fast and musical with chattering sounds.

Subalpine Warbler   Orange throat (pale in female) and white moustache. Song : slow and musical.

Whitethroat
male
female

Sardinian Warbler
female
male

Aquatic Warbler

Lesser Whitethroat

Aquatic Warbler

Whitethroat

Lesser Whitethroat

Subalpine Warbler

Sardinian Warbler

Subalpine Warbler
female
male

Spectacled Warbler *Sylvia conspicillata* 13 cm 5 in. Lives and nests in low bushes in dry open country. Sings from top of bush and in flight.

Dartford Warbler *Sylvia undata* 13 cm 5 in. Lives and nests among low bushes, especially gorse, and heather on dry open ground and hillsides. Very shy, but may sing in flight. Has generally spread its breeding range during the last few years, but could be vulnerable in Britain, partly due to cold winters and heath fires in hot summers.

Fan–tailed Warbler *Cisticola juncidis* 10 cm 4 in. Lives and nests in dense, low plants in marshes, on lake and river banks, in fields and on plains. Often very shy, but may be seen and heard singing in flight.

Willow Warbler *Phylloscopus trochilus* 11 cm $4\frac{1}{2}$ in. Found scurrying and flitting about in woods, among scattered trees and bushes, and in parks and gardens. Usually nests on the ground among bushes. Virtually identical to chiffchaff, except for song.

Chiffchaff *Phylloscopus collybita* 11 cm $4\frac{1}{2}$ in. Found in same places and as restless as willow warbler, but prefers areas with trees. Nests above ground. Virtually identical to willow warbler, except for song.

Wood Warbler *Phylloscopus sibilatrix* 13 cm 5 in. Lives and nests among woods and forests. Very active, singing as it moves through the leaves and flies from tree to tree.

Bonelli's Warbler *Phylloscopus bonelli* 11 cm $4\frac{1}{2}$ in. Lives in woods and forests, usually on hills and mountainsides. Nests on the ground among trees.

WHAT TO LOOK FOR

Spectacled Warbler   Like whitethroat, but pinker breast and darker head. Song: high, short and unvarying warble.

Dartford Warbler   Red-brown breast, cocked tail. Song: short musical phrases with varying pauses.

Fan-tailed Warbler   Streaked crown and back; small size with short tail. Song: repeated 'cheep cheep' sounds.

Willow Warbler   Grey-green back. Yellowish underside, white eye-stripe, legs usually pale. Song: liquid warble of descending notes.

Chiffchaff   Like willow warbler, but legs always dark. Song: repeated 'chiff chaff' sounds.

Wood Warbler   Yellow throat and breast, yellow eye-stripe. Song: liquid trill followed by a few long notes.

Bonelli's Warbler   Like willow warbler, but greyer above, whiter beneath and with yellowish rump. Song: short trills.

FLYCATCHERS

Family Muscicapidae

These birds are well named, for they are most likely to be seen sitting watchfully on a perch and then suddenly darting out to capture a fly or some other flying insect or swooping down to the ground to make a catch there. They often return to the same perch to wait for the next meal.

Spotted Flycatcher *Muscicapa striata* 14 cm 5½ in. Found at the edges of woods, among scattered trees, and in parks, orchards and gardens. Nests on buildings and tree trunks, often behind creepers. Flicks its tail as it perches. Only young birds are spotted; the adults are lightly streaked instead.

Pied Flycatcher *Ficedula hypoleuca* 13 cm 5 in. Found in woods, parks and gardens. Nests in hole in tree or wall, also in nest boxes. Flicks tail, but does not often return to same perch after chasing insects.

Collared Flycatcher *Ficedula albicollis* 13 cm 5 in. Lives in same places and behaves in same way as pied flycatcher. In spring and summer the male's plumage varies. In Italy and central Europe, the western form (*Ficedula albicollis albicollis*), which has a white collar, is found. The eastern form (*Ficedula albicollis semitorquata*), which is found in eastern Europe, lacks the white collar.

Red–breasted Flycatcher *Ficedula parva* 11 cm 4½ in. Found in woods and parks, usually feeding among leaves in trees but sometimes chasing insects. Nests in hole in tree or wall and also on tree trunk. The male looks rather like a small robin, except that it has white on the sides of its tail.

WHAT TO LOOK FOR

Spotted Flycatcher Grey-brown with lightly streaked breast and head.

Pied Flycatcher Male in summer: black back and white underside with white wing patch. Male in autumn and female: brown back with white wing patch.

Collared Flycatcher Male in summer: like pied flycatcher but white collar (western form only) and white forehead. Male in autumn and female: very like pied flycatcher.

Red-breasted Flycatcher Orange (male) or buff (female) throat; white tail edges.

Spotted Flycatcher

female (and male in autumn)

Collared Flycatcher

male, western form (summer)

Red-breasted Flycatcher

male

female

Pied Flycatcher

female (and male in autumn)

male (summer)

| Spotted Flycatcher | Pied Flycatcher | Collared Flycatcher | Red-breasted Flycatcher |

GOLDCRESTS
Family Regulidae

Goldcrests are active little birds that flit through bushes and trees, hunting for insects. In the winter, they may join flocks of tits seeking food. Two species are found in Europe, and they are the smallest European birds.

Goldcrest *Regulus regulus* 9 cm 3½ in. Found in woods and forests, especially in conifer trees; also in hedges, low bushes and undergrowth in winter. Builds basket-like nest of moss, often hung in conifer tree or among ivy.
Firecrest *Regulus ignicapillus* 9 cm 3½ in. Found in same places as goldcrest, but has no preference for conifer trees. Nest may be hung in bushes or creepers as well as in trees.

ACCENTORS
Family Prunellidae

Accentors are small birds that root about on the ground or among low plants seeking insects and spiders to eat, and also seeds in winter. Two species are found in Europe.

Dunnock or **Hedge Sparrow** *Prunella modularis* 15 cm 6 in. Found in woods, bushy countryside, hedges, parks and gardens, where it shuffles through flower beds. Resembles female house sparrow but is recognized by its narrow bill and dark grey head and underside. Nests in hedges, bushes and low plants.
Alpine Accentor *Prunella collaris* 18 cm 7 in. Lives on rocky mountain slopes, though may descend for the winter. Nests in holes in rocks.

A hard-working dunnock feeds a hungry young cuckoo hatched from an egg left in its nest.

WHAT TO LOOK FOR

Goldcrest Tiny; orange (male) or yellow (female) stripe on crown.

Firecrest Like goldcrest, but black and white stripe over eye.

Dunnock Grey head and breast with brown back.

Alpine Accentor Spotted throat and streaky flanks.

PIPITS AND WAGTAILS

Family Motacillidae

Pipits and wagtails are small birds that spend most of their time on the ground in search of insects. Pipits look like several other streaky brown ground birds, such as buntings and larks, but they can be recognized by their narrow beaks and slender bodies. Wagtails have long tails, which they wag up and down all the time.

Tawny Pipit *Anthus campestris* 16 cm 6½ in. Lives on dry, open, often sandy ground, also in fields. Nests in low plants on ground.

Meadow Pilpit *Anthus pratensis* 15 cm 6 in. Found in all kinds of open country – moors, fields, dunes, grassy slopes – and in winter in marshes and along rivers, often at the coast. Makes its nest on the ground hidden among low plants. May be seen and heard singing as it makes short flights rising from and returning to ground.

Tree Pipit *Anthus trivialis* 15 cm 6 in. Lives in light woods and clearings and among scattered trees and bushes. Nests among low plants on ground. May be seen and heard singing in short spiral flight rising from a perch.

Water Pipit *Anthus spinoletta spinoletta* 16 cm 6½ in. Lives in mountains in spring and summer, nesting in holes in rock. Descends for winter, usually living near water.

Rock Pipit *Anthus spinoletta petrosus* 16 cm 6½ in. Belongs to same species as water pipit, but lives at coast, often among rocks. Nests in rock crevices.

WHAT TO LOOK FOR

Tawny Pipit   Sandy unstreaked breast and faintly streaked neck.

Meadow Pipit   Pale breast with dark streaks; brown legs.

Tree Pipit   Breast buff with dark streaks; pink legs.

Water Pipit   Summer: unstreaked breast with grey back. Winter: like rock pipit, but white eye-stripe.

Rock Pipit   Dark and streaky all over; dark legs; grey edges to tail (white in other pipits).

Tree Pipit

Meadow Pipit

winter

summer

Rock Pipit

Water Pipit

Tawny Pipit

Tree Pipit   Water Pipit   Rock Pipit   Tawny Pipit   Meadow Pipit

summer

winter

White Wagtail

winter

summer

Pied Wagtail

White Wagtail

Pied Wagtail

Grey Wagtail

Yellow Wagtail

male
(summer)

female

male
(winter)

**Grey
Wagtail**

male

**Yellow
Wagtail**

female

White Wagtail *Motacilla alba alba*
18 cm 7 in. Often found in open country,
usually near water, and also on farms
and in villages and towns. Nests in
holes and on ledges among rocks
and on buildings. In winter, large
groups sleep on buildings and in trees
in cities and towns.

Pied Wagtail *Motacilla alba yarrellii*
18 cm 7 in. Form of white wagtail
found mainly in British Isles. Lives and
nests in same places as the white
wagtail.

Grey Wagtail *Motacilla cinerea* 18 cm
7 in. In spring and summer, found by
streams and rivers, mostly in hills and
mountains, where it nests in hole in
wall or rock beside water. In winter,
moves to lowland rivers and lakes,
sewage farms and coast.

Yellow Wagtail *Motacilla flava* 16 cm
6½ in. Found in marshes and fields,
usually near water. Nests on the
ground, among grass or crops. Several
forms with different head patterns and
different names live in Europe. They all
have their own regions but where
these meet, intermediate forms may be
seen. In southern Scandinavia and
central Europe, the blue-headed wagtail (*Motacilla flava flava*) is found.
Britain is the home of the yellow
wagtail (*Motacilla flava flavissima*).
The Spanish wagtail (*Motacilla flava
iberiae*) lives in Spain, Portugal and
southern France. In Italy and Albania,
the ashy-headed wagtail (*Motacilla
flava cinereocapilla*) is found, and the
blackheaded wagtail (*Motacilla flava
feldegg*) lives in south-east Europe.
Each kind may sometimes stray from
its own region.

WHAT TO LOOK FOR

White Wagtail Black and white with
very long tail; grey back.

Pied Wagtail As white wagtail, but
black back in spring and summer.

Grey Wagtail Grey back with yellow
underside; black throat (male in summer
only).

Yellow Wagtail Green-brown back and
bright yellow underside (pale in female).

Yellow Wagtail Head Patterns

Blue-headed Wagtail Blue-grey
crown, white stripe over eye, yellow
throat.

Yellow Wagtail Olive and yellow
head.

Spanish Wagtail Grey crown, white
stripe starting from eye, white throat.

Ashy-headed Wagtail Grey head, no
stripe over eye, white throat.

Black-headed Wagtail Black head,
no stripe over eye, yellow throat.

WAXWINGS

Family Bombycillidae

Waxwings are unusual birds because they do not have particular homes. Except when nesting, they continually wander in flocks from place to place, looking for fruits, berries and insects to eat. They may be seen in one place for a short time and then not again for years.

Waxwing *Bombycilla garrulus* 18 cm 7 in. Found in woods, parks and gardens, busily eating berries and fruits. Nests in Arctic and spreads into Europe in winter in search of food.

SHRIKES

Family Laniidae

Shrikes are like small birds of prey. The shrike darts after its prey and snaps it up in its hooked beak. The victim is then usually taken to the shrike's 'larder', a sharp thorn or barbed wire fence where it is impaled so that the shrike can tear it apart – a habit that has earned the shrike its other name of butcherbird.

Great Grey Shrike *Lanius excubitor* 24 cm 9½ in. Found at edges of woods, among scattered trees and bushes and in hedges and orchards. Nests in trees and bushes.
Lesser Grey Shrike *Lanius minor* 20 cm 8 in. Found among scattered trees and bushes. Nests in trees.
Woodchat Shrike *Lanius senator* 18 cm 7 in. Found in scattered trees, bushy countryside, orchards and woods. Nests in trees.
Red–backed Shrike *Lanius collurio* 18 cm 7 in. Found in bushy places and among brambles and thickets. Nests in bushes and small trees.

WHAT TO LOOK FOR

Waxwing   Large crest; yellow tip on tail.

Great Grey Shrike   Black and white with grey back and crown.

Lesser Grey Shrike   As great grey shrike but black forehead.

Woodchat Shrike   Chestnut crown with white wing patch and rump (female paler than male).

Red-backed Shrike   Male: grey crown with chestnut back and wings. Female: plain brown back with bars on breast.

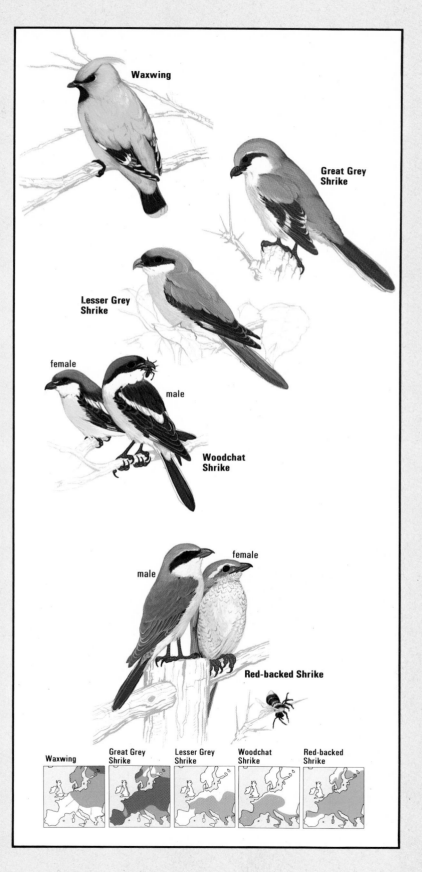

Waxwing

Great Grey Shrike

Lesser Grey Shrike

female   male

Woodchat Shrike

male   female

Red-backed Shrike

| Waxwing | Great Grey Shrike | Lesser Grey Shrike | Woodchat Shrike | Red-backed Shrike |

STARLINGS
Family Sturnidae

Starlings like each other's company and live in flocks that in winter may contain thousands of birds. They wander over the ground, busily pecking here and there for food. They chatter constantly, often copying other sounds.

Starling *Sturnus vulgaris* 21 cm 8½ in. Found throughout the countryside and also in towns, where flocks sleep on buildings and in trees. Nests in holes in trees or ground, on buildings and in nest boxes. As spring arrives, it loses the white spots of its winter plumage because the white tips of its feathers wear away. Also, the beak, which is dark in winter, turns yellow.
Spotless Starling *Sturnus unicolor* 21 cm 8½ in. Lives and nests in same kinds of places as starling. In spite of its name, it is slightly spotted in winter.

FINCHES
Family Fringillidae

Like tits, finches are generally among the most well-known and liked of birds, for they often come to gardens and parks, adding a touch of colour with their bright plumage. They are less likely to be seen in the summer when they are nesting.

Greenfinch *Carduelis chloris* 15 cm 6 in. Often seen among scattered trees and bushes, in fields, parks and gardens. Clings to net bags or wire baskets of nuts to feed, like tits. Nests in trees and bushes.
Hawfinch *Coccothraustes coccothraustes* 18 cm 7 in. Lives in woods, orchards, parks and gardens, but may hide away among leaves, especially in Britain. Nests in trees and bushes. Has huge bill that can crack open hard seeds.

WHAT TO LOOK FOR

Starling Summer: slightly-speckled glossy black with green-purple sheen. Winter: black with white spots.

Spotless Starling Summer: as starling but unspeckled deep black. Winter: as starling but small spots.

Hawfinch Huge beak above small black bib; wide white wingbar.

Greenfinch Green-brown with yellow edges to wings and tail (female paler than male).

Goldfinch

male and
female (winter)

Twite

female (summer)

male
(summer)

female

male

Siskin

male

female

Linnet

| Goldfinch | Siskin | Linnet | Twite |

Goldfinch *Carduelis carduelis* 13 cm 5 in. Lives and nests in same places as greenfinch, but does not come to feed on nuts. Often seen climbing over thistles or on high perch. Badly named, as gold is only seen clearly on wings in flight.

Siskin *Carduelis spinus* 12 cm 4¾ in. Found in woods, usually nesting in conifer trees and, in winter, feeding in alder and birch trees. Also seen in parks and gardens.

Linnet *Acanthis cannabina* 13 cm 5 in. Nests in low bushes, thickets and hedges, usually in open country but sometimes in parks and gardens. Roams over fields, rough pastures, and marshes in winter.

Twite *Acanthis flavirostris* 14 cm 5½ in. Lives on moors and hills in summer, nesting among heather and bushes and in stone walls and rabbit burrows. Descends for winter and roams over open fields, marshes and seashores, where it can often be seen in large flocks.

WHAT TO LOOK FOR

Twite Streaky brown back, head and breast, but unstreaked throat; yellow beak (winter only); pinkish rump (male).

Goldfinch Red patch on face; wide yellow wingbar.

Siskin Male: yellow-green with black crown and chin. Female: grey-green with streaky breast, yellow tail edges.

Linnet Male: red forehead and breast (pale in winter), grey wing patch. Female: as twite but streaky throat and grey wing patch.

Serin

female

male

female

male

Bullfinch

male

female

Redpoll

Arctic Redpoll

female

male

female

male

Pine Grosbeak

Bullfinch

Pine Grosbeak

Redpoll

Arctic Redpoll

Serin

Redpoll *Acanthis flammea* 13 cm 5 in. Usually found in woods, but may be seen in parks and gardens. Nests in trees and bushes; often seen in alder and birch trees in winter together with siskins. Scandinavian redpolls are light in colour.

Arctic Redpoll *Acanthis hornemanni* 13 cm 5 in. Nests in Arctic. Usually seen in winter in woods, in company with redpolls.

Serin *Serinus serinus* 11 cm 4½ in. Found at edges of woods and in orchards, parks and gardens. Nests in trees and bushes.

Bullfinch *Pyrrhula pyrrhula* 15 cm 6 in. Found in woods, orchards, hedges, parks and gardens. Nests in trees, bushes and hedges. Raids fruit trees for their buds.

Pine Grosbeak *Pinicola enucleator* 20 cm 8 in. Lives and nests in woods, especially among conifers and in birch woods. Largest of all European finches. May be seen in flocks outside the breeding season. Usually rather tame in nature. Named grosbeak for its heavy bill.

WHAT TO LOOK FOR

Pine Grosbeak Red (male) or green and gold (female) with two white wingbars; heavy hooked bill.

Redpoll Red forehead and black bib; pink breast (male only).

Arctic Redpoll As redpoll but white rump.

Serin As siskin, but no yellow edges to tail and no black crown in male; also yellow rump and yellow (male) or streaky (female) forehead and breast.

Bullfinch Black crown and bright red (male) or brown-pink (female) breast.

188

female

male
(summer)

Chaffinch

male
(winter)

male

female

Parrot Crossbill

male

Crossbill

female

female

male
(summer)

male
(winter)

Brambling

Chaffinch

Brambling

Crossbill

Parrot
Crossbill

Crossbill *Loxia curvirostra* 16 cm 6½ in. Lives and nests among conifer (especially spruce) trees in woods and forests. The tips of its bill are crossed so that it can cut open fir cones to get at the seeds. When cones are scarce, it may spread in search of food, reaching the British Isles, France and Italy in great numbers.

Parrot Crossbill *Loxia pytyopsittacus* 17 cm 6¾ in. Lives and nests mainly among pine trees, feeding in same way as crossbill. Less likely to spread in search of food. Gets its name from the way it holds a cone while opening it, rather as a parrot holds a fruit while eating it (though crossbill performs same action).

Chaffinch *Fringilla coelebs* 15 cm 6 in. Often found in woods, among scattered trees and bushes, and in fields, hedges, orchards, parks and gardens. Nests in trees and bushes; spreads to more open country in winter.

Brambling *Fringilla montifringilla* 15 cm 6 in. Nests in trees in woods, and spreads to fields, parks and gardens in winter, often with chaffinches and other finches. Found especially in beech trees.

male female

Black-headed Bunting male

female

Yellowhammer

Corn Bunting

Cirl Bunting

male

female

male

female

Cretzschmar's Bunting

| Cretzschmar's Bunting | Corn Bunting | Yellowhammer | Black-headed Bunting | Cirl Bunting |

BUNTINGS
Family Emberizidae

Buntings are small seed-eating birds like finches, and have similar stout bills to crack open seeds. Buntings are most likely to be seen feeding on the ground in winter, often in groups, and also singing from a perch in spring and summer.

Several buntings, especially the females, look rather like other streaky brown ground-living birds, such as larks, pipits and sparrows. However, only buntings and sparrows have stout bills, and sparrows (page 192) have distinguishing marks that make them easy to recognize.

Corn Bunting *Emberiza calandra* 18 cm 7 in. Found in open fields and on rough ground with scattered bushes. Hides its nest in grass or low bushes. May be seen perching on a post, wall or telegraph wires.

Yellowhammer *Emberiza citrinella* 16 cm 6½ in. Found in clearings and at edges of woods, among scattered bushes, and in fields and hedges. Nests on the ground or in a low bush or hedge. Sings throughout spring and summer, repeating its famous phrase that seems to say 'little bit of bread and *no* cheese' – in fact, a group of short notes and a long one.

Black-headed Bunting *Emberiza melanocephala* 16 cm 6½ in. Lives among scattered trees and bushes; may come to gardens. Nests in low plants. Not the only bunting with a black head.

Cirl Bunting *Emberiza cirlus* 16 cm 6½ in. Found among scattered trees and bushes and in hedges, where it nests near ground.

Cretzschmar's Bunting *Emberiza caesia* 16 cm 6½ in. Found in dry and rocky places with scattered bushes; may visit gardens. Nests on ground.

WHAT TO LOOK FOR

Corn Bunting Large, streaky brown.

Yellowhammer Male: yellow head and underparts, chestnut rump. Female: streaky pale yellow head and breast, chestnut rump.

Black-headed Bunting Male: black head and yellow breast. Female: unstreaked buff underside with yellow patch under tail.

Cirl Bunting Male: black throat. Female: as female yellowhammer but olive rump.

Cretzschmar's Bunting Male: blue-grey head with rusty-coloured throat. Female: streaky brown with rusty-coloured throat.

Snow Bunting

female
male (winter)
male (summer)

Lapland Bunting

female
male (summer)
male (winter)

Ortolan Bunting

female
male

Rock Bunting

male
female

Reed Bunting

female
male (summer)
male (winter)

Rock Bunting
Ortolan Bunting
Reed Bunting
Lapland Bunting
Snow Bunting

Reed Bunting *Emberiza schoeniclus* 15 cm 6 in. Lives mainly in reed beds and swamps but also among bushes and hedges, where it nests on or near the ground. Spreads to fields in winter, and may come to bird tables in gardens.

Lapland Bunting *Calcarius lapponicus* 15 cm 6 in. Nests on ground in mountains and Arctic tundra. Moves to seashore and fields and moors near coast in winter.

Snow Bunting *Plectrophenax nivalis* 16 cm 6½ in. Nests in crevices in rocks, usually high up in mountains. Spreads in winter to open coasts, hills and fields. Usually seen in winter in flocks known as snowflakes, from the way the little white birds dance through the air.

Ortolan Bunting *Emberiza hortulana* 16 cm 6½ in. Found among scattered trees and bushes, often in hills; also in fields and gardens. Nests among low plants on or near the ground.

Rock Bunting *Emberiza cia* 16 cm 6½ in. Lives in mountains on rocky slopes and among scattered trees and bushes, also in vineyards. Nests on the ground or in a low bush. Moves to lower altitudes in winter. Usually seen on the ground, but also in trees. Often flicks open its tail when feeding on ground, showing white edges to tail.

WHAT TO LOOK FOR

Reed Bunting Male: black (summer) or brown (winter) head and throat with white moustache and collar. Female: streaky brown with white moustache.

Lapland Bunting Male: chestnut nape; black head and throat with buff eye-stripe (summer only). Female: as female reed bunting but chestnut nape.

Snow Bunting Large white wing patch with either white head (male in summer), or sandy head (male in winter), or grey-brown head (female).

Ortolan Bunting Male: green-grey head with yellow throat. Female: streaky brown with yellow throat.

Rock Bunting Male: grey head with black stripes. Female: streaky brown with greyish throat.

Spanish Sparrow — male, female

Tree Sparrow

House Sparrow — female, male

Italian Sparrow (male)

Snow Finch

Rock Sparrow

House Sparrow · Spanish Sparrow · Tree Sparrow · Snow Finch · Rock Sparrow

SPARROWS
Family Ploceidae

No bird is better known than the house sparrow, which lives with man almost everywhere. Sparrows are small streaky brown birds with stout bills, rather like several buntings but having special marks that are easy to recognize.

House Sparrow *Passer domesticus* 15 cm 6 in. Found in city centres and squares, parks and gardens, farms and fields. Nests under eaves, in holes in walls and rocks, and in nest boxes; also builds domed nest in creepers, bushes and trees. In Italy, Corsica and Crete, the Italian sparrow (*Passer domesticus italiae*) is found. It is a form of house sparrow with different head colours. It has a chestnut crown and white cheeks.

Spanish Sparrow *Passer hispaniolensis* 15 cm 6 in. Found in woods and among scattered trees and bushes. Nests in trees and bushes, often in old nests of other birds. Less common in towns than house sparrow and tree sparrow.

Tree Sparrow *Passer montanus* 14 cm 5½ in. Found in woods, among scattered trees and bushes, and in fields and gardens. Nests in holes in trees. Also lives and nests in towns and villages like house sparrow, especially in southern and eastern Europe.

Snow Finch *Montifringilla nivalis* 18 cm 7 in. Lives on bare mountain slopes and summits, nesting in crevices. Spends winter lower down, often visiting huts and houses. Belongs to sparrow family, in spite of its name and bunting-like appearance.

Rock Sparrow *Petronia petronia* 14 cm 5½ in. Found in rocky and stony places; sometimes in gardens and among buildings. Nests in holes in rocks and trees.

WHAT TO LOOK FOR

Snow Finch White wings with black tips, grey head and dark chin (female duller than male).

House Sparrow Male: grey crown and black bib. Female: streaky back with plain light breast; dull eye-stripe.

Italian Sparrow Male: chestnut crown with black bib; no cheek spot. Female: as female house sparrow.

Spanish Sparrow Male: as male Italian sparrow but with large black breast patch. Female: as female house sparrow but streaky flanks.

Tree Sparrow Chestnut crown with black spot on cheek (both sexes).

Rock Sparrow Pale with stripes on head, spots on tail, yellow spot on breast.

Glossary

Albumen The white of an egg. It cushions the growing embryo inside the egg and also helps to feed it.

Amphibian A class of animals including frogs, toads and newts.

Bib The part of a bird's plumage just beneath the beak. It is also called the chin.

Bill Another word for a bird's beak.

Bird Of Prey Generally, any bird that seeks animals to eat. Usually, a member of the order of birds consisting of vultures, eagles, hawks, buzzards, kites, harriers, ospreys and falcons. Owls, belonging to a different order, are also known as birds of prey.

Breed To produce young.

Breeding Season The time of year when birds nest and raise their young. In Britain and Europe, the breeding season extends from early spring through to late summer.

Brood A group of young birds that are raised at the same time from the same clutch of eggs.

Burrow A hole in the ground or a bank in which a bird nests. Some birds dig their own burrows while others use existing holes.

Call A special sound made by birds to indicate danger, to threaten intruders or to keep a group of birds together. Calls are short sounds and are different from songs.

Camouflage A camouflaged bird has plumage that looks like its surroundings, for example like leaves or grass. Camouflage helps birds to hide when danger threatens.

Chick A young bird that is able to leave the nest and walk or swim, but cannot yet fly.

Class A fundamental division of the animal kingdom. Birds are one class. Others are insects, crustaceans, reptiles, amphibians and mammals.

Classification A system of naming birds by placing them in groups to express their affinities, so that similar birds are included in the same group. Different kinds of groups include class, order, family, genus and species.

Clutch A batch of eggs laid by a female bird.

Cock Another word for a male bird, especially a chicken.

Colony A group of birds that gather together to breed.

Courtship The activities of a male and female bird at the beginning of the breeding season. Courtship brings the two birds together so that they

may form a pair and raise young.

Crest A patch of feathers on the top or back of a bird's head that can be raised and lowered.

Crown The top of a bird's head.

Dabbling A dabbling bird is an aquatic one that lowers its head to feed at the surface of some water, and sifts through the surface water to find food. The term is usually applied to surface-feeding ducks.

DDT A chemical that kills insects, but has proved to be harmful to birds and other animals. The letters stand for dichloro-diphenyl-trichloroethane.

Display A courtship activity of a bird. A display may involve showing off colourful patches of feathers, making a special pose or posture, singing or dancing. There are also aggressive displays made towards intruders and competitors for food and territories.

Diurnal Bird A bird that is active by day and sleeps by night.

Down The fluffy feathers that cover a young bird. Adult birds also have down feathers next to their skin (beneath the contour feathers).

Egg Tooth A small projection on the beak of a baby bird. It helps the bird to break out of its shell as it hatches.

Embryo The developing young bird inside an egg.

Evolution Evolution is a gradual change in the nature of living things over millions of years. Different kinds of living things evolve because the environment of living things changes. The different kinds of birds that now live in the world can be explained by the process of evolution.

Family One of the groups in classification. A family contains birds of related genera (see genus), and related families make up an order.

Feral Bird A bird that was once tamed or kept captive by man, but has now returned to the wild. Birds such as Canada geese that escape from park lakes, for example, become feral birds.

Field Guide A book that contains information on all the birds living in a particular region. It is essentially a guide to identification.

Fledge A bird fledges when it learns to fly. A young bird that can fly but has not left the nest is called a fledgling.

Game Bird Any bird shot for sport by hunters, but especially the grouse and pheasant and partridge families.

Genus One of the groups in classification. The plural is genera. Birds of closely-related species make up a genus, and related genera make up a family.

Habitat The physical surroundings of a bird, for example woodland or marshland.

Hen Another word for a female bird, especially a chicken.

Hide A portable tent or a construction in which a birdwatcher can observe a bird closely while remaining unseen.

Hormone A natural chemical in the body that influences behaviour.

Imprinting Birds learn much behaviour from their parents in their first days of life. This kind of learning is called imprinting. It helps a bird to learn its own identity, and to behave in the right way to survive.

Instinct Birds perform almost all actions by instinct, that is, without thinking. This ability is handed down from a bird's parents, and is as hereditary as its body shape and plumage.

Interbreeding Birds of subspecies that are slightly different can breed with each other. This is called interbreeding.

Introduced Bird A kind of bird that has been taken from its home range and brought somewhere else to live. Mandarin ducks, for example, have been introduced to Britain and Europe from China.

Irruption A sudden spread of birds outside their normal home range, usually caused by shortage of food.

Latin Name The genus and species and other classification groups of birds are given names in a form of Latin because this can be understood throughout the world. More correctly called scientific name because some involve words derived from other classical languages, for example Greek.

Migrant A bird in migration.

Migration The journeys that a bird may undertake every year between separated breeding and wintering ranges.

Moulting Losing old feathers and growing new ones.

Nestling A young bird that lives in a nest.

Nidicolous Bird A bird that has young which live in the nest for some time after hatching.

Nidifugous Bird A bird that has young which are able to leave the nest soon after hatching.

Nocturnal Bird A bird that is active by night and sleeps by day.

Observatory A bird observatory is a special building for birdwatchers, placed in an area where interesting birds (especially migrants) are to be seen. Usually coastal.

Omnivorcus Able to eat any kind of food, either plant or animal.

Order One of the groups in classification. An order contains birds of related families, and the related orders of birds make up a separate class (Aves) of the animal kingdom.

Peck Order When different birds meet, for example when feeding, they may arrange themselves in a peck order in which some birds dominate others.

Perching Bird Generally, any bird that can perch on a branch. Usually, a member of the order of perching birds and songbirds (Passeriformes), which contains most small- to medium-sized land birds.

Pigments The substances in eggs and feathers that give them colour.

Plumage The feathers that cover a bird's body.

Pollution The dumping by man of harmful waste materials on the land, in rivers or lakes, in the sea, or in the air. Pollution may also be caused by using materials that later turn out to be harmful, for example DDT.

Population The total number of birds of one particular kind in a certain area or region.

Predator Any animal that hunts other animals for food.

Preening The action of cleaning feathers with the beak or feet.

Prey Any animal hunted by a predator.

Primary Feathers The major wing feathers at the end of a wing. Together with the secondaries they comprise the main flight feathers.

Range The area of land or sea over which a particular kind of bird can normally be found; this may vary between summer and winter.

Reptile A class of animals including snakes and lizards.

Ringing Placing a numbered ring around a bird's leg in order to trace its movements and life span when it is later recovered.

Roost A place where birds sleep. 'Roosting' is another word for sleeping. Some birds roost solitarily, others communally.

Scientific Name The more correct term for what is often called the Latin name.

Seabird A bird that normally makes its permanent home at sea or at the seashore. Seabirds include fulmars, shearwaters, petrels, gannets, cormorants, skuas, gulls, terns and auks.

Secondary Feathers The major wing feathers in the centre of the wing.

Song A particular set of sounds that a bird (normally a male) uses to claim a territory and attract its mate during the breeding season. A song is made up of a repeated phrase of notes. A bird may have several different songs.

Songbird Generally, any bird that can sing. Usually, a member of the order of perching birds and songbirds, many of which are good at singing.

Species Groups of male and female birds that breed among themselves and produce fertile young comprise the same species. Closely related species comprise a genus in the groups of classification.

Subspecies Birds of the same species that are slightly different yet can still breed together freely.

Talons The sharp claws possessed by birds of prey.

Territory A piece of land that a bird or pair of birds consider their own during the breeding season, and which they will defend against intrusion by other birds of the same kind. Some species also defend winter feeding territories.

Vane The main part of a feather.

Vertebrate An animal with a backbone.

Wading Bird Any bird that likes to wade in shallow water or mud to find food. Birds that live in damp places like marshes and probe the wet soil for food may also be known as wading birds. The principal wading birds are plovers, sandpipers and herons.

Waterfowl A collective name for ducks, geese and swans. But covers in addition other birds, such as coots and flamingoes, which live by water.

Wildfowl The name for ducks, geese and swans exclusively.

Wingbars Strips of white or bright colour on the wings of a bird.

Yolk The yellow part of an egg, used as food by the embryo.

Bibliography

Austin & Singer *Birds of the World* Hamlyn

Brunn & Singer *The Hamlyn Guide to the Birds of Britain & Europe* Hamlyn

Campbell & Watson *The Oxford Book of Birds* Oxford

Fitter *Collins' Guide to Birdwatching* Collins

Gooders *The Bird Watcher's Book* David & Charles

Gooders *Where to Watch Birds in Europe* Andre Deutsch/Pan

Hammond & Everett *Birds of Britain and Europe* Pan

Heinzel, Fitter & Parslow *The Birds of Britain & Europe* Collins

Keith & Gooders *Collins' Bird Guide* Collins

Peterson, Mountfort & Hollom *A Field Guide to the Birds of Britain and Europe* Collins

Perrins *Birds* Collins

Saunders *RSPB Guide to British Birds* Hamlyn

Sparks *Bird Behaviour* Hamlyn

Tuck & Heinzel *A Field Guide to the Seabirds of Britain and the World* Collins

Index

Page numbers in *italics* refer to illustrations.

Acknowledgements

The author and publishers wish to thank the following for their help in supplying photographs for this book on the pages indicated:

Dr. N. Collar 74; Brian Hawkes 10-11, 19, 26 *centre*, 32, 34, 35, 36, 40 *centre*, 47 *bottom*, 54-55, 57, 65 *top left*, 69, 74, 93 *bottom left*, 98, 107, 110, 111, 112, 116 *bottom*, 118; Eric and David Hosking 5, 8-9, 12-13, 14-15, 20-21, 25, 26 *top*, 30-31, 37, 38 *top*, 39, 40 *top*, 42, 44, 45 *bottom right*, 47 *top*, 48, 50 *top*, 58, 60 *top*, 61 *centre*, 62, 63, 71, 75, 78-79, 82-83, 87, 94, 101, 114 *top*, 119, 120-121; J. Jeffery 50-51; P. Morris 20 *top*, 21 *centre*, 22 *top left*, 28-29, 77, 108; N.H.P.A. 6-7, 16, 20 *bottom left*, 22 *top right*, 26 *bottom right*, 29 *top*, 31 *bottom left*, 33, 38 *centre left*, *bottom left*, 41, 43, 45 *top*, *bottom left*, 52, 60 *bottom*, 61 *bottom right*, 65, 72, 76, 84, 86, 89, 93 *centre left*, 103, 114 *bottom left*, 115, 116 *top right*.

Front cover: Brian Hawkes. Back cover: Stephen Dalton/N.H.P.A.

Picture Research: Tracy Rawlings

Artwork: Sarah De'Ath/Artist Partners; Hayward Art Group; Chris King/Temple Art.

The author and publishers would also like to thank André Deutsch Limited for their help in supplying information, taken from *Where To Watch Birds In Europe,* by John Gooders, for the preparation of the map on pages 104/105.